INN PERSPECTIVE

INN Perspective

A Guide to New England Country Inns

Jane Anderson

Drawings by Peter J. B. Vercelli

HARPER & ROW, PUBLISHERS

NEW YORK, HAGERSTOWN, SAN FRANCISCO, LONDON

The quotation on page v appeared in the March 1932 issue of *Harper's* magazine.

The quotation on page 223, "If Once You Have Slept on an Island," is from *Taxis and Toadstools* by Rachel Field. Copyright 1926 by The Century Company. Reprinted by permission of Doubleday & Co., Inc.

FIRST EDITION

Designed by Lydia Link

Library of Congress Cataloging in Publication Data

Anderson, Jane, 1944–
    Inn perspective.
    1.   Hotels, taverns, etc.—New England.   I.   Title.
TX907.A66   647'.9474   74–1785
ISBN 0–06–010138–5
ISBN 0–06–010137–7 pbk.

76 77 78 79 80 10 9 8 7 6 5 4 3 2 1

New England is a finished place. . . .
It is the first American section to
be finished, to achieve stability in
the conditions of its life. It is the
first old civilization, the first
permanent civilization in America.

BERNARD DE VOTO,
"New England: There She Stands"

Contents

Author's Note

————————•··◆◇◆··•————————

Most people know my father as Leroy Anderson, the composer, but in our family he was also a great planner of trips. When my father took my mother, my three brothers, and me along on trips, he was the tour guide. Whether he was traveling as a guest conductor to concerts or taking us on a vacation, my father planned where we would stay, suggested relevant books to read, and drilled us on how to behave in train stations, airports, hotel lobbies, and concert halls. His rule about luggage was "Travel light and never take more than you can carry yourself." No one took this advice more to heart than he did. On his last trip to Europe, he went to Iceland, where he was an interpreter for the Army in the Second World War because he was fluent in Scandinavian languages and Icelandic. "I'm only taking an overnight bag," he said. Among the contents were two shirts, extra socks, a warm suit, a tie, a second pair of shoes, and powdered soap, string, and clothespins to use to wash out his belongings. When he returned, I asked him about the packing. "I did that perfectly," he said. Then he paused. "I think I could have taken just one shirt instead of two."

My father often wondered aloud about how I packed for my trips to New England inns. He surveyed my cardboard box files, my books about the region, and the small bulletin boards dotted with multicolored map tacks representing the 419 inns I contacted and the 236 inns I visited. "How do you manage to pack all those things into one Volkswagen Beetle?" he asked. My mother had just one remark about my driving: "Put Jane at the wheel of a car, send her to town, and she'll come back with 2,000 miles on the car." I traveled more than 35,000 miles (my family claims it was closer to 50,000) in all six New England states during spring greening, summer sunshine, fall foliage, and winter snows.

Before visiting the inns, I gathered an arsenal of material relating to New England and inns. My father-in-law, the restaurateur, Luigi B. Vercelli, of the Savoy Hotel, consented to come from London and give me a cooking course to help me evaluate restaurant meals. My husband, Peter Vercelli, who did the drawings for this book, is an architect. We traveled to many inns together, as we have over the past nine years, and I took notes and he took photographs from which he drew the inns.

In trying to decide which inns to include, I found myself influenced as much by their environs as by their ambiance, their food, their furnishings, and the warmth of their welcome. For that reason, you will find some places included that are not inns in the pure sense of the word. In many instances, I should have liked to describe attractive drives in more detail within the vicinity of an inn. For the readers who are interested, I recommend an excellent book called *Back Roads of New England* by Earl Thollander. It is published by Clarkson N. Potter, Inc., 419 Park Avenue South, New York, N.Y. 10016.

Writing a book about inns suggests a pleasant excursion into nostalgia, but even the most picturesque New England villages and the loveliest inns are vulnerable to the effects of decisions made far away. Rhode Island, for instance, was enormously popular around the turn of the century, but the construction of I-95, which followed the destruction of the '38 hurricane, changed all that. Now travelers speed through America's smallest state en route to Cape Cod, and in the exhaust are left inns that have seen better days. In Rhode Island alone I stopped and looked at twenty-two inns, not counting those on Block Island, of which you will find only one in the section on mainland Rhode Island.

A word of explanation about the organization of the book: within each state the inns are listed west to east in Connecticut and Massachusetts and south to north in Vermont, New Hampshire, and Maine. Each state except Rhode Island has a general introduction, and I have saved the islands for last, as a separate section. Since my definition of an island is a place you reach by boat, I have chosen to leave Mount Desert and Westport islands attached to their peninsulas in Maine.

The reader should note that all population figures are according to the 1970 census. In addition in the text, inns have private bathrooms only if specifically mentioned. For honeymooners or the young at heart, I have singled out New England's "most romantic bedrooms." Most have a double bed and a private bathroom as well as exceptional furnishings or a bed canopy or a private porch or a working fireplace, more for atmosphere than anything else. A table at the back of the book provides a handy reference for information about each inn.

In writing the final manuscript, I consulted many people to whom I am grateful for information and advice. Among those I wish to thank most wholeheartedly are Hugh Van Dusen of Harper & Row, and Geraldine Van Dusen. For his counsel on writing, I am indebted to James V. Healion, Connecticut bureau chief, United Press International. I, however, am solely responsible for the content. I will welcome comments and suggestions for future revision, which may include other inns time prevented my reviewing in this edition. Any reader may write to me c/o the Trade Department, Harper & Row, 10 East 53rd Street, New York, N.Y. 10022.

Finally, many people have asked me if I was accorded special treatment by innkeepers because I was writing a book about their inns. I thought it would be best if I paid my own way and, in turn, was treated as a casual guest so I could write, without obligation to anyone but my readers, "Inn Perspective."

April 1976

Preface

Hospitality consists in a little fire, a little food, and an immense quiet.

RALPH WALDO EMERSON
Journal [1856]

You will find inns in this book that are hidden down dirt roads, surrounded by rolling pastures and little brooks; inns set in Christmas-card villages where the wood is stacked high by the door and the glow of a welcoming light at dusk shines through the frost-embroidered windows. There are inns with antiques and braided rugs and alphabet samplers on the walls and homemade pies for dessert. In these inns you can spend the night in any one of about forty bedrooms with canopy beds. There are over one hundred bedrooms and cabins with working fireplaces, from the pine-scented Maine woods to the Litchfield and Berkshire hills, where the mountain laurel blooms the last weekend in June as if the bushes were sprouting snowballs.

There are fancy inns with plain food, and plain inns with fancy food. Some inns are very expensive and others are economical, especially if you want to bring your entire family. Some inns invite children; others exclude them. Some inns are large and formal, with the atmosphere of a resort; others are tiny and personal, with room for ten or twelve people.

There are inns in the mountains with glorious views and inns on the sea with private beaches. Some inns are nostalgic and out-of-the-way; others are pleasant stopovers for the night and easy to find. In the best tradition of New England hospitality, inns are homes away from home. They are friendly places that produce a reluctance to leave and a desire to return.

During the 1700s stagecoach stops provided food and shelter for travelers in a hurry. Today motels and motor inns are to us what stagecoach inns and taverns were in the eighteenth century. Inns are for travelers who are not in a hurry. Go to a New England motel and you could be anywhere in America. But drive to a New England inn when the leaves are copper-speckled in the fall, have dinner in a cozy, candlelit dining room, take a walk in the moon-drenched night afterward, settle in for an evening in front of a crackling fire, and fall asleep in a four-poster canopy bed, and you are definitely in New England every moment of your stay.

New England inns are offshoots of Great Britain's inns in many ways, but the American contribution to innkeeping is the American plan—a flat rate paid for dinner, one night's lodging, breakfast, and lunch—which goes back to New England in the 1830s and 1840s. At this time, travelers began using inns for stays longer than one night, so a comprehensive fee made sense. The "American" part of the plan was the New England tradition of letting strangers serve themselves from food placed on a central table. English travelers, even in the 1700s, always commented on this. They were accustomed to dining at separate tables or in their own rooms, but in America the guests pulled up their chairs to the same table.

In 1776 Samuel Johnson said, "There is nothing which has yet been contrived by man by which so much happiness is produced as by a good tavern or inn." But Johnson was speaking of English inns, where the tradition was privacy. And only two years later, in 1778, he said, "I am willing to love all mankind, except an American." The chances are excellent he would have detested the American tradition of fellowship.

You will find that this legacy of American goodwill is still shared over many dining-room tables in New England inns, where guests often eat together after being seated by the innkeeper. If you feel this is the sort of thing you too can do without, there are many inns that have separate tables in the dining room.

Only a handful of inns still operate on the American plan, but the Modified American plan—which means the price consists of dinner, a night's lodging, and breakfast—is very popular. The automobile preceded the Modified American plan, allowing travelers to explore country roads during the day. More than half the

inns in this book offer box lunches, because people like to meander at will and stop for a picnic among New Hampshire's silver
birches or near a covered bridge in Vermont.

When you pack for a trip to New England's inns, you will
want to take some maps. To write for free state maps, here are
the addresses:

Connecticut: State Highway Department, Wolcott Road,
Wethersfield, Conn. 06109

Maine: State Development Office, State House, Augusta,
Maine 04330

Massachusetts: Massachusetts, Box 1775, Boston, Mass.
02105

New Hampshire: Office of Vacation Travel, P.O. Box 856,
Concord, N.H. 03301

Rhode Island: Tourist Promotion Division, Rhode Island
Department of Economic Development, 1 Weybosset Hill, Providence, R.I. 02903

Vermont: Information Travel Division, Vermont Development Agency, 61 Elm Street, Montpelier, Vt. 05602

What is there to do at New England inns? Many inns provide facilities for activities of one kind or another. You will find
the specifics in the description of each inn. In general, though,
village inns do not offer activities on the premises, so when you
stay in a New England town, here are suggestions for things to do.

· If a town meeting is being held during your visit, go. A few
people will turn around when you walk into the Town Hall and
study you long enough to conclude that they do not know you
and you must be visiting. Then they will carry on with their
discussion about new buildings in town, the upkeep of town
roads, what to do about the overcrowded school, and how to
attract or keep away industry. You can usually determine
whether the meeting will be routine or controversial by arriving
at the Town Hall ahead of time. If clusters of people gather
outside exchanging opinions before the meeting has even begun,
the chances are you will be in on an important meeting. If people
arrive at the Town Hall and immediately walk inside, nodding
curtly to those they know, the chances are the meeting will be
routine.

• Go to the town bulletin board, usually located near the post office, and study the notices of nearby events. These notices are also posted in the front windows of general stores. You may find that church suppers, county and church fairs, antique shows, and auctions are being held nearby. In the summer the area may boast concerts, plays, and square dances.

• Take a walk around town after dinner. If you see a building lit up inside and surrounded by many parked cars outside, something interesting is probably going on. Following this advice, my husband and I have been to square dances, church services, and concert rehearsals.

• If there is a parade scheduled in town during your stay, make a point of going to it. New England's Memorial Day parades in small towns are usually delightful; so are the Fourth of July parades.

• Finally, pack your curiosity, enthusiasm, and a friendly smile. Traveling to New England inns is great fun because each inn is a new adventure and offers an individual statement about hospitality, whether you are in salt-scrubbed Maine or smelling the trailing roses on white-picket fences of Cape Cod or listening to the snow melt from the eaves in maple-sugar season in Vermont, when the days are warm and the nights are cold. New England has islands, too, and a trip to any one of them will probably be memorable.

Henry Adams wrote, "Every man carries his own inch-rule of taste, and amuses himself by applying it, triumphantly, wherever he travels." We have carried our own inch-rule of taste and no doubt you will carry your own. So consider this book, as we do, a little conversation between travelers and, most of all, have a wonderful time.

Connecticut

In the ordinary business of life, industry can do anything which genius can do, and very many things which it cannot.

HENRY WARD BEECHER
Proverbs from Plymouth Pulpit
[1887]

There is an old New England maxim that goes, "Use it up, wear it out; make it do, or do without." Over the years, Connecticut's Yankees have used it up, worn it out, and made it do, but rarely have they done without. Call it ingenuity, call it being practical, call it business acumen, call it the drive to make a fast buck. Whether you consider them shrewd or frugal, the people in New England's southernmost state have traditionally been in the forefront of inventing, manufacturing, promoting, and selling things.

Most of those things have been small in size—from thimbles and flutes to clocks and guns. But the figures alongside the dollar signs have been another story. Today Connecticut, the third smallest state in the nation, has the highest per capita personal income in the forty-eight contiguous states. In 1974, when the state's estimated population was just over three million people, the average per capita income in Connecticut was $6,455 as compared with the national average of $5,448.

Connecticut is the gateway to New England. It is bordered by New York, Massachusetts, Rhode Island, and Long Island Sound. Although Connecticut has half a dozen industrial cities, it is hard to believe this when you are walking along the dirt roads in rural areas, listening to the geese honk overhead in late September, watching the leaves turn yellow, orange, and red. Then it

1

is easy to forget that Connecticut is sandwiched between New York City to the southwest and Boston to the northeast.

"It's a great place to visit, but I wouldn't want to live there" is something you might say about a lot of states. Well, the reverse is also true. There are places better to live in than to visit, and Connecticut is one of them. Ask people why they like Connecticut and they will tell you, "It's a vibrant state, full of activity and friendly people. You can get to Boston or New York easily—if you have to go there—and you can also live in the countryside. On weekends you can go skiing in Vermont or the Adirondacks. And you don't have to have ten generations under the ground before people will talk to you."

If you look at it from a traveler's point of view, you have to use some initiative to enjoy Connecticut fully. This is the only New England state where if you just drive through on the interstate highways, you are apt to feel you could be anywhere in America. From the highways the state's only distinguishing features appear to be Hartford's golden-domed State Capitol building and its equestrian statue of Lafayette by Paul W. Bartlett, a sculptor born in New Haven in 1865. The statue is a replica of one presented to France on July 4, 1900, by the schoolchildren of America. Look closely and you will see the turtle beside one of the horse's hooves. Old-timers say the sculptor added the turtle to symbolize the length of time it took for him to be paid for the work.

There are those in Connecticut who would use the same turtle symbol to describe the Penn Central Railroad: they are Connecticut's commuters. At a May 4, 1939, press conference, Leverett Saltonstall said, "The real New England Yankee is a person who takes the midnight train home from New York." But do not be fooled by the rumor that Connecticut is merely the master bedroom for New York City's commuters who flood Manhattan by day and come slowly home to Connecticut at night. The New York part of Connecticut is Fairfield County. The rest is just Connecticut.

There are picturesque pockets in each section of the state where you will find wooden-steepled villages and narrow country lanes as inviting as any in New England. But the two most scenic areas are Windham County in the northeastern corner and Litchfield County in the northwestern corner. Windham County has

Connecticut's smallest town, Union (population 443), and more stone walls than anywhere else in the state.

In Litchfield County, U.S. 7 from Bull's Bridge in Kent north to Canaan is an especially pretty drive. It takes you past two of the state's three covered bridges, the Sloane-Stanley Museum in Kent, where old farm implements are imaginatively displayed, and the Kent Falls State Park. North of Cornwall Bridge the road meanders along the lovely Housatonic River, where fishermen wade in high rubber boots, and people in red canoes maneuver around the rocks.

The night signal used by the Green Mountain Boys, three mournful hoots of an owl, never rolled through the Connecticut hills in the eighteenth century. But Litchfield County is where Ethan Allen and many of his relatives and friends came from. Allen was New England's Paul Bunyan who led the Green Mountain Boys (among them were Seth Warner and the memorably named Remember Baker from Roxbury, and Matthew Lyon from Woodbury) in their bloodless capture of Fort Ticonderoga. The Allen family lived in Roxbury, Litchfield, Cornwall, and Salisbury before moving to Vermont. And Ethan Allen's first wife, Mary Bronson, was from Woodbury. Not all of Allen's contemporaries considered him a hero. The Reverend Nathan Perkins, a West Hartford Congregational minister, traveled through Vermont in 1789. In his diary he wrote, "Arrived at Onion-river falls & passed by Ethan Allyn's grave. An awful Infidel, one of the wickedest men yet ever walked this guilty globe. I stopped & looked at his grave with a pious horror."

Connecticut's industrial character today was determined by something that happened in 1798. It was a practical idea that marked a turning point in both the state and the nation. The man who started it all was graduated from Yale College, class of 1792. In Georgia by April 1793, he had invented the cotton gin, which made slavery in the South profitable. Then in 1798 he tried something new in New Haven that made industry in the North profitable. His name was Eli Whitney, and his idea of interchangeable parts was simple. It came to be called mass production.

On June 14, 1798, Eli Whitney signed a contract with the federal government for delivery of 10,000 muskets in twenty-eight months. He built a factory in Whitneyville (outside New Haven) and started producing firearms. His concept was to manufacture each of the musket's parts separately and then to assemble them afterward. The parts were interchangeable, and the machines were so simple that unskilled workers could operate them. The principle of mass production meant that the heyday of the individual craftsman was over. Quality may or may not have suffered but quantity was here to stay.

"Invention breeds invention," Ralph Waldo Emerson wrote. During the 1800s Connecticut proved Emerson was right. Its towns and villages produced, among other things, mousetraps, pins, looms, ivory combs, brass buttons and shoe buckles, tacks, almanacs, cookbooks, coffee mills, friction matches, ink, inkstands, hooks and eyes, sleigh bells, fishhooks, spectacles, candlesticks, applewood fifes, hinges, and latches. Even the Shakers got into the act. In 1802 in Enfield they sold the first packaged garden seeds in America.

Eli Whitney's guns were followed by clocks, covered bridges, and chairs. In 1807 Eli Terry of Plymouth Hollow contracted with the Porter Brothers of Waterbury to make 4,000 hang-up wooden clock movements at four dollars each. Before that, clock movements were brass and they cost twenty-five dollars apiece to make. The Porter brothers supplied the lumber, and the work was done by mass production. Terry's partnership with Seth Thomas and Silas Hoadley dissolved, and in 1814 Terry alone designed and built the enormously popular thirty-hour pillar-and-scroll clock with wooden movements.

In 1820 an architect named Ithiel Town, born in Thompson in 1784, patented a bridge design so simple that it could be built by any carpenter. He called it the Town Lattice Truss. It was an uninterrupted series of criss-cross diagonals that formed a diamond pattern. A competitor called it "a garden trellis fence," but it worked and was widely used. About seventy of New England's covered bridges are built this way and are still standing, including the Bull's Bridge in Kent and the West Cornwall Bridge.

After Eli Terry and Seth Thomas made the clock a common household item, and after Ithiel Town designed a bridge anyone could build, Lambert Hitchcock gave the citizenry chairs. In 1826 he started manufacturing stenciled chairs in Riverton that could be shipped in parts and assembled at their destination. On August 17, 1831, Hitchcock advertised in *The Hartford Courant* that he had "on hand a large and elegant assortment of Chairs, made after the latest and most approved patterns." The advertisement ended, "Two or three Young Men from 16 to 20 years of age, of industrious and correct habits, who will abstain from the use of ardent spirits, can have steady employment as above."

Those Connecticut clocks and chairs, and all the other items small enough to be called "Yankee notions," found their way into homes across America because of the peddler. The peddlers were the nineteenth-century's traveling salesmen. They rode on stage-coaches, walked with their wares in sacks on their backs, and stayed at New England inns, where they took orders for dry goods and notions, boots and shoes, coffee mixers, hardware, medicines, soap, horse nails, spectacles, buggy whips, tea and spices, and garden seed. In Grafton, Vermont, at Phelps Hotel (now The Old Tavern at Grafton), the guests' occupations were listed in the registry book, which can still be consulted. A button peddler, spelling his product backwards, wrote, "Snot tub." And one man, W. L. Bailey of Springfield, inscribed this self-description for posterity: "Trader in watches and great lover of girls and beechnuts." In May 1868 one judge and three lawyers named Stoddard, Wheeler, Birely, and Walker registered with this explanation: "Ober and Davis, fence trouble."

In 1833 a Scotsman named Thomas Hamilton wrote a widely circulated book, *Men and Manners in America*. This is how he described the peddlers: "The whole race of Yankee peddlers in particular are proverbial for dishonesty. They go forth annually in the thousands to lie, cog, cheat, swindle, in short, to get possession of their neighbor's property in any manner it can be done with impunity. Their ingenuity in deception is confessedly very great. They warrant broken watches to be the best time-keepers in the world, sell pinchbeck trinkets for gold; and always have a large assortment of wooden nutmegs and stagnant barometers."

The extent to which Connecticut peddlers traveled was summed up by an Englishman, G. W. Featherstonbaugh, who wrote in the 1840s, ". . . here in every dell in Arkansas and in every cabin where there is not a chair to sit on, there is sure to be a Connecticut clock." The peddlers were responsible for that, and they also gave Connecticut the nickname, the Nutmeg State.

In 1859 Bartlett's *Dictionary of Americanisms* said, "NUTMEG STATE. A nickname given to the State of Connecticut in allusion to a ridiculous story that wooden nutmegs are there manufactured for exportation." Whether anyone actually ever made wooden nutmegs and sold them to unsuspecting customers, Connecticut's reputation for cleverness in manufacturing and marketing was widespread. And after the peddlers had filled people's homes with "Yankee notions," it was a Connecticut man, Linus Yale of Stamford, who invented the first cylinder lock in 1848. Now the owners of those possessions could shut their doors for safe-keeping.

Finally, in 1866 a fifteen-year-old boy in Bridgewater had an idea that changed marketing. On July 4 Charles Bridgewater Thompson ran a classified advertisement in a newspaper offering some fine stationery for a quarter—and with it a set of free jewelry. He bought the stationery and the jewelry on credit, but he sold it all in no time and cleared more than one hundred dollars from the one advertisement. And so the idea of the premium was born. During the 1870s Thompson started America's first mail-order business in his home town, attracting customers with more premiums such as face creams, healing lotions, dolls, lanterns, air guns, hoes, and pruning shears.

Here are some Connecticut museums, including those that honor the state's tradition of invention and manufacturing. All charge an admission fee or a trolley-ride fee except where indicated:

Bristol: American Clock and Watch Museum, 100 Maple Street; more than six hundred items dating from 1790, most manufactured in Connecticut; open April to November, Tuesday through Sunday, 1 to 5.

East Haven: Branford Trolley Museum, River Street; more than eighty-five classic trolleys displayed, three-mile shoreline ride; open mid-June to Labor Day, weekdays 10 to 5; open April to December, weekends.

Essex: Valley Railroad, Railroad Avenue; vintage steam train carries passengers on hour-long round trip to Chester; open June to September, daily 10 to 5; open May and October, weekends 1 to 5.

Kent: Sloane-Stanley Museum, U.S. 7 north of town; early American craft and domestic tools, displayed in attitudes of use; grounds include ruins of Kent Iron Furnace; open Memorial Day to end of October, Wednesday through Sunday, 10 to 4:30.

Riverton: Hitchcock Chair Museum, Conn. 20; extensive collection of rare nineteenth-century Hitchcock furniture; open May to December, Tuesday through Saturday, 10 to 5.

Terryville: Lock Museum of America, 114 Main Street; collection of 12,000 locks and keys from the nineteenth century, most made in Terryville area; open May to November, Tuesday through Sunday, 1:30 to 4:30, or by appointment.

Warehouse Point: Connecticut Electric Railway Trolley Museum, Conn. 140 east of town; more than thirty refurbished trolleys dating from 1892 carry passengers on three-mile ride; open all year, weekends and holidays, 1 to 5; open summer, Tuesday through Friday, 11 to 4.

Windsor Locks: Bradley Air Museum, Conn. 75 at Bradley International Airport; vintage airplanes from the Second World War to the present; open all year, weekends and holidays, 10 to 6; open June to October, daily, 10 to 6; closed Christmas Day and in inclement weather.

Even the weather in Connecticut has been spoken of in terms that describe the people—those ambitious, ingenious manufacturers—as much as anything else. When Mark Twain gave a speech at a dinner of the New England Society in New York on December 22, 1876, he said, "There is a sumptuous variety about the New England weather that compels the stranger's admiration—and regret. The weather is always doing something there; always attending strictly to business; always getting up new designs and trying them on people to see how they will go. But it gets through more business in spring than in any other season. In the spring I have counted one hundred and thirty-six different kinds of weather inside of twenty-four hours."

Twain, who spent his boyhood years in Hannibal, Missouri, built a whimsical house in Hartford in 1874 with nineteen rooms and eighteen fireplaces for $131,000. This is where he wrote *The Adventures of Tom Sawyer* in 1876 and *The Adventures of Huckleberry Finn* in 1883. (His house at 351 Farmington Avenue and the adjacent Harriet Beecher Stowe House at 73 Forest Street are open June to August, Monday through Saturday, 10 to 5; September to May, Tuesday through Saturday, 10 to 5; all year, Sunday, 2 to 5; closed major holidays.)

In the late nineteenth and early twentieth centuries, a wave of Irish and Italian immigrants found work in Connecticut's mills and factories, raised families, and stayed. Now Connecticut is predominantly a Catholic state. In 1974 a Democrat, Ella Tambussi Grasso, whose parents were immigrants from northern Italy, became the first woman to be elected governor in her own right in the United States. She was also the first person of Italian extraction to be elected governor in Connecticut.

In 1975 Connecticut's General Assembly debated the question of what to name as the state's animal. When Sen. David Neiditz, a Democrat from West Hartford, suggested Homo sapiens, people snickered and laughed. In the end the endangered sperm whale was given the honor. But think of Eli Whitney and mass production, think of Eli Terry and Seth Thomas and the Connecticut clocks, of Ithiel Town and the Town Lattice Truss, of Lambert Hitchcock's stenciled chairs, and of the peddlers with their Yankee notions. Think of the people who started enterprises alongside rivers and streams and left Connecticut a tradition of rarely doing without. When you consider that legacy, Homo sapiens would have been an appropriate choice.

In keeping with its history of making do, Connecticut has a lot of inns in old buildings that were first used for a completely different purpose. In Woodbury, The Curtis House was a minister's home. The Old Riverton Inn in Riverton was a stagecoach stop. The Kilravock was a country estate in Litchfield. The Mayflower Inn in Washington was built to be a grammar school. And in Norwalk, The Silvermine Tavern was a speakeasy during Prohibition.

Our favorite Connecticut inn for imaginative food is The Hopkins Inn in New Preston, which also has a splendid view. The most elegant inn in Connecticut is The Kilravock in Litchfield. The best all-around inn is The Mayflower in Washington.

THE SILVERMINE TAVERN

Norwalk, Connecticut

Norwalk, to say the least, is neither a village nor a town. It is Connecticut's seventh largest city, with a population of 79,288. But Norwalk does have an unusually attractive residential section in what used to be the village of Silvermine, an hour's drive from New York City. And it has The Silvermine Tavern.

The Silvermine, a speakeasy during Prohibition, is open all year, but it is closed on Tuesdays from October through May. There are fourteen bedrooms, each with a private bathroom. The inn serves lunch and dinner (and Sunday brunch) daily for guests and the public. A Continental breakfast is available for inn guests only.

The inn has two of New England's most romantic bedrooms, T-2 in the main building and G-6 above the tavern's gift shop. Room T-2 has a little balcony overlooking the duck pond above the waterfall that once supplied power for an old mill. From the balcony you have a view of the shedding sycamore trees that line the river banks. This room has a four-poster double bed with a fishnet canopy top. So does the bedroom above the gift shop.

The Silvermine Tavern is very popular as a restaurant that can seat as many as several hundred people in its high-ceilinged dining rooms. These rooms are filled with an enormous number of fascinating old kitchen utensils displayed on the walls, along with American primitive portraits of stern-faced men and women. During our visit a June bride and groom, attended by six bridesmaids in pale-pink gowns and wide-brimmed straw hats, had an afternoon wedding reception here.

Compared with the bedrooms and the inn's furnishings, the food is ordinary. The dinner entrees include fried chicken, Boston scrod, broiled ham, sirloin steak, and baked stuffed filet of sole. The inn also has a shore dinner of clam chowder, steamed clams, soft shell crab, and boiled lobster. The ice cream used in many of the desserts, such as the ice cream pie, the meringue glacé, and the topping for the Indian pudding, is made in the inn's kitchen.

The Environs: The crossroads outside The Silvermine Tavern used to be the center of an industrial area with a mill, a country store, a grocery store, a butcher shop, a post office, a blacksmith shop. During the 1920s artists began moving here. They formed the Silvermine Guild, which features art exhibits, workshops, and concerts. Now Silvermine is a residential area where the corners of Norwalk, Wilton, and New Canaan converge. When you stay here in the summer, you can drive to the Westport Summer Theatre or to the Stratford Shakespeare Festival.

The reason Norwalk has so few seventeenth- and eighteenth-century buildings is that the town was burned on July 11, 1779, by British soldiers and Tories acting under Gov. William Tryon of New York. When the flames died down and a count was taken, this is what was burned: eighty-seven barns, eighty houses, seventeen shops, five vessels, four mills, and two churches. In his report of the action, published in a London newspaper, Governor Tryon referred to the Tories as "The king's American regiment."

Scenic Drive: Conn. 106 north to Ridgefield. In Ridgefield stop at the cemetery along the main street. Not far from the sidewalk there is a stone tablet commemorating a 1777 battle fought in Ridgefield, one of the few on Connecticut soil. The touching epitaph is a footnote to the kinship felt between many Americans and British at the time. It says, "In defense of American Independence At the battle of Ridgefield, Apr. 27, 1777 Died Eight Patriots Who were Laid in These Grounds Companioned by Sixteen British Soldiers; Living, Their Enemies, Dying, Their Guests. In Honor of Service and Sacrifice, this Memorial is Placed For the Strengthening of Hearts."

Directions to the Inn: From New York, take the Merritt Parkway to exit 38. Turn left at the end of the ramp, take another left by the firehouse at the streetlight, and drive to the inn along Silvermine Ave. From Boston, take I-95 to the Merritt Parkway to exit 40. Take U.S. 7 south, turning right at the first light onto Perry Ave. Continue on Perry Ave. for about 1.5 miles and bear left at the fork.

THE CURTIS HOUSE

Woodbury, Connecticut

Welcome to Woodbury in western Connecticut, where, as The Curtis House brochure puts it, "New England really begins."

At the meetings of The Old Woodbury Historical Society, The Curtis House is the building referred to as "the Anthony Stoddard house," in honor of its first owner, an immensely popular and influential town minister for sixty-one years. This large clapboard inn has not been owned by anyone named Stoddard since 1799. Today the sign by the inn's front door says simply,

"Built before 1736," because that was the year when the Reverend Stoddard deeded "about one acre of my homelot" to his son Eliakim "with ye Mansion thereon." That deed in the Woodbury Land Records is the first reference to the "Mansion" that is now The Curtis House.

This inn opened to paying guests in 1754, and it was a stagecoach stop in the days when an inn also functioned as a post office, a tavern, a livery, a place to eat and sleep, and a meeting hall where townspeople could gather in the second-floor ballroom. Today The Curtis House, like several other New England inns, serves as a banquet hall for local clubs, as a taproom where townspeople sometimes stop for a drink, as a very popular restaurant that can seat as many as 350 persons, and as a hostelry for travelers.

The Curtis House is open all year except on Christmas Day. There are eighteen bedrooms in the inn and a veneer-paneled annex next door. The inn serves lunch and dinner daily both to guests and the public.

Of the fourteen old-fashioned bedrooms in the inn itself, eight have private bathrooms and four-poster beds with unbleached muslin canopy tops. The rooms are furnished with maple bedsteads, small desks, television sets, nonworking fireplaces, and quaint flowered wallpaper patterns.

The disadvantage to staying here is that The Curtis House does not serve breakfast, and you must drive along Main Street to a coffee shop or diner before downing your first cup of coffee or tea. The inn's strong point is that you can still get a lot for your money here.

The dinner menu offers about twenty-five entrees and a lot of desserts. During our visit the inn was having, among other things, roast stuffed turkey, broiled bluefish, fried chicken, grilled hickory-smoked ham, broiled scrod, and broiled filet mignon. We had an onion soup made from scratch, fresh poached salmon, which was tender and moist, with Newburg sauce, mashed potatoes that tasted reconstituted, and a good apricot pie for dessert. The wine list had about twenty domestic and imported wines.

The Environs: The Curtis House is on Woodbury's busy Main Street, which is also U.S. 6. This is one of New England's most interesting and picturesque main streets because for almost two miles the houses, shops, and five churches represent the entire spectrum of this region's architectural styles from the seventeenth century to the twentieth. Antique collectors know Woodbury well because this town of 5,869 people has over thirty antique shops. But Woodbury is sometimes overlooked by travelers who have heard of Litchfield more often and go there first.

In some ways Woodbury is more interesting than Litchfield, where the substantial homes set back from the broad streets have a homogeneous, prosperous air. In Woodbury the relationship and scale of the buildings on Main Street, once an Indian trail, is varied and visually pleasing. The town exudes the atmosphere of an extended village rather than a preserved museum.

Here is a short tour that will introduce you to the town and to New England:

• From The Curtis House, go north on Main Street and turn down Hollow Road. On your left you will see the red Hurd House, owned by the Old Woodbury Historical Society. Notice the gable roof and the molded cornice at the eaves on the front and rear. It was built in the Georgian style during the early colonial period between 1674 and 1740. This was the home of John Hurd, named Woodbury's town miller on August 28, 1681.

• Across from the Hurd House you will see the nineteenth-century sawn-picket fence in front of the Jabez Bacon House, a private home. Bacon was a fabulously successful merchant who owned ships and warehouses, profited during the Revolution, and left an estate of 200,000 pounds sterling. He had this impressive Georgian gambrel-roofed house with a central chimney and pedimented dormers built for him in 1760, reputedly by a man named Roswell Moore who, like Bacon, was twenty-eight years old in 1760.

Notice the one-story servant quarters on the east side. This is where Matthew Lyon, one of the most volatile, outspoken, and restless Irishmen to call Connecticut home for a while, started life in America. He lived here as an indentured servant.

Lyon was born on July 14, 1750, in County Wicklow, Ireland, and came to America in 1765 when he was fifteen. In exchange for his passage, he became an indentured servant to Bacon, who traded him for a pair of Devon steers to Hugh Hannah of Litchfield. Later, Lyon married a niece of Ethan Allen's, served at Ticonderoga with the Green Mountain Boys, and worked as a laborer on a farm in Arlington, Vermont, belonging to Vermont's governor, Thomas Chittenden. After Lyon's wife died in 1783, Lyon married Chittenden's daughter. In 1797 he was elected to Congress as an anti-Federalist from Vermont.

On January 30, 1798, Connecticut's Rep. Roger Griswold

criticized Lyon's military record on the floor of the House of Representatives. Lyon's temper got the best of him and he spat in Griswold's face. On February 15, Griswold retaliated by hitting Lyon on the head with a stout hickory cane. On October 9, 1798, Lyon, prosecuted for his opposition to the new Sedition Laws, was sentenced to four months in Vermont's Vergennes prison and to a $1,000 fine. But he was re-elected while serving his jail term and apparently arrived in Congress just in time to cast the deciding vote electing Thomas Jefferson president over Aaron Burr.

Lyon moved from Vermont to Kentucky and represented his new state in Congress from 1803 to 1811. Then he moved to Arkansas and was elected to Congress in 1822, earning the distinction of having been the only man ever to be elected to Congress from three different states. Before he could take his Arkansas seat, he died at age seventy-five.

In the servant quarters in the nineteenth century, Collis P. Huntington, who pioneered the Central Pacific Railway, served as an apprentice to the Curtis family, who had bought the business and the property from Bacon's widow.

• Bacon used the red house next door to his own as his store. It was built between 1674 and 1740. A large warehouse in the rear was destroyed by fire. The store is now a private home.

• Continue west on Hollow Road to The Glebe House, the birthplace of the American Episcopal Church. This is where the Reverend Dr. Samuel Seabury, a Tory who was jailed in New Haven during the Revolution, was elected to be sent to England for consecration as America's first bishop. On November 14, 1784, he was consecrated in Aberdeen by three Scottish prelates. The Glebe House, built in the Georgian style in 1672, is open to the public Wednesday through Sunday. It is well worth a visit.

• From The Glebe House, turn northeast on Sycamore Road past the Old Burying Ground, where the gravestones date from 1678 and the ancestors of President Ulysses S. Grant and General William T. Sherman are buried.

• Continue to St. Paul's Episcopal Church. Construction of the church began in 1785 at the end of the late colonial period (1741–88). It was built on this site because the established Congregational Church gave a small corner of its burying ground to the Episcopalians for their church. St. Paul's interior is elegantly simple. Notice the stained-glass window in the chancel. It was placed in the church so that the sun could stream through it at Easter time.

• Across from St. Paul's Church is the commercial structure housing three stores, built during the pre–Civil War period (1829–65) in the Greek Revival style. It is at the northern end of what is known here as Greek Revival Row.

• Next to the stores, and set back from the street, is the Woodbury Town Office Building, an example of the Italianate style. This two-story brick structure with a hip roof and cupola was built in 1866–67.

• As you return to The Curtis House, you will pass the six clapboard houses along Greek Revival Row. They have gable roofs and variations in trim.

The Curtis House claims to be Connecticut's oldest continuously operated inn. When it opened, it was called The Orenaug Inn. Since then, it has been named The Woodbury Hotel, The Woodbury Inn, Foot's Tavern, Kelley and Foot's Hotel, Kelley's Hotel and Livery, and The Curtis House. It is still The Curtis House, because people have become used to the name. Over the years it has been owned by four different Curtises, none of them related.

Scenic Drive: Main Street, Woodbury.

Directions to the Inn: From New York, take I-84 east to exit 15 and U.S. 6 north to Woodbury. From Boston, take I-90 west to I-86 west to I-84 west to exit 17 and Conn. 64 west to U.S. 6 north to Woodbury. The inn is on U.S. 6.

THE MAYFLOWER INN

Washington, Connecticut

You might not think much about it when you sign a guestbook at an inn, but it is the leather-bound registration books of a century and more ago that history buffs use to reconstruct who stayed at inns, why they stayed, and how they liked it.

In some ways the entries have changed a lot over the years. When a man was asked to register in the 1800s, it was common for him to sign his name in lavish script with words like these tacked on: "and wife, 2 horses, 1 coachman." Often he would add the name of the state from which he had come, not mentioning the town.

If you look at the old guestbooks of The Mayflower Inn, you will not find any entries like that. This brown-shingled inn nestled in the Litchfield Hills was only founded in 1920. What historians will discover one day, though, are the Mayflower Logs. In these carefully preserved bound volumes, the earliest guests not only wrote their names but often made drawings, inscriptions, and water-color paintings as well.

The Mayflower Inn has long been popular with parents of students at The Gunnery, a private boys' preparatory school across Conn. 47. But the only indication of the inn from the road is a green sign in lovely script beside a shimmering pond with white swans. A narrow winding road leads you up a hillock where the three-story inn is secluded on thirty-five acres of woods, with brooks, mature maple trees, and attractive landscaped lawns and gardens.

The inn is open all year, serving three meals daily both to guests and the public. Box lunches are put up on request. There are a total of twenty-five old-fashioned bedrooms in the main inn and two separate buildings.

This cozy retreat has three of New England's most romantic bedrooms. Here these are the rooms with working fireplaces. In the Colton Cottage, the suite consists of a large sitting room with a fireplace, a bedroom with a double bed, and a private entrance. There is also a working fireplace in a room for one person in this cottage. In the main inn there are two bedrooms with working fireplaces. The bedrooms throughout the inn are furnished simply, with antique furniture, desks, fresh flowers, and white curtains and bedspreads.

When we stayed at The Mayflower, there were ten entrees for dinner, including veal goulash with noodles, broiled scrod, calf's liver with bacon, chicken in a red wine and mushroom sauce, and New York sirloin steak. We started dinner with a freshly made cream of mushroom soup loaded with thinly sliced mushrooms. The menu also offered fruitcup with sherbet, pâté maison, baked French onion soup, and marinated herring.

Among the desserts were chocolate mousse, several fruit pies, cheesecake, ice cream, and crêpes au citron filled with a thin, hot, lemon mixture. The crêpes were folded like small fans on the plate and sprinkled with a pinch or two of granulated sugar.

The inn's wine list is varied with both imported and domestic (New York State) wines. You can have a drink before dinner by a roaring fire in the tiny library, where the bar is secreted behind a paneled wall.

The Environs: For some delightful scenery a stone's throw from the inn, go back down the narrow driveway, cross Conn. 47, and turn up Conn. 199 to Ferry Bridge Road on the right side. This leads you to the Steep Rock Reservation, a park with many walking trails. Steep Rock is a cliff overlooking the Shepaug River, which curves around a promontory called the Clam Shell. Often, rock climbers practice on Steep Rock. From the cliff you may see people riding horseback on the trails below. Once in early April we saw someone swimming in the river. The water is extremely cold.

You can walk along the old Shepaug Valley Railroad bed and through the train tunnel within the park. It is no longer used, but it is still intact. This train bed was said to have covered the most crooked stretch of railroad in the United States. It went from Litchfield to Hawleyville, a distance of about twenty-five miles as the crow flies. In the process the train track made 175 curves equivalent to 17 complete circles.

Some of the most interesting museums in New England are the little ones in small towns. The Gunn Memorial Library Historical Museum is not open all the time but it is just up Conn. 47 from the inn at the corner of Wykeham Road. It is a charming museum. The items given by Washington residents and the Indian artifacts uncovered in archaeological digs conducted in town will give you a keen sense of local history. If you go to the museum, walk into The Gunn Memorial Library next door, where the ceilings are hand-painted.

The town of Washington, including Washington Depot, New Preston, and Marble Dale, has a population of 3,121. The town center, several miles north of the inn, is called the Depot. It sits in a valley beside the peaceful Shepaug, a branch of the Housatonic River, which overflowed and swept away much of the village in the raging flood of August 1955. When you drive into the Depot on Conn. 47 from the inn, notice the Salem Evangelical Covenant Church on the right side of the road. The church's stone steps marked the cresting point of the Shepaug in 1955. All the red-brick buildings housing the stores, the pharmacy, the banks, and the gas station were built after the flood.

Did George Washington sleep in Washington, Connecticut? The answer is Yes, but that is not why the town was named in his honor. In fact, it was not even the idea of the people who lived in what was called Judeah in 1779 to name this town Washington at all. For some reason, the residents asked the Connecticut General Assembly to name their town Hampden. But patriotic fervor was at full tide when the General Assembly met in Hartford on January 7, 1779. Several assemblymen managed to persuade representatives of the townspeople that the first Connecticut town named after the signing of the Declaration of Independence should be named for America's first president.

The Mayflower Inn was named in much the same way. It was built as a grammar school by G. Hamilton Gibson, the first headmaster of The Gunnery. After Mr. Gibson died, it was turned into an inn in 1920 by Harry Van Sinderen, a Gunnery alumnus, trustee, and benefactor. Mr. Van Sinderen named it The Mayflower because 1920 marked the tercentenary anniversary of the Pilgrims' landing at Plymouth Rock. So the inn, like the town itself, was named to commemorate great events that took place far away.

Scenic Drive: Conn. 199 toward Roxbury, Conn. 67 to Roxbury Station, and Conn. 133 to Bridgewater.

Directions to the Inn: From New York, take I-84 to exit 15 and U.S. 6 north to Woodbury. From Boston, take I-90 west to I-86 west to I-84 west to exit 17 and Conn. 64 west to U.S. 6 north to Woodbury. Follow U.S. 6 north through Woodbury to Conn. 47 to the turnoff for the inn.

THE BOULDERS INN ON LAKE WARAMAUG

New Preston, Connecticut

"Down the center two by two, bring that lady back with you!" That is what you will hear the square-dance caller say over the music at the weekly summer barn dance at The Boulders Inn.

This family-style inn, surrounded by 225 acres with trails through the woods, faces beautiful Lake Waramaug in western Connecticut. Innkeepers Jane and Dick Lowe, along with their children and grandchildren, have been running The Boulders since 1950. This compound of cottages, the brown-shingled inn, and the barn attract many returning guests, who look forward to using the tennis courts and to swimming and canoeing off the inn's 400 feet of private lake shoreline.

There are a total of twenty-four bedrooms in the inn and cottages behind the main building. Each has a private bathroom.

The Boulders is busiest during the summer, when three meals are served daily from late May through mid-September. All meals are open to the public except Monday dinner, when the inn has a cookout for houseguests. At dinner in the summer you can request a box lunch for the next day. The inn is open the rest of the year, but you must make reservations ahead. Breakfast is always available for inn guests, and full meal service is provided on some winter weekends.

At The Boulders the atmosphere is unusually friendly and homelike. The inn's guests typically greet newcomers with a smile and say, "Hello, how are you?" Often people sit outside while they have a cocktail before dinner. The inn is named for the gigantic boulders that form the building's foundations and two outside walls. During our visit we found guests seated on the boulders at the entrance as if they were chairs.

The inn's bedrooms are unpretentious, with light-green painted walls, white curtains, and white bedspreads. The cottages range from little old-fashioned white-clapboard structures to two newly built ones with motel-like interiors. Some are designed for families, with two or three rooms. One cottage has a working fireplace.

The blue-paper placemats on the dining room's plain-pine tables show a detailed map of the lake and the area around the inn. When we had dinner here, the entrees were whitefish, a cold poached salmon with pressed cucumbers, and beef tongue. Small, thin slices of a sweet brown bread made with cinnamon came with the meal, along with homemade white bread. The desserts included orange curaçao cake and a crème caramel.

The Environs: During the winter you can go skiing on the cross-country trails here, go ice skating, or go sledding. In the summer you can play tennis and badminton, and you can hike. There are eight trails behind the inn. The red-blazed Pinnacle Trail starts beside the inn and climbs to the top of a bald rock, altitude 1,200 feet. From here, you have a magnificent bird's-eye view of Lake Waramaug and the hills surrounding the lake.

We consider Lake Waramaug exceptionally peaceful and lovely. Other people have also spoken highly of it. The 1935 *Connecticut Guide* published by the Emergency Relief Commission called Lake Waramaug "one of the most beautiful in the State."

There are many scenic routes in Litchfield County, but the road around Lake Waramaug affords views as memorable as any.

You can drive, walk, or bicycle around it. At the northwestern tip the small Lake Waramaug State Park is a good place for a picnic. As you go around the lake, you pass through the corners of three towns: New Preston, which is part of the town of Washington (see The Mayflower Inn), Warren, and Kent.

Scenic Drive: Conn. 45 south to Conn. 25 east to Litchfield to Conn. 63 north to Conn. 4 west to U.S. 7 south to Conn. 45 to the inn.

Directions to the Inn: From New York, take I-84 east to exit 7; then U.S. 7 north to Conn. 25 north to Conn. 45 north. From Boston, take I-90 west to I-86 to I-84 west to exit 39; then Conn. 4 west to Conn. 118 west to Conn. 25 west to Conn. 45 north to the inn. The inn is on Conn. 45.

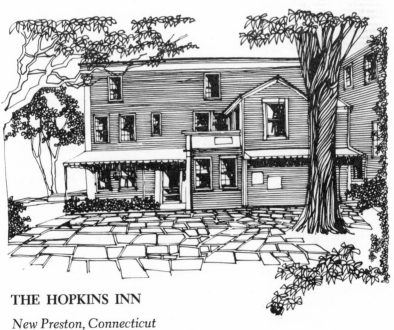

THE HOPKINS INN

New Preston, Connecticut

The Hopkins Inn serves excellent, imaginative food in a setting that is as romantic as any you will find in Connecticut.

This yellow-clapboard inn is perched on the side of a hill overlooking Lake Waramaug. In warm weather if you request a table for dinner on the outdoor terrace, you will have both a memorable meal and an unforgettable view of the colorful sail-boats skimming along the lake and of the hills surrounding it. If a terrace table is not available, make reservations indoors and ask to have a cocktail on the terrace. It is one of the loveliest places in New England from which to watch the sun set.

The Hopkins Inn is open from the beginning of May through October. Luncheon and dinner are open to the public; the inn is closed on Mondays. Breakfast is served only to house-guests. Of the eleven cheerful bedrooms, the two that overlook the lake are the front bedrooms on the second floor. Each has twin beds and a private bathroom. Room 18 on the third floor has a double bed, a blue-and-white striped ceiling, and a view of a giant maple tree.

The innkeepers are Margrit and Rudy Hilfiker, who came here in 1967 when the late Albert Stockli told Mr. Hilfiker, who once worked for Stockli, that the inn was for sale. Mr. Hilfiker spent that summer working in the inn's kitchen to determine whether to buy the inn. In 1968 the Hilfikers did.

The inn presents its menu in white chalk on a green black-board that is brought to your table. The thirteen entrees on a Saturday night we spent there included Wienerschnitzel, roast pork with a sweet paprika sauce, broiled sweetbreads, sauer-braten with spaetzle, broiled salmon, roast duck à l'orange, calf's brains, rack of lamb, and scampi à la Hopkins.

There are a lot of appetizers to choose from, such as pâté maison, smoked salmon, clams casino, eggs à la Jacques, melon, escargots, and hot barley soup. Among the dozen desserts are strawberries Romanoff, peach Melba, meringue glacé, baba au rhum, coupe aux marrons, chocolate mousse, and pear Hélène. After dinner, you can have Irish coffee, American coffee, or tea.

The inn's extensive wine list offers about thirty wines, from California Wente to Chateau Mouton Rothschild. The Hilfikers, who are Swiss, have included several Swiss wines on the list. The taproom, a cozy space, is called the Hex Bar. It used to be a laundry room. That was in the days when The Hopkins Inn was the guesthouse for The Sachem Inn, now a private home, down the road. Overnight guests ate at The Sachem Inn and then walked the few yards uphill to spend the night in this house.

The name Hopkins has been associated with this property for nearly two hundred years. Elijah Hopkins bought the land from the Indians in 1781 and built this central-chimney house in 1786. It stayed in the Hopkins family and was known as "the Hopkins place" until the Hilfikers bought it.

The Environs: When you stay at The Hopkins Inn, you can swim in Lake Waramaug off a private beach, hike in Mount Bushnell State Park, or bicycle around the lake. Every now and then at dusk, a blue haze (not pollution) envelops the lake. Each aspect of the landscape is a different shade of blue: the sky, the water, the trees, and the hills around the lake. If you photographed it, people would think you had used a blue-tinted lens.

New Preston, part of the town of Washington (see The Mayflower Inn), has a village center south of the lake on Conn. 45. If you would like to see a wonderful, solitary church made of stone with a wooden steeple, go to the village, turn by the Boys' Club, and drive up New Preston Hill. The church, built in 1824, has its pulpit at the entrance so that as you walk inside, the pews are facing you. Two attractive communities southwest of New Preston that are not on state roads are Lower Merryall and South Kent.

Although there are a variety of things to do in and around New Preston, most people who come to The Hopkins Inn have two things in mind: the food and the view. As we sat down to dinner, we overheard one woman ask another, "Did you think for a minute that you were back in Switzerland?" The woman replied, "As a matter of fact, I did."

Scenic Drive: Conn. 45 north to U.S. 7 south (past Kent Falls State Park) to Conn. 341 east to Conn. 45 south to the inn.

Directions to the Inn: From New York, take I-84 east to exit 7, U.S. 7 north to Conn. 25 to Conn. 45 north to Lake Waramaug. From Boston, take I-90 west to I-86 to I-84 west to exit 39; then Conn. 4 west to Conn. 118 west to Conn. 25 west to Conn. 45 north to Lake Waramaug. Drive north along the lake, turn left on Lake Road and follow signs to the inn.

THE KILRAVOCK INN

Litchfield, Connecticut

Ask anyone who lives in Connecticut what single town you should visit on your New England trip and the reply will probably be, "Well, have you been to Litchfield?"

Litchfield in northwestern Connecticut is best known for its village center, the first historic district designated by the Connecticut General Assembly in 1959. The well-preserved churches and large clapboard homes exude a stately, serene air along Conn. 63 just north and south of the middle of town. The Kilravock (pronounced Kil'rook) Inn is several miles west of the historic district down U.S. 202, but this inn, the most elegant in Connecticut, is just as stately, just as serene as the homes in town, and it is secluded as well.

Drive along the country lane off busy U.S. 202 and the winding stone walls lead you back to the days when Americans built country estates imitating the grandeur that marked the English aristocracy before the First World War. When we arrived here in October, the pungent aroma of wood smoke curled up from one of the inn's enormous chimneys. Scarlet leaves had started to fall on the sweeping lawns around the half-timbered stone mansion, built in 1905 in an English manor-house style.

If you grew up with Nancy Drew mysteries, you may expect the huge solid-oak door to creak with foreboding as you cautiously open it, knowing that if you were Nancy Drew, your thoughts would be riveted on finding hidden staircases and secret passages and on solving the mystery of the gypsies at Black Hall. But should you think of Nancy Drew as you listen to the wind rustling in the trees and unlatch the door handle, you will forget about unsolved mysteries the moment the door swings open.

The first thing you might see as you walk into the huge central space that opens to the roof thirty feet above is a crackling fire in the fireplace and two white West Highland terriers fast asleep alongside. With smiles, innkeepers Phillips and Lis Hoyt welcome travelers to the leisurely pace of a lifestyle that invites you to unwind. There is nothing foreboding, dark, or dreary about The Kilravock Inn.

This majestic inn has twenty-three bedrooms, five of them with working fireplaces. It is open all year except during November and December. The inn serves three meals daily for houseguests, and for the public by reservation only. The dining rooms are closed for lunch and dinner on Wednesdays during the summer and fall, and on Tuesdays and Wednesdays during the winter and spring.

A meal at The Kilravock starts in the gracious living room, where you can sit on a comfortable sofa, order a cocktail, and study the wine list and dinner menu offering entrees such as roast leg of lamb, sautéed sea scallops, club steak, and roast duck. Mrs. Hoyt, who is Danish, adds Scandinavian touches both to the food and to the unusually attractive plants and bouquets. The roast duck, for instance, was stuffed with apples and prunes. The salads included sliced tomatoes with avocado and an onion and poppy seed dressing, and a Danish cucumber salad.

The Environs: When you stay here during the summer, you can swim in the inn's large pool and play tennis on the four courts. In the winter you can ski at Mohawk and Sundown ski areas nearby. Drive west from the inn on U.S. 202 and you come to the White Memorial Foundation's 4,000-acre wildlife sanctuary. There is an excellent nature museum here, twenty-seven miles of dirt roads to walk on, and a long boardwalk over a large bog. The bird-feeding station is built so that you can watch the birds only a few feet away without the birds seeing you. There is even a path for the blind where small hemlock and spruce trees have been allowed to spread their branches so that as you walk along, you can feel the pine needles softly brush by.

In Litchfield's historic district most of the houses are private homes. Two buildings that are sometimes open to visitors are the Historical Society across from Cobble Court, a restored shopping area, and Judge Tapping Reeve's Home. Judge Reeve started the nation's first regular law school in the house next to his home on South Street in 1774. From this tiny school were graduated 101 members of Congress, 34 state chief justices, 40 judges of higher state courts, 28 senators, 14 state governors, six cabinet members, and three Supreme Court justices.

Litchfield, population 7,399, is picturesque any time of year. But at the height of the foliage season the orange, yellow, and rust-colored leaves contrast with the white churches and homes and bring the village alive. The colors punctuate the 146 acres of lawns and woodlands at The Kilravock Inn, where we studied the field of corn husks behind the inn and thought of Stephen Vincent Benét's description of Connecticut's autumn. In *John Brown's Body* he wrote,

> Here was October, here
> Was ruddy October, the old harvester,
> Wrapped like a beggared sachem in a coat
> Of tattered tanager and partridge feathers,
> Scattering jack-o-lanterns everywhere
> To give the field-mice pumpkin-colored moons.

Scenic Drive: Conn. 25 east to Conn. 63 north to Conn. 4 west to Conn. 128 (through Cornwall Center and West Cornwall's covered bridge) to U.S. 7 south to Conn. 45 south to Conn. 341 east to Conn. 25 east to the inn.

Directions to the Inn: From New York, take I-84 east to exit 7 to U.S. 7 north to Conn. 25 to the turnoff to the inn on the left side of the road. From Boston, take I-90 west to I-86 to I-84 west to exit 39 to Conn. 4 west to Conn. 118 west to Conn. 25 west to the turnoff to the inn west of Litchfield village.

THE WHITE HART INN

Salisbury, Connecticut

In Connecticut's most northwestern town you will find The White Hart Inn at the crossroads of U.S. 44 and Conn. 41, near New York State and Massachusetts.

As New England inns go, The White Hart is what we think of as "a standard inn." There is nothing especially unusual or imaginative about the inn, which is very popular as a restaurant that can seat up to 230 people at once. But The White Hart is set in the center of picturesque Salisbury, population 3,573, and it is a convenient stopover for travelers touring western New England.

At The White Hart, open all year, there are twenty-two bedrooms, each with a private bathroom. These are located in the main inn, in the attractive annex, and in an adjacent motel. The old-fashioned rooms are furnished with subdued wallpaper patterns, small desks, and white candles in glass candleholders. Three simple meals are served daily for guests and the public. A gift shop called The New England Country Store occupies a lot of space on the inn's first floor, not far from the taproom.

The Environs: In the fall The White Hart Inn attracts visitors who enjoy the foliage along the many scenic roads. During the winter skiers often make this their home base and decide, once they are here, whether to drive to Catamount Ski Area in Hillsdale, New York, or to Butternut Basin or Otis Ridge, both in Massachusetts' Berkshire Hills. Snow conditions can vary a great deal on either side of the mountainous ridge.

Since The White Hart is a village inn, you can park your car outside and walk along the main street, browsing in the inviting shops and in the Housatonic Bookstore. This is a beautiful bookstore in an old white house with black shutters and a nice wood-paneled door. Walk to the fountain beside the church and you will probably find hikers and visitors, young and old, filling their containers with the pure spring water. There are, at the most, two or three of these springs left in Connecticut, and this is the only one with such a lovely setting.

If you would like to hike and be rewarded with the best view in Connecticut, ask the inn to make you a box lunch. Put it in your day pack, fill a canteen, wear wool socks and boots, and follow these directions: Drive north on Conn. 41 for about three miles, watching on the left for the blue-blazed Under Mountain Trail. Park along the road, follow this trail 1.89 miles, turn right on the white-blazed Appalachian Trail and continue .85 miles to the Bear Mountain summit. From the forty-foot cairn on the top, you will have a splendid panoramic view of three states. Look east and south and you will see the sparkling Twin Lakes in the Housatonic Valley. To the west lies New York State and to the north the Berkshire Hills. They say that on a clear day you can see as far north as Mount Greylock.

Salisbury is not far from U.S. 7, which is still the primary north-south route from southwestern Connecticut to northwestern Vermont. It is a pretty drive from U.S. 7 west along U.S. 44 to the inn. If you take Conn. 41 north from the inn, you have views of the stark Taconic Range paralleling the road to the west. The Appalachian Trail runs along the ridge of these mountains, which include Connecticut's highest peak, Bear Mountain, 2,316 feet in altitude.

Scenic Drive: U.S. 44 west to Conn. 41 south to Conn. 361 south to Conn. 4 east to U.S. 7 north to Conn. 126 north to U.S. 44 west to Salisbury.

Directions to the Inn: From New York, take the Taconic Parkway north to the exit for Millbrook and follow U.S. 44 east to Salisbury. From Boston, take the Mass. Turnpike west to exit 2; follow signs to U.S. 7 south to U.S. 44 west to Salisbury.

THE OLD RIVERTON INN

Riverton, Connecticut

When John Kenney left his West Hartford shoe store one April day in 1946 to "go a-fishing," as he put it, he hoped to catch a trout from the West Branch of the Farmington River. He did not get the trout. Instead, he spent the afternoon at The Old Riverton Inn, and he came up with a notion that has since put this village back on the map.

What was Kenney's idea? To manufacture again the stenciled chairs designed and produced here between 1826 and 1840 by Lambert Hitchcock. Even as he sat in The Old Riverton Inn that day, poring through books for facts about the town and Lambert Hitchcock, Mildred and James Zucco were restoring and remodeling what had once been The Jesse Ives Tavern. But Kenney had no way of knowing that the timing was auspicious.

In fact, however, the factory and the inn had been companions from the start, just as their respective builders, Hitchcock and Ives, had been. When one prospered, so did the other. And when one started a gradual decline, the other eventually followed suit. In 1946 the inn, once a stagecoach stop, was getting a new coat of paint and so, in time, would the dilapidated factory.

To make a long story short, Kenney saw his dream realized. Now Riverton is known for the handsome white-brick factory with red trim, old-fashioned signs, a weather vane, and a stream of stenciled Hitchcock reproductions. And right across the river from the factory and showrooms, Mildred and James Zucco are still welcoming guests at The Old Riverton Inn.

This is an informal inn with twelve pleasant bedrooms, each with a private bathroom. The most spacious rooms here, furnished with flowered wallpaper, small desks, and nonworking fireplaces, tend to be those with twin beds. The inn is open all year. It is closed on Mondays and Tuesdays and on Christmas Day. (Sometimes it also closes for a month during the winter when everyone who works here takes a vacation at the same time.) The inn serves lunch and dinner daily to guests and the public. Breakfast is available only for houseguests. Box lunches are put up on request.

The Old Riverton is especially popular at lunch, when you may find the dining room occupied almost exclusively by women who have come to Riverton for a day's outing. Mrs. Zucco once overheard a visitor during the fall-foliage season remark to a friend, "I have no idea where we are, but isn't it nice?" Most people come here on purpose, though. They are in Riverton to see the factory, to visit the Hitchcock Museum in the stone church nearby, to enjoy the drive along the river on the way, and to eat at The Old Riverton.

The inn has an extensive, reasonably priced menu for lunch, with entrees such as baked stuffed pork chop, ham or cheese omelets, corn fritters and bacon, chicken-salad plate, Beef Stroganoff, baked stuffed shrimp, broiled Boston scrod, beef burgundy with wild rice, and broiled stuffed filet of sole. The desserts usually include several pies, a peppermint-stick sundae, and a variety of ice creams. The inn has a wine list and serves cocktails. Jackets are required in the dining room. The house salad dressing, commonly called "French," is made and bottled for sale at the inn.

The Old Riverton is perhaps best known for its candlelit buffet dinner, which has been served (at modest prices) every Wednesday from 5 to 8:30 since December 1946, except for two Wednesdays during and after the August 1955 flood.

The Environs: The Hitchcock Chair Company factory, closed on Sundays, is open on Wednesdays from 9 to 9 and the rest of the week from 9 to 5. Sometimes you can watch the weavers making chair seats out of real fiber rush. There are attractive displays of "seconds" on chairs, tables, cabinets, desks, bedsteads, mirrors, and tinware, all with various stencil designs.

Riverton, legally part of the town of Barkhamsted, has its own post office, which was built in the 1960s by the chair company. The post office bears the name "Riverton" and then, in parentheses, "Hitchcocks-ville." The village's original name was Hitchcocks-ville, but it was changed to Riverton in 1865 because mail to residents of Hitchcocks-ville sometimes wound up in Hotchkiss-ville, a section of Woodbury.

Even if you do not stop at the chair factory, be sure to step inside the John Tarrant Kenney Hitchcock Museum in the Old Union Church. The memorabilia of Hitchcock's life and times are imaginatively displayed in a wonderful space decorated with hand stenciling. (The museum is open on Saturdays only from December 1 through April 30, and daily except Sundays and Mondays the rest of the year.) Most New England nineteenth-century churches were made of wood, but this one was built in 1829 of hand-cut granite. Both Hitchcock and Ives were on the church building committee. Hitchcock was married to Eunice Alford here on October 30, 1830, and Ives is buried in the plot behind the church.

For an extremely rewarding hike, drive or walk south from the inn along the road beside the river to the site of the Barkhamsted Lighthouse. Follow the trail that turns off here and climbs 299 stone steps to the Overlook, where you will have a view of the Farmington Valley and the hills twenty miles away. Just north of the Overlook, Chaugham Lookout provides a fifteen-mile view of the valley in which Riverton sits. The hike is about two miles round trip.

If you come to Riverton on the third Saturday in April, the first day of Connecticut's fishing season, you will find anglers casting their lines in the Annual Fishing Derby from 6 to 10 A.M. It is sponsored by the chair company in commemoration of the day in 1946 when John Kenney went "a-fishing." Whoever catches the largest fish wins a Hitchcock chair.

Scenic Drive: Conn. 20 north to Hartland, West Hartland, and East Hartland to Conn. 179 south to Conn. 219 south to Conn. 318 to Conn. 181 to the right hand turnoff through Peoples State Forest to Riverton.

Directions to the Inn: From New York, take I-84 east to Conn. 8 north to Conn. 20 to Riverton. From Boston, take the Mass. Turnpike to the Westfield exit, follow Route 10 south to Granby, Connecticut, and Conn. 20 west to Riverton. In Riverton, follow signs to the chair factory and continue over the river to the inn.

THE GENERAL LYON INN

Eastford, Connecticut

Nathaniel Lyon's likeness graces the sign in front of this homey, white-clapboard inn with the traditional dark-green shutters typical of New England towns. Cozy and informal, the inn sits in one of Connecticut's least developed areas, Windham County, at the center of the "town with six corners" that used to be a stagecoach stop. In 1970 Eastford's population was 922.

You will have a sense of history in Eastford because this is where Nathaniel Lyon, the first northern general killed in the Civil War, was born. But Lyon was idolized here as a career army officer even before he died at age forty-three a thousand miles from home at Wilson Creek, Missouri. After the August 10, 1861, battle, the news of Lyon's death was sent to his hometown by telegraph. The operator who received the message was inexperienced, but he understood and the news spread through town like brushfire.

It was raining the night Lyon's body was brought home for burial in September, but men, women, and children turned out anyway, carrying lamps, lanterns, and candles to light the way to the church. The next day, about fifteen thousand people came to Lyon's funeral. According to a *Hartford Courant* newspaper story at the time, Lyon "left practically all his property, about $30,000, to the government for which he gave his life."

The General Lyon is a small inn with simple home cooking, seven plain, old-fashioned bedrooms, and three bathrooms. The bedrooms are furnished with antiques and have wide sloping floorboards. The one room with a double bed is in the guesthouse or annex. If you are looking for good value you will find it here. The inn is open all year, serving lunch and dinner daily to the public and breakfast to houseguests only. On request the inn will put up box lunches.

The inn's dining room is charming, with lace tablecloths, African violets in the center of each table, and cut herbs in little vases. Mrs. John Bowen, the innkeeper's wife, makes the soups from scratch. Among the most popular soups is an English eighteenth-century beef marrow ball soup. The dumplings are made of sieved marrow, eggs, dried bread, and herbs. On the Saturday when we visited, the inn was having fruitcup, beet soup, rib roast with Yorkshire pudding, and half a dozen other entrees. Mrs. Bowen maintains the New England tradition of serving baked beans every Saturday night. The desserts range from hot deep-dish apple pie to Indian pudding and ice cream.

Liquor has been an issue in Eastford for many years. In 1875 when the question of whether to grant a license to sell liquor was put to vote at a town meeting, the "yeas" and "nays" seemed so equal that a hand vote had to be taken. The official tally was one hundred "no" and ninety-one "yes." The liquor license was denied. Even when Eastford was "wet," Lieutenant Lyon and others would enjoy a drink in the inn that was called Temperance Tavern. Since Eastford is a dry town today, you must bring your own wine or liquor to the inn.

Temperance Tavern was named The Eastford House when Waldo and Beatrice Kennedy bought it for $600 in 1918. The Kennedys changed the name after Judge James Tatem stopped by one day. "If you'll change the name from The Eastford House to The General Lyon Inn, I'll give you the lye stone from Lyon's birthplace down the road," he said. The Kennedys liked the idea, and today you will find the lye stone, once used for making soap, at the foot of the steps to the dining-room entrance.

After they changed the name, the Kennedys received an unexpected house-warming gift. It was from General Lyon's grandnephew, who decided to repay a favor the Kennedys had done for him. While they ran a store in town for two years, the Kennedys had given him bones for his dogs free of charge. In 1919 the grandnephew presented them with a package. In it was a teapot that had belonged to the general's mother. (You will see the teapot on the dining-room mantel.) Mrs. Kennedy ran The General Lyon from 1918 until 1975, an innkeeping stint of fifty-seven years.

The Environs: For a delightful side trip, drive to the Vernon Stiles Tavern in the picturesque village of Thompson, about a mile east of Conn. 52. This inn is a lovely, out-of-the-way place to visit for lunch or dinner daily except Tuesday. It is on the Thompson common (at the juncture of Conn. 193 and 200) next to a white-steepled church designed by Ithiel Town. One of the men on the church-building committee that selected Town in 1815 was John Nichols, part owner of a cotton factory and a brick factory, who built the handsome white-brick mansion, now privately owned, across from the inn.

Scenic Drive: Conn. 169 from Woodstock south to Canterbury.

Directions to the Inn: From New York or Boston, take I-86 to exit 100. Follow U.S. 44 east and Conn. 198 north to Eastford. The inn is at the center of town.

Rhode Island

THE WEEKAPAUG INN

Weekapaug, Rhode Island

All along the New England coast people still tell stories about where they were and what happened to their property in the hurricane of 1938. When the hurricane struck the southern Rhode Island shore at Weekapaug on September 21, 1938, the summer season at this resort had just ended. As the winds howled and the white-capped waves crashed against the fine sandy beach, the five people working in the inn that day were rescued through deep water before mid-afternoon. Between 3:30 and 3:50 P.M. two thirty-foot tidal waves hit The Weekapaug Inn. It had been a gracious hotel where people came for the entire summer since Frederick C. Buffum, Sr. built it right on the beach in 1899. The severe storm chewed off the front of the inn, carrying about a dozen bedrooms into the Atlantic Ocean and washing away all the outbuildings.

Once Frederick C. Buffum, Jr. had surveyed the damage, he decided to rebuild the inn back from the beach. The question was, Where would the money come from? There was no flood insurance at the time and no federal aid forthcoming. But the community of Weekapaug had been built around The Weekapaug Inn and local banks responded to a local cause. They came through with financing, and ground was broken in February 1939. In four short months this spacious, three-story brown-shingled inn was built. There was just one drawback. The Buffums had to open their summer season one week late that year.

Today The Weekapaug Inn is open from mid-June through early September, serving three meals daily to guests and the public and putting up box lunches on request. This is a large place. It has eighty bedrooms, each with a private bathroom. Some cottages are available on the American plan during the season; you can also stay in the cottages (and families often do) on a no-food basis before and after the season.

Although many of Rhode Island's beach hotels never fully recovered from the 1938 hurricane, The Weekapaug Inn bustles with the activities of a friendly staff, starting with the bellboy who greets you by name when you first arrive. Most guests, between fifty and eighty years old, congregate in the three large living rooms on the inn's second floor, exchanging news of the past year and addressing even long-time acquaintances as "Mr." and "Mrs."

In the large, low-ceilinged dining room, dinner consists of six courses: appetizer, soup, fish, entree, dessert, and cheese. In addition, relishes, rolls, a vegetable, a potato, salad, and coffee come with the meal. All the portions are small, so you can eat everything and not feel uncomfortable afterwards. When we visited, the entrees were roast ribs of beef, broiled scallops, baked spring chicken, and an omelet with a creamed lobster filling. For the fish course, the broiled Block Island flounder was memorably fresh and served with melted butter and sliced almonds. The inn does not have a liquor license, but there is a bar upstairs where drinks are mixed for those who have brought their own provisions.

In the dining room the hostess will introduce you to the busboy and waitress to whom you have been assigned. After dinner you will find your bed has been turned down, and after breakfast you will find that your bed has already been made and that fresh towels have been placed in your bathroom.

The bedrooms are furnished in a plain manner, with small desks, beige-painted walls, wooden chairs with cushions, white bedspreads, and white candles in glass candleholders. Many rooms look out on the inlet, which acts as a buffer zone between the inn and the Atlantic Ocean, a matter of yards away. In each bedroom there is a small, neat card above a white buzzer. It says, "Ring once for Bell-Boy, Twice for Ice Water, Three times for Chambermaid." For all these services, the atmosphere here is deceptively casual, as if all the work behind the scenes were merely so much pleasantry.

Many people stay at The Weekapaug Inn for as long as three or four weeks each summer, whereas others come for a week or a weekend. Since there are so many returning guests, the overall feeling is like that of a genteel, friendly club. In one living room a woman asked another, "Did you bring your photographs of the family this year?" "Oh, dear," said the second, "I meant to pack them and forgot." "And a good thing, too," said her husband. "You packed everything else in the house."

The Environs: Besides swimming in the Atlantic Ocean, you can play tennis here on the inn's courts, go fishing and sailing, and play golf at an eighteen-hole private course four miles from the inn. The beach at Weekapaug is a lovely undeveloped stretch of sand that extends for miles. Some guests like to go to Mystic Seaport in Connecticut for the day. Others look forward to the inn's annual lawn-bowling tournaments. (Wooden plaques on the living-room walls record the names of tournament winners and runners-up since 1959.)

Scenic Drive: Along the ocean to Watch Hill.

Directions to the Inn: From New York, take I-95 to exit 1 marked R.I. Beaches to R.I. 3. Take R.I. 3 south to R.I. 216 south to R.I. 91 south. At Dunn Corner continue straight to Weekapaug. From Boston, take I-95 to exit 1 to R.I. 3.

Massachusetts

and the History of Innkeeping

Classics which at home are drowsily read have a
strange charm in a country inn. . . .

RALPH WALDO EMERSON
English Traits [1856]

Massachusetts, from the Berkshires to Cape Cod, is the geographical and cultural hub of New England. It is this region's most populous state, with 5,689,170 people. Boston, known for baked beans, banking, Harvard University, and the Boston Symphony Orchestra (affectionately called the BSO), is New England's major city and metropolitan area, the eighth largest in the nation. Boston is also where the transportation trends in New England were established first and where the tradition of northern innkeeping began.

When Gov. William Bradford, who came on the *Mayflower*, recalled the Pilgrims' landing in 1620, he wrote, "They had no friends to wellcome them, nor inns to entertaine or refresh their weatherbeaten bodys." It was not long before the Massachusetts settlers had inns, and from the beginning the American inns provided a lot more than refreshment.

Until 1639 the only "postmasters" were ship's captains who brought mail from overseas and received a penny for each letter, collected from the sender or the addressee. In 1639 the General Court of Massachusetts stated that if you wanted to send a letter, you could deposit it with anyone you chose, but from then on all incoming mail would be delivered to one place in Boston. That place was Richard Fairbanks' Tavern. In New England, inns were used as post offices for more than 150 years. In 1773 a

British postal inspector, Hugh Finlay, complained about the careless way letters were kept on tavern tables and bars so that anyone could sift through the mail.

In the 1600s New England inns were called "ordinaries," and they were built not so much for travelers as for the townspeople. Sometimes religious services were conducted in the inn until a church or meetinghouse could be built. Other times, the church was built first, and licenses to keep inns were granted on the condition that the inn be sited near the church. Before and after Sunday services, parishioners gathered and drank in the inn. The idea was that the inn was a warm place in the winter to wait for church services to begin and to stop on the way home. But in the mid-1600s so many parishioners went to the inn before church began and never got to church at all that the General Court of Massachusetts ordered inns within a mile of a church to close during church services.

In Vermont some parishioners went one step further. They took their cider to church with them: a resident of one town remembered, "I have known even ministers of the Gospel who made no secret of taking a glass of grog before entering the pulpit to preach; and many of their hearers carried their flasks of cider brandy in their pockets to church, and they were freely and fearlessly passed around at intermission, with the understanding that if it assisted the minister to preach, it also assisted them to hear and understand."

During the 1600s people traveled only if they really had to, and they did it on horseback or with a horse and cart. Still, the General Court in Connecticut in 1644 ordered each town to name someone "to keepe an Ordinary for provision and lodgeing in some comfortable manner, that such passengers or strayngers may know where to resorte." The court required stabling for two horses and suggested a spare room. Any town that did not comply within a month had to pay a monthly fine. In 1656 the General Court of Massachusetts passed a similar law.

Around 1700 the word *ordinary*, to mean an inn, was not used much anymore. People called inns *taverns*. They drank in them (mostly drinks made with rum), they signed land deeds in them, they used the upper rooms as temporary jails, they held court in tavern parlors at noon, and the town selectmen met in them.

Taverns in New England became the center of a community's business and social activities, just as plantations were in the South. When a plantation owner knew a traveler was approaching down the road, he would often send someone to the tree-shaded entrance to invite the passing stranger to stay the night. It was a good way for a plantation owner to keep in touch with news from far away, and it established the tradition of hospitality at home in the South.

In New England the first turning point in the history of inns was the coming of the stagecoach. It appeared in the early 1700s and dominated transportation on land until the railroad arrived. On May 13, 1718, a stagecoach started running from Boston to Rhode Island. For more than one hundred years, stagecoach drivers, wearing bearskin caps and greatcoats made of buffalo skin, stopped at New England taverns for passengers, luggage, mailbags, and students going to college. Their coaches clattered over "corduroy" roads made of logs and slowly crossed small streams and muddy lowlands. In 1765 *The New England Almanack* gave two stagecoach routes from Boston to Hartford. The distances were listed from tavern to tavern. As the roads improved after about 1750, people traveled more on business, but not for pleasure.

As the Revolutionary War approached, inns were where people gathered to exchange opinions over a glass of flip. In Massachusetts the Sons of Liberty met in the Liberty Tree Tavern in Boston. On April 18, 1775, the Minute Men rallied at Buckman Tavern. After the Battle of Lexington, the soldiers reassembled at the Red Horse Tavern (now the Wayside Inn) in Sudbury and at the Black Horse Tavern in Winchester. Samuel Adams, John Hancock, and Paul Revere, among others, discussed the question of adopting the federal Constitution in the Green Dragon Tavern. The Green Dragon was used as a hospital during the war, when many taverns were recruiting offices.

During and after the Revolution the signboards in front of New England taverns came down and were repainted. When they were hung again, the names had changed. There were a lot of New England inns named The King's Arms before the Revolution. Afterward, they were renamed Washington Tavern or Hancock Tavern. In a Boston tavern named The Bunch of Grapes, an early insurance broker named John Hurd set up business. In

Hartford at another Bunch of Grapes, Noah Webster met with an aide to Col. Jeremiah Wadsworth in 1793 to discuss starting a bank in Hartford. Tavern signs depicted horses, coaches, animals such as rabbits and foxes, Indians, and, at The Bunch of Grapes, a bunch of grapes.

What was it like to stay at an inn in the stagecoach days? During the 1700s travelers at a stagecoach stop ate at the same table, and in isolated areas there was usually a set menu for dinner. In Maine guests might be served baked lobster. Near the Connecticut River during the spring they would have eaten fresh shad. Other times, the taverns served boiled meats such as mutton, ham, beef, and ox tongue. Roast meats were also offered, but boiled meats were more popular. For breakfast, a country inn might have fried salt pork or corn-meal mush. At a city tavern, though, the menu often included eggs, potatoes, bread, boiled beets, steak, and pie.

Early travelers reported that in the middle of the night the innkeeper would sometimes arrive, holding a candle, with another traveler who would climb in the other side of your bed. The Marquis de Chastellux wrote at the time that "it very commonly happens that after you have been fed, a stranger of any condition comes into the room, pulls off his clothes and places himself, without ceremony, between your sheets."

Sometimes travelers who kept journals wrote about the innkeepers, rather than the food or lodging. In 1791 John Lincklaen wrote, "Sunday, October 2nd. By the laws of Vermont it is not permitted to travel on this day, but we risked being arrested, & started for Burlington Bay, where happily we arrived at Col. Keyes. He is obliged to keep tavern by the situation of the place, is truly amiable, has been well educated & had many attainments. We are very comfortable at his house, & very glad to spend some days here to refresh ourselves & recover from the fatigues & the bad roads we have just come through."

But even the "amiable" Colonel Keyes was capable of losing his temper. Two years earlier, in 1789, the Reverend Nathan Perkins wrote, "At Burlington Bay Col. Stephen Keyes whipped bruised & almost killed a Dr. Stephens last month because he brought in a high bill for attending his father-in-law, Col. Sheldon, when sick there the winter past." The Reverend stayed with ministers during his Vermont trip on horseback but sometimes stayed with families willing to take a lodger. Once, when he got lost in the woods and his horse sank into the mud to his belly, he traveled on until "I found a little log hut & put up there. Could get no supper—my horse no feed—Slept on a Chaff-bed without covering—a man, his wife & 3 children all in the same nasty stinking room."

If northern Vermont was unrefined in the 1790s, all that had changed by the time an Englishman named James S. Buckingham arrived in Danville, Vermont, by stagecoach from Montpelier in 1838. He wrote, "The driver of our first stage from Montpelier, like all we have yet seen in America, was remarkably kind to his horses. Though he drove faster and steadier than any who had yet driven us, he never used his whip to touch the horses, but merely smacked it in the air, and talked to the animals as though he believed they understood every word he said."

This is how Buckingham described the Danville inn: "We reached Danville at seven o'clock. The inn at which we stopped was a very humble one, but clean in every part. We retired early and slept in the first curtained bed since our leaving England a year ago. We had seen four-post beds with curtains, in private houses, but in no hotel or boarding-house, not even in the depth of winter, till this at Danville."

But even as James Buckingham fell asleep in a four-poster curtained bed in Danville in 1838, a new trend had started in Boston. It was the railroad, and it overtook the stagecoach very quickly. In 1832 there were 106 stagecoach lines from Boston. Only three years later, in 1835, the Boston and Lowell, the Boston and Providence, and the Boston and Worcester railroads opened for business. Stagecoaches continued to run, especially in northern New England, but the railroads were here to stay. On January 7, 1843, Ralph Waldo Emerson of Massachusetts was at Barnum's Hotel in Baltimore when he wrote in his *Journal*, "The railroad, which was but a toy coach the other day, is now a dowdy lumbering country wagon. . . . The Americans take to the little contrivance as if it were the cradle in which they were born."

As the railroad tracks were laid, they carried a new concept with them. It was travel for pleasure's sake, and it resulted in the country hotel. In New England, people began to travel in earnest for pleasure after the Civil War ended in 1865. Usually, they packed their luggage, took the train, and went somewhere for several weeks, if not the entire summer. Some of New England's most popular destinations in the 1870s were Bar Harbor, Maine; Nantucket Island off Massachusetts; Newport, Rhode Island; Lenox in the Massachusetts Berkshire Hills; Mount Mansfield, Vermont's highest peak; and the White Mountains in New Hampshire.

In the late 1800s many inns were called hotels. One hotel, built in 1884 in Deerfield, Massachusetts, was not named for over a year. But a local correspondent who sent news to *The* [Greenfield, Massachusetts] *Gazette and Courier* included sporadic comments about the hotel's progress. The first item appeared on May 26, 1884: "J. D. Bradley from Bridgeport, Conn., has opened a hotel in the building erected by George A. Arms near the post office and will have a livery stable in connection." The reporter said nothing more about the hotel (now The Deerfield Inn) until mid-summer, but there was plenty of news about the weather. It was terrible. There were late spring frosts, a summer "drouth," and a grasshopper plague.

But the visitors came anyway. On July 14, the newspaper reported, "The old street is filling up with summer visitors. . . . Bradley has a good business at the new hotel." Those grasshoppers must have given people a lot to talk about. This is what the Deerfield correspondent had to say about them:

[*July 21, 1884*] The grasshoppers have got over the Conway line and are clearing the fields of all crops as they go.

[*July 28, 1884*] The ravages of the grasshoppers are every day becoming more wide-spread. . . . In many places the fields are left as clean of vegetation as a floor, and it is doubtful if the grass starts up again.

By September, some Franklin County farmers had already slaughtered their cattle because there was no grass for them to eat and the farmers had run out of grain. The harvests were drastically reduced that year. But the people who came for the summer stuck it out in spite of the heat and the grasshoppers. On September 1, the newspaper correspondent wrote, "The summer boarders are folding their tents and stealing away, browner and better for their stay."

Some of the most enthusiastic summer travelers in the 1800s were a group of Massachusetts gentlemen who knew each other and whose paths we ourselves have crossed at least a dozen times. They stayed in inns, primarily in New Hampshire, Massachusetts, and Vermont. When you visit New England's inns, you will come across their names, too, in books tucked away in living rooms, entry halls, and bedrooms. They are Massachusetts' authors.

In August 1868 Ralph Waldo Emerson stayed at the Mountain House on Mount Mansfield in Vermont. In the morning "a man went through the house ringing a large bell, and shouting Sunrise." Emerson was also apparently the first of the Massachusetts authors to stay at a famous nineteenth-century hostelry in the White Mountains of New Hampshire. It was Ethan Allen Crawford's inn. On July 14, 1832, Emerson spent the night here and wrote in his *Journal*, "The good of going into the mountains is that life is reconsidered." In September 1832 Nathaniel Hawthorne stayed here and later wrote "The Great Stone Face" and "The Great Carbuncle." And in 1836 the poet Henry Wadsworth Longfellow spent the night of August 26 at Crawford's inn. John Greenleaf Whittier visited the White Mountains in 1835 and again in the 1840s. He wrote the poems "Mary Garvin" and "In The Crystal Hills" about the mountains.

Henry David Thoreau kept a journal of his trip to the White Mountains in 1849. It was called *A Week on the Concord and Merrimack Rivers*. He returned to the White Mountains in 1858, but he did not stay at Crawford's. Thoreau, who lived in a cabin on Walden Pond in Concord during the 1840s, slept outdoors in New Hampshire. He later reported, "I heard that Crawford's House was lighted with gas, and had a large saloon, with its band of music, for dancing. But give me a spruce house made in the rain."

Here are some Massachusetts authors' homes you can visit today (all require admission or a donation except for Walden Pond):

Amesbury: John Greenleaf Whittier Home, 86 Friend Street; open all year except Thanksgiving and Christmas, Tuesday to Saturday, 10 to 5.

Amherst: Emily Dickinson Home, 280 Main Street; open all year on Tuesdays, 3 to 5, and from May 1 through October 1 on Fridays also, 3 to 5; reservations required; call (413) 542-2321.

Cambridge: Henry Wadsworth Longfellow House, 105 Brattle Street; open all year, daily, 9 to 4:30.

Concord: Louisa May Alcott House, Lexington Road, near Hawthorne Lane; open from mid-April through mid-November,

Monday to Saturday, 10 to 5, and Sunday, 1 to 5.

Concord: Ralph Waldo Emerson House, 1 Cambridge Turnpike; open from April 15 through November 1, Tuesday to Saturday, 10 to 5, and Sunday, 2 to 5; closed Mondays except holiday Mondays.

Concord: Old Manse, Monument Street; Emerson's grandfather built this house, and Nathaniel Hawthorne lived here; open from April 19 through May 31, weekends only; open from June 1 through October 15, daily, Monday to Saturday, 10 to 4:30, Sunday, 1 to 4:30; open from October 16 through November 11, weekends only.

Concord: Walden Pond State Reservation; 150 acres with picnic facilities, fishing, boating, nature trails, and a plaque marking the site of Thoreau's cabin.

Cummington: William Cullen Bryant Homestead; open June 15 through Labor Day on Saturdays, Sundays, and holidays only, 2 to 5.

Salem: House of Seven Gables (Nathaniel Hawthorne), 54 Turner Street; open from July 1 through Labor Day, daily, 9:30 to 7:30; open from Labor Day through July 1, daily, 10 to 4:30.

Almost all the inns we selected in Massachusetts have swimming facilities. The Craigville Inn and The Melrose Inn on Cape Cod both have a private beach. The Yankee Clipper Inn has a salt-water pool and swimming off the huge rocks. Most of the other inns have swimming pools, including The Col. Ebenezer Crafts House, which is part of The Publick House in Sturbridge.

The best Massachusetts inns for imaginative food are the Cornwall House (the restaurant is called La Méditerranée) on Cape Cod in North Truro and The Williamsville Inn on Mass. 41, a back road, in West Stockbridge in the Berkshires. The Deerfield Inn has the state's most outstanding village setting on Main Street in Old Deerfield Village. Massachusetts also has the oldest operating inn in the United States: The Wayside Inn in Sudbury.

Our favorite all-around Massachusetts inn has the best of the Bay State's two worlds: the sea and the hills. It is named for a speedy clipper ship, but it is nestled in a secluded corner of the undulating Berkshire Hills: The Flying Cloud Inn in New Marlboro.

THE IVANHOE COUNTRY HOUSE

Sheffield, Massachusetts

This is a guesthouse on the eastern side of Massachusetts' Taconic
Range along scenic Undermountain Road, which is Mass. 41.

The Ivanhoe is open all year, serving a Continental breakfast to houseguests and no other meals. There are five bedrooms,
including a double-bedded room (called Sunrise) with a working
fireplace. Innkeepers Carole and Dick Maghery put a coffee
maker and a tin of sweet cinnamon rolls outside each guestroom
at night so you can open your door, bring the tray inside, and
plug in the coffee maker whenever you wake up.

Staying here has its advantages. There is a secluded feeling
to the setting because the guesthouse nestles in the shadow of
Race Mountain. And there are so many things to do in the Berkshires—from Tanglewood in the summer to skiing in the winter—
that you often have to make reservations well ahead of time for a
weekend at an inn. If you stay at The Ivanhoe Country House,
though, you can sample the food at various inns in the Berkshires,
most of which serve dinner, if not lunch as well, to the public. Or
you can buy your own food and request a room at The Ivanhoe
with a kitchenette unit.

Drive south from The Ivanhoe on Mass. 41 for about two
miles and you will come to The Stagecoach Hill Inn, which has
no old-fashioned bedrooms but offers an interesting dinner menu.
In the winter you can have a cocktail or an after-dinner drink in

the inviting taproom, where there is a roaring fire in the fireplace and where a pianist sometimes plays light jazz.

The Environs: If you are here in the summer or fall, you can hike to Race Brook Falls not far from The Ivanhoe. Drive south on Mass. 41 less than a mile from the guesthouse. Park your car in the little roadside picnic area on the west side of the road and walk about one hundred yards south along 41. Opposite the Salisbury Road, you will see a red blaze and the words "Race Brook" on the west side of the road. Follow the red-blazed trail 1.5 miles to Race Brook Falls, a series of five beautiful waterfalls. Warning: the beginning of this trail passes through an area that is muddy after it rains. The Race Brook Falls Trail is a feeder to the Appalachian Trail that runs along the crest of the Taconic Range.

If you want to hike to the Mount Everett firetower, continue on the red-blazed feeder to the white-blazed Appalachian Trail, turn north (to the right) onto the trail, and a steep climb will bring you to the Mount Everett summit (2,602 feet), where you will have a great view of the Taconic Range, the Massachusetts Berkshires, and the mountains in New York State.

Scenic Drive: Mass. 41 from South Egremont to Salisbury, Connecticut.

Directions to the Inn: From New York, take the Saw Mill River Parkway to the Taconic Parkway, exiting at Hillsdale. Take Mass. 23 east to Mass. 41 south. From Boston, take the Mass. Turnpike west to exit 2, then Mass. 102 to U.S. 7 south to Mass. 23 west to Mass. 41 south.

THE EGREMONT INN

South Egremont, Massachusetts

Back in the days when the stagecoach ran from Hartford, Connecticut, to Albany, New York, the route took it past The Old Riverton Inn in Riverton, Connecticut, and then into the Berkshire Hills, where this inn was a stagecoach stop.

The Egremont Inn is still a convenient place for visitors to stay any time of year except for several weeks during the spring when the inn closes. The dates vary, depending on the weather. There are twenty-five bedrooms here, each with a private bathroom. The bedrooms have been remodeled so that they are air-conditioned in the summer, but the old-fashioned flavor of the rooms has been retained. They are mostly furnished with flowered wallpaper patterns, maple bedsteads, and old lamps. The inn serves three meals daily, all open to the public, and puts up box lunches on request. The Saturday night buffet from 6 to 9 is especially popular among South Egremont's 1,138 townspeople.

The Egremont Inn Country Club is not far down the road. You can use its eighteen-hole golf course and the four tennis courts. The club has a pro shop, a golf pro, and a tennis pro. Guests at the inn swim in the pool behind the inn itself. On rainy days you can read a book in front of the inn's large fireplace in the living room. If you plan a summer visit here, bear in mind that a minimum stay of two days is required on weekends during the Tanglewood concert season.

The Environs: From South Egremont, there is an excellent side trip that will take you to a spectacular waterfall, to Massachusetts' tiniest town, and to a lookout tower for a great view. Ask the inn to make you a box lunch and then drive to the juncture of Mass. 23 and 41. Go south on 41 for a few yards and take your first right. This is an unnumbered paved road. Follow the signs toward Mount Everett and Mount Washington until you come to the signs toward Bash Bish Falls. You will see a parking area on the roadside; from there, the trail downhill is very steep to the point where you can see the falls. There are sometimes many people here, so you may not have solitude. The falls, dropping 200 feet, are awesome, though, and well worth the meandering drive to get to them.

If you continue on these narrow paved back roads, following signs to Mount Washington and Mount Everett, you will come to Massachusetts' smallest town, a homely hamlet on the western side of Mount Everett. Union Church is the principal village in the town of Mount Washington, which had a population numbering fifty-two in 1970. You will know you are in Union Church when you have arrived at the church. It is next to the town hall. There are no stores or even a post office in Mount Washington, but there is a terrific view.

Mount Everett is the only mountain in the southern Berkshires you can drive up, and on a clear day the view is wonderful. Take the road to the parking area and picnic ground. From here, you can walk around Guilder Pond, which is almost covered in the summer with pink and white water lilies. A foot trail takes you the half mile to Mount Everett's summit (2,602 feet), where you will have a view to the south of Bear Mountain in Connecticut (distinguished by the cairn on top), the Twin Lakes in Connecticut, and the Berkshire Hills to the north.

Scenic Drive: Mount Everett.

Directions to the Inn: From New York, take the Taconic Parkway north to the exit for Mass. 23 east. Follow Mass. 23 east to South Egremont. From Boston, take the Mass. Turnpike west to exit 2, then Mass. 102 to U.S. 7 south to Mass. 23 west to South Egremont.

THE FAIRFIELD INN

Great Barrington, Massachusetts

For many years this rambling inn has been a landmark on Mass. 23 just over the South Egremont town line on the way to Great Barrington. In 1975 the white clapboards, red doors, and black shutters got a new coat of paint, and the interior was remodeled by the inn's new owners, Hugh James Macbeth and Laurent James Nicastro.

Now The Fairfield Inn is a pleasant and convenient stopover in the Berkshire Hills, where you can spend the night in one of the inn's two four-poster canopy beds. There are eleven bedrooms here, each with a private bathroom. The inn is open all year, serving breakfast and dinner daily both to houseguests and the public. The inn puts up box lunches on request.

In the summer, dinner is served on the terrace behind the inn. After the temperature drops in September, you can dine indoors in a cozy wood-paneled room or in the more formal blue-and-white dining room where classical music, such as the minuet from Mozart's fortieth symphony, plays on the intercom. Before dinner, cocktails are served in the dimly lit lounge. There is also a bright living room with white-wicker furniture and vivid yellow cushions alongside large healthy plants.

During our visit the dinner menu was presented on a blackboard that the waitress brought to the table. The appetizers were melon with Madeira, fruit with kirsch, shrimp in dill sauce, tomato stuffed with crabmeat, clam chowder, and chilled consommé Madrilène. The entrees were roast duck with cherries, chicken cordon bleu, roast leg of lamb, baked stuffed shrimp, broiled red salmon, roast pork with prunes, and strip steak. For dessert, the inn was having pecan pie, strawberry tart, and various ice creams. The wine list includes domestic and imported wines.

The Environs: During the warm months you can walk across the road to the Egremont Inn Country Club, where there are tennis courts and an eighteen-hole golf course. Behind The Fairfield Inn there is a fresh-water pool. Get in your car and you have a tremendous range of places to visit and things to do in the Berkshires.

In the summer there are concerts at Tanglewood in Lenox, the summer home of the Boston Symphony Orchestra, and dance recitals at Jacob's Pillow in Lee. The Hancock Shaker Village is on U.S. 20 west of Pittsfield. For an admission fee, you can visit this restored village of nineteen buildings. One is a circular stone barn (circumference 276 feet) in which all the stalls face the outer walls. This was once a prosperous community of 5,000 acres set in Hancock, itself a Baptist town.

Two miles west of Stockbridge, off Mass. 183, the Chesterwood Studio, where Daniel Chester French fashioned his sculpture of Abraham Lincoln (now at the Lincoln Memorial in Washington, D.C.), is open to the public. The 150-acre estate, the gardens, and the chestnut-beamed barn housing French's work are owned by the National Trust for Historic Preservation.

The Berkshires are studded with antique shops of all kinds, ranging from expensive stores to flea markets. Lists of dealers are available at the tourist information booths in Great Barrington and Stockbridge. You can also write to the Berkshire County Antique Dealers Association, Box 323, South Egremont, Mass. 01258.

The Berkshires are very popular during the summer because of all the cultural acitivities here. In the fall, the foliage attracts the most visitors, but in early September Great Barrington, the shopping center for the southern Berkshires (population 7,537), is the annual destination for fair-goers. The Barrington Fair started in 1842 in the center of Great Barrington, where horses were exhibited on Main Street and cattle near the Congregational Church. The fair has its own grounds now and it is one of Massachusetts' major agricultural fairs.

Scenic Drive: Mass. 41 from South Egremont south to Salisbury.

Directions to the Inn: From New York, take the Saw Mill River Parkway to the Taconic Parkway, exiting at Hillsdale. Follow Mass. 23 east to the inn. From Boston, take the Mass. Turnpike west to exit 2, then Mass. 102 to U.S. 7 south to Mass. 23 west to the inn.

THE FLYING CLOUD INN

New Marlboro, Massachusetts

"What's your favorite inn in the Berkshires between, say, Salisbury, Connecticut, and Williamstown, Massachusetts?" That was the question put to us recently, and it was easy to answer—The Flying Cloud. "The Flying Cloud. How do you get there?" we were asked. "'Well, that's a little harder to answer," we said.

For people who have skied at Otis Ridge or Butternut Basin on Mass. 23, finding this bucolic retreat will not be too difficult. But if you are not familiar with the pretty winding roads in this section of Massachusetts, getting to The Flying Cloud may not be the simplest thing in the world. Once you are there, though, your efforts will be well rewarded.

The Flying Cloud is open from the second week of May through the end of October, and from about December 20 through March 17. Besides its ten cozy bedrooms, six with private bathrooms, The Flying Cloud has good food, serving breakfast and dinner to guests, and lunch, including box lunches, on request. The inn will also put up box dinners for those who wish to attend any of the evening events in the area.

This wonderful, secluded hideaway has a congenial atmosphere, lovely furnishings, and a countryside setting that exudes gentility. From the outside, the white-clapboard house looks plain, but inside each antique has been placed with loving care, and this attention to detail is evident from the moment you step over the threshold.

Among other things here, you will find one of New England's most romantic bedrooms. It is Room 1, with a four-poster bed, a tailored yellow canopy, a red patchwork quilt, and two reading lamps attached to the bedposts. Room 1 shares a bathroom with Room 2, also on the inn's first floor. Unless you feel you must have a private bathroom, we suggest you ask for Room 1 and just pack your bathrobes. Otherwise, all the bedrooms are unusually good-looking, with substantial antiques and charming wallpaper. If you bring your children, you might want to ask for the inn's dormitory space with bunk beds.

Whatever time of year you come here, you are bound to work up an appetite, and that is what the inn expects. The dinner menu is set, the food is simple, and there is plenty of it. When we visited the inn, the main course was roast lamb with flat buttered noodles and a delicious purée of carrots, potatoes, and cream. The appetizer was toast points spread with a tuna fish, egg, and anchovy mixture. The homemade whole-wheat rolls were excellent. The salad was fresh greens and sweet red-onion slices. For dessert, there was a moist chocolate cake made with sour cream.

Innkeeper David R. Schwarz has a keen interest in wines and offers about twenty imported varieties on the inn's list. If you like a glass of port after dinner, you can have it on the screened-in porch during the summer or in the gracious living room beside a winter's roaring fire.

The inn is set on 200 acres of gentle meadows and woods, with four miles of walking trails on the property. There are two tennis courts, an all-weather court, and a very good clay court, with instruction available. If you bring your bicycle, you can ride along the country lanes near the inn. They are relatively flat, pretty in an understated way, and attract very little traffic. In front of the inn there is a fresh-water spring-fed pond where you can take a swim after playing croquet, badminton, or volleyball.

The inn was named some years ago for the American clipper ship *Flying Cloud*. This ship was built in East Boston by Donald McKay (1810–80), a master craftsman who perfected a type of graceful three-masted, square-rigged clipper ship designed for speed. The *Flying Cloud*, 41 feet wide and 21 feet in depth, had a deck about 230 feet long and weighed some 1,800 tons. She set a record on her maiden voyage in 1851, going from New York around Cape Horn to San Francisco in eighty-nine days. That record was never broken.

Donald McKay designed and built more than ninety sailing ships. In 1921 Samuel Eliot Morison described three of them, including the *Flying Cloud*, in his *Maritime History of Massachusetts*. Morison wrote, "Never, in these United States, has the brain of man conceived, or the hand of man fashioned, so perfect a thing as the clipper ship. . . . The Flying Cloud was our Rheims, the Sovereign of the Seas our Parthenon, the Lightning our Amiens; but they were monuments carved from snow. For a brief moment of time they flashed their splendor around the world, then disappeared with the sudden completeness of the wild pigeon."

You might think it peculiar to name such a pleasant, relaxed inn after a fast clipper ship, especially this far from the ocean. We wondered about it ourselves. But then we took a walk through the fields around the inn, which come alive in June with a profusion of flowers: daisies, red clover, yellow water-buttercups, and Indian paintbrush, that rust-colored flower. Standing on the open hillside, we looked down at the inn and it seemed tiny. Suddenly we realized why the retired Naval lieutenant commander who named the inn chose The Flying Cloud: the inn sits amid these meadows as if it were a clipper ship on the open seas. It is beautifully situated on a small hill with the high-grassed fields rolling away rhythmically like billowing waves on the ocean.

Like many New England inns, The Flying Cloud functioned as a farm long before it became a hostelry in 1946. But it seemed to us to be as appropriate a place as any to honor the memory of Donald McKay. After all, McKay, born in Shelbourne County, Nova Scotia, was himself brought up on a farm.

The Environs: During the summer there are many concerts, art exhibits, and dance performances in the Berkshires, including Tanglewood, where the Boston Symphony performs, and Jacob's

Pillow, the dance theater. In the winter the inn's rates include the use of cross-country skis, snow-shoes, sleds, and a toboggan. (And do not forget to pack your ice skates.) If you love downhill skiing, Otis Ridge and Butternut Basin are not far away. Otis Ridge has a particularly fine ski program for children. You can also drive to Catamount and Bosquet ski areas.

Scenic Drive: Campbell Falls via New Marlboro, then to Bartholomew's Cobble via Ashley House.

Directions to the Inn: From New York, take I-684 to I-84 east (or the Merritt Parkway exit 52) to Conn. 8 north to U.S. 44 west to Conn. 183 north 14.5 miles to the turnoff (marked by a sign) on the left to the inn. From Boston, take the Mass. Turnpike to exit 2, then Mass. 102 south to U.S. 7 south to Mass. 23 east to Mass. 57. Beyond the village of New Marlboro, take the right fork through Sandisfield State Forest 2 miles to the inn.

THE RED LION INN

Stockbridge, Massachusetts

They say that travelers coming to this busy town in the Berkshires for the first time often think they recognize people they know. After a while of wondering why, it dawns on them that this is

Norman Rockwell's town (population 2,312) and that some townspeople have been models for Rockwell's paintings.

The enormous, all-white Red Lion Inn, Main Street's most prominent feature, occupies a good portion of Rockwell's winter scene *Christmas in Stockbridge, Mass.* When he painted it, though, the inn's windows were darkened because it was not open in the winter. Now it is open 365 days a year, has 106 bedrooms (more than half with private bathrooms), and serves three meals daily to houseguests and the public. The inn puts up box lunches on request.

There are two dining rooms here: one is formal, with nicely separated tables, fresh flowers, and waitresses wearing black uniforms and white aprons. The other is Widow Bingham's Tavern, where you can reserve the intimate booth, enclosed on three sides, that seats four and dine in a more informal atmosphere.

We ate in the more formal dining room, where the soups of the day were cream of eggplant and turkey Creole. The eighteen regular entrees included a vegetable platter, baked stuffed jumbo shrimp, veal scaloppini Marsala, Châteaubriand for two, and baked striped bass. The fish had been baked with slices of Spanish onion, green pepper, and tomato. Dinner came with scalloped potatoes and fresh, thin asparagus tips. The Hollandaise sauce on the asparagus was hot, delicious, and had a proper hint of lemon. The wine list here offers about thirty-five selections, mostly French.

There are a lot of large resort hotels throughout New England that give the feeling the moment you walk inside that they have seen better days. The Red Lion Inn is not among them. The living room where you enter is gracious, with Oriental rugs, antiques, and pieces of pewter and china. The bedrooms are furnished simply but are entirely pleasant, with small desks, small-sized arm chairs, and white-wicker headboards in the double-bedded rooms.

Some of the bedrooms are in what the inn calls its "motel." These are the rooms kept open during the winter months. The definition of this will give you an idea of just how refreshingly old-fashioned The Red Lion is. The "motel" occupies one wing of the inn. The only difference between the "inn" and the "motel" is that the motel rooms have small television sets. Otherwise, they are the same. All have room telephones and many are furnished with Norman Rockwell prints.

For the best rooms in the inn, ask for one of the eight

bedrooms with direct access to a porch. The porches are on the second and third floors at about eye level with the maple trees lining U.S. 7. Of these, four (Rooms 11, 12, 24, and 25) are especially light and sunny with bay windows. Two bedrooms have canopied beds.

During the summer, Stockbridge is enormously popular because it is so close to Lenox, where the Boston Symphony Orchestra performs at Tanglewood, and to Lee, the home of Jacob's Pillow, the dance theater. When you stay at The Red Lion, you can swim in the outdoor pool behind the inn. You should come prepared in the summer for a bustling Stockbridge, where the diagonal parking spaces, typical of western Massachusetts towns in which the main street coincides with U.S. 7, are full.

The Environs: Stockbridge is less busy the rest of the year, but Main Street is just as picturesque in the winter as in the summer. You can visit The Old Corner House, a block from The Red Lion, any day but Tuesday, from 10 to 5. This white-clapboard former home is a museum for Norman Rockwell's paintings, and the tour is definitely worthwhile.

One painting on exhibit here is *The Discovery*, portraying a young boy who has just discovered a Santa Claus costume in his parents' chest of drawers. Reproductions have made this moment of youthful, wide-eyed surprise familiar to many people, but several members of our tour group expressed surprise themselves when they saw the canvas. The Santa Claus beard has real hair on it, and the wall behind the chest of drawers is textured with a layer of sand.

Scenic Drive: The unnumbered road heading north across from the inn.

Directions to the Inn: From New York, take the Saw Mill River Parkway to the Taconic Parkway to N.Y. 23 east to U.S. 7 north to the inn. From Boston, take I-90 west to exit 2 to Mass. 102 to Stockbridge.

THE WILLIAMSVILLE INN

West Stockbridge, Massachusetts

If you are looking for an inn in the Berkshires and your first requirement is imaginative food, The Williamsville Inn is where you want to go. This is a cozy clapboard inn off the beaten path in the hamlet of Williamsville (population 900), and yet it is only four miles south of exit 1 on the Mass. Turnpike.

There are sixteen bedrooms altogether here. The inn is open all year, serving breakfast every day and lunch and dinner daily except Tuesdays to guests and the public. The inn makes box lunches on request.

Come on the weekends and you will probably meet innkeeper Chandler Warren, who works four days a week as a lawyer in New York City and who generally arrives here on Thursday nights to supervise the kitchen. Cooking is his great love, and his culinary achievements are rewarded by the inn's guests who make comments in the "remarks" column of the guestbook such as, "Even better than promised" and " 'Le Pavillon' in the Berkshires."

It is unusual to find a southern New England inn where the menu does not include juice, shrimp cocktail, and fruitcup among the appetizers. Instead, our choices for the first of four courses were pâté maison, asparagus Hollandaise, quiche Lorraine, eggs à la Russe, baked stuffed mushrooms, and chicken liver pâté. The soups here were refreshingly different. We sampled the watercress soup and the turnip vichyssoise—a smooth cold soup with a chicken stock base, leeks, potatoes, turnips, salt, white pepper, and heavy cream. We plan to order the artichoke soup on our next visit.

The entrees were boeuf Bourguignon; blanquette de veau; poulet Marchand de Vin; Coquilles St. Jacques; a shell steak broiled with crushed black pepper, Tabasco, Worcestershire sauce, and butter, and flambéed in cognac; and filet of grey sole poached in wine and baked in a light cheese soufflé sauce. Light, dry saffron rice came with the meal, along with chunks of hot baked eggplant presented with a little thick tomato sauce. There were no crackers or store-bought rolls in the bread basket but warm small-sized popovers.

The salads on the à la carte menu were a green salad, spinach and bacon salad, and Doug's Caesar Salad for two. (Doug is Douglas Bersaw who oversees the inn in Mr. Warren's absence.)

The wine list here is extensive with thirty-eight wines, all French, ranging in price from $2.75 to $800 for a 1929 Château Mouton Rothschild (Pauillac). The taproom is inviting, with small wooden tables, an entry space wallpapered with old sheet-music covers, and light jazz over the intercom.

If you think you have no room for dessert, you may change your mind when presented with the choices: a rich cheesecake, homemade apple pie, chocolate mousse, lemon angel pie, peach Melba, and two flaming desserts, Cherries Jubilee and Bananas Foster. The Bananas Foster consists of butter, banana liqueur, cinnamon, dark-brown sugar, a sliced banana—all flambéed with brandy.

Compared with the food, the rooms here are less imaginative. They offer a variety of accommodations, from old-fashioned rooms in the main inn to more modern ones in a building behind the inn. Room 4 in the main inn has a working fireplace and a double bed.

The Environs: Behind the inn there is a swimming pool, a clay tennis court, and a trout pond. You can hike on Tom Ball Mountain, which rises in back of the inn. The mountain, 1,930 feet in altitude, is wooded with mostly deciduous trees and it is totally undeveloped, forming an appealing backdrop for the two dozen houses in Williamsville. Tom Ball, a Revolutionary scout, was the mountain's first owner, and his property, known as the Tom Ball

Farm, included The Williamsville Inn. The inn, built in 1794, is now the second oldest building in the hamlet.

Scenic Drive: U.S. 7 to Williamstown.

Directions to the Inn: From New York, take the Saw Mill River Parkway to the Taconic Parkway, exiting at Hillsdale. Follow Mass. 23 east through Great Barrington to Mass. 41 north. The inn is five miles north on Mass. 41. From Boston, take the Mass. Turnpike west to exit 1. Turn left on Mass. 41 south and continue for four miles to the inn.

THE VILLAGE INN

Lenox, Massachusetts

When the Boston Symphony Orchestra was invited to perform in Lenox in 1936, Serge Koussevitzky, the conductor, agreed to play six concerts. They were held in a huge tent (capacity 5,000 people), and even these first concerts were broadcast over radio with Olin Downes as commentator. It was during an all-Wagner program in 1937 that a dramatic summer cloudburst interrupted the concert and destroyed the tent. So money was raised (over $100,000) to build the present music shed (capacity 6,037), and today these popular summer concerts are known as the Tanglewood Music Festival.

When the Tanglewood concerts were just beginning, The Village Inn on Church Street, a side street in the center of town, was open all year, charging four dollars a day for three meals and lodging. This cozy, cheerful inn is still open all year, and although today's rates would have seemed unthinkable in 1936, The Village Inn is a relatively good buy in expensive, summertime Lenox. There are nineteen small but bright bedrooms, with flowered wallpaper patterns and crisp white curtains. The rooms have a fresh feeling you do not find in many Lenox inns. The Village Inn serves three meals daily (the restaurant is closed on Sunday nights). All meals are open to the public.

There is a friendly atmosphere at The Village Inn, tucked between clapboard buildings, fronted by a postage-stamp-sized lawn, and owned by innkeepers Richard and Marie Judd. As you step across the narrow porch past the flag, a vine arbor, three hanging pots of pink petunias, and wind chimes, you will enter a snug hallway where there is an exquisite standing mirror made of mahogany.

In the informal dining room there are usually half a dozen entrees, such as Yankee pot roast with buttered noodles, chicken breast à la Kiev, tenderloin steak, filet of sole, roast top beef sirloin, and lobster Newburg. The inn's desserts include fresh-baked hot apple pie with ice cream, Indian pudding, cheesecake, parfaits, and a variety of sherbets and ice creams. Next door, the inn's pub, Poor Richard's Tavern, is open daily from 11:30 A.M. until 1 A.M. (on Sundays it opens at 1 P.M.). You can have wine, draft beer, and other alcoholic drinks, as well as hot sandwiches, in this former horse stable.

The Environs: Lenox (population 2,208) is busiest during the summer because most of the thousands of concert-goers drive through the center of town on their way to Tanglewood. This 210-acre estate was given to the orchestra by descendants of William A. Tappan, who was Nathaniel Hawthorne's friend. Tappan named the estate after Hawthorne's *Tanglewood Tales.* At Tanglewood you can sit in the music shed or listen to the concerts from the lawn. Many people bring their own box lunches (these are also sold on the grounds), wine, and blankets and chairs to sit on. When you walk through the entrance gate, you will see people of all ages, dressed casually, strolling around the lawns. Tickets for seats in the music shed are sold ahead of time, but you can buy single lawn tickets several hours before a concert. You can also buy tickets to the Saturday morning rehearsals here, and they are often even more interesting and enjoyable than the concerts.

Lenox is also popular during the fall-foliage season, when the peak of color usually occurs about October 10. The Berkshires are inundated with cars, however, especially on state-numbered roads. If you want to avoid the bumper-to-bumper weekend traffic, your best bet is to get a Massachusetts State map and drive along unnumbered roads. Even at that, you will not be alone in the Berkshires, summer or fall.

When you stay at The Village Inn, you should walk along Main Street to the Lenox Library. It is the former county courthouse (from 1787 to 1868 Lenox was the county seat until it moved north to Pittsfield), built with a round, open cupola in 1816. Inside, there is a section of shelves with books written by Berkshire residents. If the weather is lovely during your visit, you can sit in the library's shaded gardens, where there are seats for readers.

No matter how you approach Lenox, you will come to the crossroads of U.S. 20 and Mass. 183. (Tanglewood is about a mile from The Village Inn just off Mass. 183 west.) At the crossroads you will pass the historic Curtis Hotel. This is where Franklin D. Roosevelt vacationed for several weeks during his first presidential term. He sat on the massive veranda each day, chatting with passers-by.

Scenic Drive: At the juncture of Mass. 183 and Mass. 7A in Lenox, take the unnumbered road south to Stockbridge.

Directions to the Inn: From New York, take the Taconic Parkway north to Mass. 23 east to U.S. 7 north to Lenox. Go east on U.S. 20 for one block, turn down Church Street, and you will see the inn on the right side. From Boston, take the Mass. Turnpike to exit 2 and U.S. 20 to Lenox. Church Street is one block east of The Curtis Hotel.

THE DEERFIELD INN

Deerfield, Massachusetts

When The Deerfield Inn opened its doors in 1884, it was welcomed by late spring frosts, a summer heat wave, and a grasshopper plague in July. But people came to the inn anyway, set in one of New England's most appealing, picture-postcard towns, and they have been coming ever since.

At The Deerfield Inn there are twelve bedrooms, each with a private bathroom. They are unpretentious, with mostly maple furnishings, but they are pleasant in a homey way. The inn is open all year except December 23, 24, and 25. It serves three meals daily but is closed for lunch on Monday. All meals are open to the public. Box lunches are made on request.

The dining room has a gracious air, with chandeliers, white-linen tablecloths, hurricane lamps, and wallpaper with a pattern made expressly for the room from a piece of old fabric portraying flowers and birds. The regular menu offers, among other entrees, beef en brochette, boneless chicken breast cordon bleu, roast duckling, shrimp in mushrooms with garlic butter, broiled lamb chops, grilled Boston scrod, sirloin steak, and sautéed lobster chunks. Sometimes the inn offers rabbit or venison.

Each afternoon at four, innkeeper George W. Butler says, "We get out our silver service and serve tea in the Beehive Parlor with petits fours and fancy cookies. We charge seventy-five cents."

The parlor is named for the unusual beehive pattern of the wallpaper.

The Environs: This inviting inn sits right in the middle of Old Deerfield Village, where you can visit eleven historic buildings open to the public all year except during three weeks at Christmas time. The late eighteenth-century and early nineteenth-century homes, silver shop, fabric hall, tavern, and printing house are located, for the most part, along the mile-long main street. This is only partly a museum town, though, because there are private homes, two schools (Deerfield Academy and Bement School), a post office, and The Deerfield Inn alongside the historic buildings.

For the setting alone, you should put Old Deerfield on your itinerary for a New England trip. Drive or walk along the main street during the day and you will notice the unusual Connecticut Valley two-leaf front doors on some houses. Not all the buildings are showpiece material; as a result, the main street has added architectural variety and charm.

The Deerfield Inn is owned by Historic Deerfield, Inc., which also owns the buildings open to the public in Old Deerfield Village. There is an admission charge to each building, with combination tickets available at reduced rates from May through September. The Information Center is across from the inn and the post office.

Memorial Hall on Memorial Street is a museum with something for everyone: a collection of early American furniture, pewter, iron, tin and woodenware, farm tools, craftsmen's tools, old tavern signs, American paintings, and musical instruments. The museum has on display the Indian House Door that withstood the French and Indian assault during the Massacre of Deerfield in 1704. A force of 200 French soldiers and 140 Catholic Indians killed 49 people, including several children, and captured another 111 men and women. They took the prisoners to Montreal, but not before burning most of the town. It was the most successful Indian raid staged against an American frontier town. The better part of the village was built after 1704, and preservation of the eighteenth-century buildings has been going on now for about a century.

Apart from its history and the charm of its main street, Old Deerfield Village is special because it does not have the deadness of a re-created town. It is a setting out of the past, with well-manicured lawns and blooming crab-apple trees and dogwood in May. But 3,850 people live in Deerfield, which includes Old Deerfield Village. So children ride bicycles down the street, dogs bark by day and howl by night, and The Deerfield Academy uses the common for school activities. The presence of the twentieth century here makes the old buildings, by contrast, more interesting.

Scenic Drive: Main Street, Old Deerfield Village.

Directions to the Inn: From New York, take I-84 east to I-91 north to the exit for Routes 5 and 10. Follow Routes 5 and 10 north to the turnoff for Old Deerfield Village. From Boston, take Mass. 2 west to Greenfield and Routes 5 and 10 south to the turnoff for Old Deerfield Village.

THE PUBLICK HOUSE and
THE COL. EBENEZER CRAFTS HOUSE

Sturbridge, Massachusetts

This is the home of Old Sturbridge Village, a 250-acre re-created town of the period from 1790 to 1840, complete with costumed guides, a white-steepled church, and a lattice covered bridge, designed by Ithiel Town, that was moved from Dummerston, Vermont, in 1951 at a cost of $13,540.08.

The Publick House is 1½ miles from Old Sturbridge Village along Mass. 131. It is located across from the common in Sturbridge itself, a town of 4,878 residents. The Publick House, open all year, is a very large place best known for its studied colonial atmosphere and its five dining rooms that can seat several hundred people at a time. The Publick House serves breakfast, lunch, late luncheon, dinner, and supper every day, with all meals open to the public. There are twenty-one bedrooms, including two suites, and nineteen bathrooms.

The bedrooms are furnished with wall sconces (electric candles are inside), white-tufted bedspreads, and attractive reproductions of antiques. On top of the chest of drawers in our bedroom, two apples and two small napkins had been placed on a china plate. The wallpapers throughout the inn are of the American patriotic variety, with subdued small figures of eagles, stars, flags, and scroll-flowers in tidy stripes. The disadvantage to staying here is that Mass. 131 is a busy road, and at night you may also hear the sounds of traffic from I-86, routed out of sight to the rear of the inn.

That is not a problem at The Col. Ebenezer Crafts House, though, where we suggest you make reservations first for your visit to Sturbridge. Like The Publick House, which runs it, The Col. Ebenezer Crafts House is open all year. It is located 1.4 miles from The Publick House, on Fiske Hill Road, in a three-story gray-clapboard building built in 1774. There are nine bedrooms, including two suites, and seven bathrooms. Meals are not served here, although coffee and buns are available in the morning.

To stay at The Col. Ebenezer Crafts House, you make reservations by contacting The Publick House, where you go first to check in and receive a detailed map to the guesthouse. The guesthouse is named in honor of the first tavern keeper at The Publick House. He was Col. Ebenezer Crafts, who ran The Publick House after it was built in 1771. In 1788 Colonel Crafts, having sold his property in Sturbridge, moved to Craftsbury, Vermont, which is also named for him.

The bedrooms here are homey and well kept, with an assortment of antiques and newer furniture. One twin-bedded room on the third floor has a sweeping view of Worcester County. Because it is off the beaten path, this guesthouse has all the personal flavor missing at the much larger Publick House, and it has a delightful pair of innkeepers, Ruth and Everett Brown.

"Just last night," Mr. Brown said to me, "a couple turned up on their way south from Canada. They had stayed with us when they were driving north. Well, they got out of their car and said, 'It's like coming home again.'"

If you stay here during the summer, bring your bathing suit. There is a twelve- by forty-five-foot swimming pool behind the guesthouse. Near the living room, where you can relax by the two fireplaces, there is a brick-lined interior hold. Ask the Browns to show it to you. Slaves are said to have been hidden here on the "underground railroad."

Since the guesthouse (and The Publick House) operate on the European plan, you can stay at the guesthouse and eat elsewhere or go to the Publick House for your meals. The dinner menu at The Publick House is extensive, with entrees such as baked lobster pie (lobster chunks in a Newburg sauce with seasoning), Rock Cornish game hen, sautéed chicken livers, broiled scrod, baked stuffed shrimp, roast prime ribs of beef, and a fancy French Canadian meat pie called Tourtière. When we ate here, the entrees came with green beans that tasted canned, fresh summer squash cooked too long, and a lukewarm baked potato.

The overall flavor of the dining rooms and the menu is summed up by the way in which the daily specialty is announced. The menu stated, "Each evening the Innkeeper causes to have prepared a dish of his own fancy." A card on the table followed up with these words, "The Innkeeper's Whim for This Evening: Grilled Center Cut Ham Steak, Glazed Brandied Peach." Among the desserts were peanut-butter ice cream pie, chocolate-chiffon cake, grapenut pudding, strawberry-chiffon pie, and "winter snowball surprise."

The wine list is varied, concentrating on French and California wines.

The best meal here is breakfast. You can have eggs any style, griddle cakes, hot, deep-dish apple pie with cheddar cheese, a breakfast tenderloin steak and egg, a single lamb chop with scrambled eggs, home-fried potatoes, kippered herring, red-flannel hash with a poached egg, and hot cider.

The Environs: Old Sturbridge Village, open all year, is especially popular among families with school-age children who enjoy watching costumed craftsmen at work in the blacksmith and tinsmith shops. One ticket admits you to all the village's buildings, which include a one-room lawyer's office, an early nineteenth-century corn barn, the Hapgood Carding Mill, and the village meetinghouse. The town is organized around a common where, when we visited in May, dozens of baby lambs were grazing on the field grasses, passively permitting small children to pat them.

Scenic Drive: A visit to Old Sturbridge Village.

Directions to the Inn: From New York, take I-95 or I-84 to I-86 north of Hartford and continue to Sturbridge. From Boston, take the Mass. Turnpike to exit 9. The Publick House is on the Sturbridge common on Mass. 131.

LONGFELLOW'S WAYSIDE INN

Sudbury, Massachusetts

"The Inn radiated the atmosphere of older New England. Lights gleamed from the windows across snow-covered fields and the faint tinkle of sleigh bells added to the old time touch. Within was a typical New England dinner and later, after Mr. Ford had fiddled and the party had danced, they played old games: 'Tucker' and 'Puss in the Corner' and 'Drop the Handkerchief.'"

That was the Associated Press' account of Henry Ford's debut as the landlord of The Wayside Inn, and on February 9, 1924, it was national news. Not only that, Henry Ford's housewarming made the Saturday front page of at least two New England newspapers. When you visit The Wayside Inn, you will find the ballroom where the man who manufactured Model-T's liked to host square dances and play his fiddle, a $75,000 Stradivarius.

The Wayside, America's oldest operating inn, has ten bedrooms, each with a private bathroom. It is open all year, except on Christmas Day. Many people make their pilgrimage to New England's shrine among inns for a meal. The inn serves three meals daily to guests and the public; reservations for breakfast are required if you are not staying here, and reservations for lunch and dinner are recommended.

When we stopped at the inn for lunch, the very reasonably priced menu offered, among other things, Yankee pot roast and a baked potato, Wayside Inn chicken pie and cranberry sauce,

London broil, a tomato stuffed with chicken salad and garnished with egg wedges, broiled chopped sirloin of beef, and Wayside Inn country sausage with an apple ring. The inn served a dozen desserts, including a fresh-baked blueberry pie with ice cream, Indian pudding, deep-dish apple pie, pecan pie with whipped cream, and strawberry shortcake.

During our visit a summer wedding was held in the formal garden. The bridesmaids fluttered across the manicured lawn in solid pink, yellow, green, and lavender dresses with matching wide-brimmed silky hats. The bride and her father walked alone, arm in arm, through the inn's main door and turned down the unpaved road in front. As they walked in step, saying nothing, a string quartet in the garden began playing and the guests smiled expectantly. Visitors to the inn that bright, blue-skied day lingered discreetly outside the garden hedge as the bride and groom bowed their heads toward each other and the minister began, "Dearly beloved."

Henry Wadsworth Longfellow put this inn, twenty miles from Boston, on the literary map when he wrote *Tales of a Wayside Inn*. One of these poems, "Paul Revere's Ride" starts, "Listen my children, and you shall hear / Of the midnight ride of Paul Revere." Many years after the group of poems was published in 1863, the inn was renamed Longfellow's Wayside Inn.

It could have been renamed after Henry Ford. He bought the inn to preserve it, bought 5,000 acres around the inn to protect its environment, bought old stage coaches and fire engines to display in the barn, moved a schoolhouse from Sterling to Sudbury, and in 1929 built a church and a grist mill on the grounds for $25,000. Finally, he had a $380,000 four-lane highway built a safe distance from his inn. He sold that to the state of Massachusetts for $1.

During the 1920s Henry Ford bucked the tide of a Charleston-crazy decade and organized square dances at The Wayside Inn. He publicized old-fashioned dancing so effectively that even Radcliffe College added a course in Early-American dancing to its curriculum. The country fiddling and the square dances and the jigs were Henry Ford's answer to New Englanders who watched him because he was a celebrity and a trendsetter.

Ford's inn started in 1661 as John How's Black Horse Tavern. The tavern had two rooms: one upstairs and one downstairs. For nearly two hundred years the How family was responsible for adding to the tavern, but it took Michigan-born Henry Ford to preserve the New England tradition the How family had built. Three years before he died in 1947, Ford deeded the inn and the property around it to the Wayside Inn Corporation.

Most people come to The Wayside Inn because it is a monument to the past and because it is New England's most famous inn. It honors a poet in its name but might not be in existence if it were not for a car manufacturer named Ford. Even if The Wayside Inn were not old or famous, it would still be a picturesque place for a wedding.

Directions to the Inn: From New York, take I-84 east to I-91 to the Mass. Turnpike east to I-495 north to U.S. 20 east for eight miles to the inn. From Boston, take the Mass. Turnpike to Mass. 128 north to exit 49 to U.S. 20 west for eleven miles (follow Weston-Marlboro signs in rotary) to the inn.

THE YANKEE CLIPPER INN

Rockport, Massachusetts

"This play is called 'Our Town.' It was written by Thornton Wilder. . . . The name of the town is Grover's Corners, New Hampshire—just across the Massachusetts line: longitude 42 degrees 40 minutes; latitude 70 degrees 37 minutes."

That is the narrator speaking at the beginning of *Our Town*, the Pulitzer Prize-winning play, produced in 1938. Wilder placed his story, now part of New England tradition, in New Hampshire. But if you look on the map for Grover's Corners and find the longitude and latitude, you wind up here, just off Rockport, Massachusetts.

The Yankee Clipper Inn is several miles north of Rockport on the way to Pigeon Cove. There are three buildings here with a variety of accommodations, from small, old-fashioned bedrooms in The Bulfinch House (where travelers register) to wall-to-wall carpeted rooms with picture windows and ocean views in The Quarterdeck. The most highly prized bedrooms in the inn are those with sitting rooms or private decks and ocean views.

The inn has twenty-six bedrooms, each with a private bathroom. There is a forty-foot heated salt-water pool on the inn's grounds and, for good swimmers, a diving board and ladder lead from the rocks at the shore's edge into the Atlantic Ocean. The inn is open from April through October, serving three meals daily for houseguests, and meals to the public by reservation only. Box lunches are made on request.

Before dinner, the guests here, many of them retired people who return each year for as long as three or four weeks, gather in the paneled living room. During our stay a waitress came through ringing a chime to announce the dinner hour. The guests were then seated at the tables on the enclosed porch, where dinner began with a lovely dish of fresh melon pieces. The entrees were broiled lamb chops, fresh scrod, sirloin steak, and boiled lobster. Fresh spinach came with the meal, along with French fries and a salad consisting of asparagus tips presented with lettuce and sweet red-onion slices. The desserts included delicate cream puffs filled with freshly made custard. Since Rockport is a dry town, alcoholic beverages are not served at the inn. (Gloucester, about five miles away, is not dry.)

The Environs: While you are packing a book or two in your suitcase, bring along your camera as well. Most visitors to Rockport enjoy photographing or painting their own version of Motif Number One. It is an old fishing shed off Bearskin Neck, which you have undoubtedly seen somewhere, if only on a jigsaw puzzle.

Rockport is a very popular town on the Atlantic Ocean north of Boston. Settled in 1690, it was a fishing village until the artists who came here to paint the boats, wharves, piles, rocks, and attractive buildings gradually displaced the fishermen. Now this town of 5,636 residents swells each summer, when enthusiastic visitors come here to browse in the shops and art galleries, many of them on Bearskin Neck.

Bearskin Neck is a long, wharflike piece of land jutting into the ocean. Many of the buildings are converted shacks, and the narrow lanes, closed to traffic, make this a colorful pedestrian mall. In front of the brown- and gray-shingled shops with white trim, there are little rock gardens, window boxes, and wooden tubs overflowing with purple petunias, pink phlox, and geraniums.

Rockport has much of the flavor of Maine, at least the flavor of fishing villages that have undoubtedly always been picturesque but now cultivate that charm for the benefit of visitors. The view from the dining-room porch at The Yankee Clipper Inn reminded us of Maine too. From it, you look out across Sandy Bay at Rockport and Bearskin Neck against the backdrop of the setting sun.

Scenic Drive: Mass. 127 and 127A around Cape Ann.

Directions to the Inn: From New York, take I-95 to I-91 north to I-86 north to the Mass. Turnpike east to Mass. 128 north to Gloucester, then left on Mass. 127 to Rockport. From Boston, take U.S. 1 north to Mass. 128 north to Mass. 127 left to Rockport. The inn is on Mass. 127, which circles Cape Ann.

CAPE COD

If the Pilgrims, who came to Cape Cod in 1620 and found un-spoiled beauty, were to return today and see what the twentieth century has done to this sixty-five-mile-long peninsula, they might dust off the stocks for immediate use. Or, if they drove near Hyannis along Route 28, lined with drive-in restaurants, unattractive gas stations, and neon lights, they might be tempted to take the *Mayflower* back to England.

People who love the Cape, much like those who are partial to Martha's Vineyard, tend to be summer residents or visitors who return year after year to rediscover the idyllic nooks and crannies where beauty and solitude can still be found. To say that the Cape is popular during the summer is putting it mildly. It is so popular that we have heard weekend radio broadcasts describing the extent of traffic to and from Cape Cod as if it were a megalopolis inundated with commuters going to and from work.

A primary reason for its high standing among many visitors is the Cape Cod National Seashore. Of the Cape's approximately three hundred miles of shoreline, about fifty are within the National Seashore, which includes parts of Chatham, Orleans, Eastham, Wellfleet, Truro, and Provincetown. The National Seashore headquarters are in Wellfleet, just off Route 6. The roads are jammed with traffic on some summer weekends, but it takes a lot of people to fill a beach, and by any standards the National Seashore is New England's most outstanding stretch of sand. For example, from Race Point in Provincetown, at the peninsula's tip, to Nauset Inlet at Orleans, the beach stretches for thirty-three continuous miles.

Advocates of Cape Cod are not only in love with the beaches. If you ask them why they cannot wait to return, they will smile wistfully and talk about the spiritual refreshment they feel after a trip to the Cape. They will tell you about the blueness of the ocean, about the briny air, the towering sand dunes, the white-capped surf. They will talk of out-of-the-way ponds, of secluded salt marshes, and of fresh fish. They may ask you if you have driven along Route 6A, considered the Cape's most scenic road, which passes through picturesque, trim villages where cultivated roses cling to white-picket trellises and fences.

And when they talk of Cape Cod smells, they may bring up

the subject of bayberries. The bayberry's generic name is *Myrica*, which derives from the Greek word meaning perfume. You will find they grow in profusion on bushes with dark-green leaves that give off a distinctive, rich fragrance when you crush them. The bayberries themselves are nutlets covered with a wax that makes good candles.

And that is not to mention the salt-spray rose. When the breezes are relatively calm, the pink and white salt-spray roses, sometimes called wrinkled roses, fill the air with a sweet, delicate scent immediately recognizable to connoisseurs of the small, red fruit they produce called rose hip. Rich in vitamin C, the rose hip was consumed by New England sailors to prevent scurvy. Now it is most often used to make jelly. You will know the salt-spray rose by its hairy stems, its wrinkled leaves, and its lovely fragrance.

Ironically, the Cape, where the Pilgrims first set foot on American soil, was the last New England area, along with Nantucket and Martha's Vineyard off its southern shore, to come into existence. Once the last glacier that covered New England started to recede, sand was swept by the ocean's currents in a northerly direction to shape Cape Cod and the Massachusetts islands. The peninsula was carved like a bent arm that juts out from the southeastern Massachusetts mainland into the Atlantic Ocean.

The Cape is rich in seafaring history, but it also towers as a spawning ground for artists. Among its literary visitors was Ralph Waldo Emerson, who often came here and wrote about one trip in a *Journal* entry dated September 5, 1854. He wrote that he had been "to Nauset Light on the back side of Cape Cod. Collins, the keeper, told us he found obstinate resistance on Cape Cod to the project of building a lighthouse on this coast, as it would injure the wrecking business. He had to go to Boston, and obtain the strong recommendation of the Port Society."

Today, Nauset Beach, south of Nauset Light at the Cape's elbow, is still a refuge, not for people in the wrecking business, but for beachcombers and bird watchers who come to enjoy the thundering surf along what the National Park Service calls "the outstanding shoreline of the North Atlantic."

There are hundreds of motels and cabins in which to stay on Cape Cod, along with many modernized inns where the dining rooms have the atmosphere of old-fashioned inns, but the bedrooms consist of motel units alone. The five inns we have chosen to tell you about on the Cape offer a wide variety of alternatives for your taste and your pocketbook.

The Craigville Inn is among New England's best buys; The Country Inn is open all year; The Melrose Inn still operates on the American plan; The Holden Inn is in picturesque Wellfleet; and the Cornwall House is romantically sophisticated.

No matter where you stay on the Cape, you will never be far from the beach, and once you have braced yourself against the summer traffic, arrived at a beach, spread your towel on the dunes, and smelled the salt-spray roses, you may decide Monica Dickens was right when she wrote, "Cape Cod is still one of the most magically beautiful places on earth."

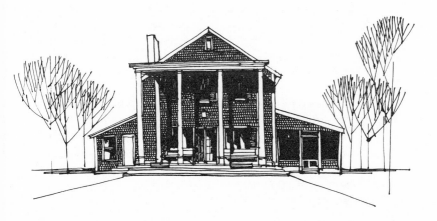

THE CRAIGVILLE INN

Craigville, Massachusetts

This inn, an inexpensive and informal place to stay, is located in one of New England's most unusual villages. In Craigville, which seems to have the dimensions of a decorative doll house, the roads are narrow lanes, the cottages are trimmed with fanciful Victorian gingerbread, and the village green has two shuffleboard sets, a volleyball net, and a post office. The post office, among the region's smallest, is open only during the summer. It is perfectly square and picturesque, with window shutters, flower boxes, and a weather vane.

The village is grouped around the inn, its separate guest-houses, and a church, which are part of a complex called the Craigville Conference Center, operated by the Massachusetts Conference of the United Church of Christ. The Center's build-ings—the inn, a manor house, a lodge, and cottages—are close together, with brown shingles, blue shutters, white trim, and flower boxes filled in spring and summer with bright-red gera-niums.

The Craigville Inn is an unpretentious, friendly place, with functional furnishings, plain food, a private beach, and rates that will please families on tight vacation budgets. There are sixty-three bedrooms, all with twin beds; some walls are painted, others have woodlike paneling. Three meals are served daily, family style, at long pine tables in the two dining rooms. There is one sitting for lunch and one for dinner. If you want to eat meals without staying the night, you may do so, but you cannot spend the night without paying for dinner and breakfast. It is open to the public (all denominations) all year, and its informality makes it a good destination if you are traveling with children.

The inn and the church, hidden on a hillock behind a grove of trees, are used for conferences and retreats, mostly on week-ends from September through the end of June. Even during these off-season months, the inn is open to the public. As the brochure puts it, "We welcome guests during this season, but there are times when accommodations may not be available on weekends. Usually, we can take guests from Sunday to Friday. Meals are available by reservation when we are serving conference and retreat groups."

The Environs: Craigville, one of more than a dozen villages in the town of Barnstable, has a long beach overlooking Nantucket Sound, and part of the beach is for the inn's guests. Many people bring their bicycles and use them to ride to the beach.

Barnstable is Massachusetts' largest town (60.16 square miles). It is also the Cape's most heavily populated town (19,842 residents), and it stretches across Cape Cod from shore to shore. Among the other communities in Barnstable are Hyannis, the Cape's shopping center; Hyannisport; and small settlements with names like Marston's Mill and Wianno. Barnstable also has three of Cape Cod's most attractive ponds: the 56-acre Lovell's Pond, not far from Route 28; the 114-acre Hamblin Pond in Marston's Mill; and Mystic Lake-Middle Pond, 249 acres in area.

Directions to the Inn: From New York, take I-95 north to Providence and I-195 to Mass. 25 to U.S. 6 east to exit 5 or 6. From Boston, take Route 128 to Route 3 to Sagamore Bridge at the Cape Cod Canal, and Route 6 (Mid Cape Highway) to exit 5 or 6. Follow signs for Centerville and Craigville. When you arrive at Craigville Beach, look for the Center's entrance about one hundred feet beyond the beach house. Follow signs to the inn.

THE COUNTRY INN

Harwich Port, Massachusetts

They say Cape Cod is even more striking and beautiful in the winter when the dunes are white-capped with ice and the wharf pilings have hats of snow. We have not been there then, but if you go, one place you can settle in for the night is The Country Inn.

This is one of the Cape's smallest inns, apart from guesthouses that do not serve meals, and you will find it on Route 124 just half a mile north of the juncture of Routes 28 and 124. The inn is open all year, serving breakfast to houseguests only and dinner to guests and the public. From the outside, the inn looks deceptively plain. It is an extended, two-story Cape Cod cottage with a picket fence bordering the front. In summer there are pink rambling roses growing over the slats. Inside, there are seven bedrooms, six with private bathrooms, a taproom with a fireplace and wood paneling, and a dining room with wide, honey-colored floorboards.

Innkeeper Bill Flynn, who was a cook for a private Yonkers, New York, club for twenty-five years before buying the inn, usually has eight entrees on the dinner menu such as his chicken Country Inn, made with ginger and orange sauce. He likes to serve a fresh fish each day and bakes small loaves of bread that he brings warm to the table. Sometimes, he presents popovers and lemon bread. For dessert, Mr. Flynn has a daily special such as hot gingerbread, lemon meringue pie, or Boston cream pie.

The Environs: In the fall you can drive along Route 24 away from town and see the cranberry harvesting. Harwich (population 5,892) leads Cape Cod in the production of cranberries, used by the Indians both as medicine and food. Indians pounded the acid cranberries, which flourish in a mixture of sand and peat, into a pulp and spread it on wounds to draw the poison out. When they combined the cranberry pulp with dried meat and melted animal fat, the result was a naturally preserved food, high in concentrated nutrients.

Cape Cod is where the cranberry was first domesticated. The plant is a vine that covers a bog with a springy, tangled mat of runners and upright shoots. The cranberry vine will grow in garden soil, but it does not bear fruit well. The berries brighten the surface of the bogs between September and late October, when most of them are picked by gasoline-powered machines. The grocer-owned cooperative, Ocean Spray Cranberries, Inc., markets most of Cape Cod's cranberries.

On a rainy day in Harwich, you can visit the Brooks Library, adjoining the old Powder House on Main Street, where there is a permanent exhibit of John Rogers' sentimental American figurines. Rogers, born in Salem in 1829 and known as the "people's sculptor," made miniature statues, most about two feet high.

Directions to the Inn: From New York, take I-95 north to Providence and I-195 to Mass. 25 to U.S. 6 east to exit 10 to Harwich. From Boston take Route 128 to Route 3 to U.S. 6 east to exit 10 to Harwich. Go right on Route 124 (Pleasant Lake Avenue), cross Harwich's Main Street, and continue on Routes 124 and 39 (Sisson Road) to the inn.

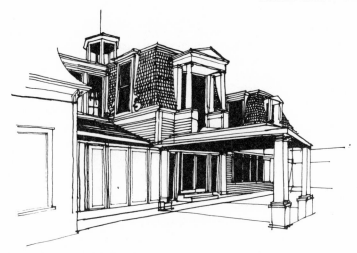

THE MELROSE INN

Harwich Port, Massachusetts

"The Melrose is something of an Horatio Alger story," said Mrs. Gladys E. Smith, who bought this yellow-clapboard inn with the striking green mansard roof in 1921.

It was a small building then, and Mrs. Smith and her late husband made many additions as their guest list grew. The design of the additions was done with care, so that the distinctive roof, which was copied, would still dominate the inn's exterior shaded by huge spreading trees along Route 28, the main street of Harwich Port. In time, the Smiths installed the unobtrusive swimming pool in back, and they acquired the guesthouses on the inn's private beach.

Now Mrs. Smith runs the inn, named by a previous owner for his hometown, Melrose, Massachusetts, with her son, C. Philip Smith. There are seventy-five bedrooms: those in the oldest part of the inn have pleasant flowered wallpaper and antiques. The rooms elsewhere, including the beach houses, are furnished in the resort style and have knotty-pine walls. You can stay here from early May through the middle of October.

If you come during the summer, you will find the inn operates on the American plan, with a picnic lunch (and thermoses filled with coffee) offered to those who do not wish to eat in the dining room at midday. All meals are open to the public. You will also discover the inn has an atmosphere reminiscent of a summer resort of the 1920s and 1930s in the large, airy, and cheerful public rooms. In the living room the sofas are antimacassared, and guests who are not reading mystery books or playing cards can gather around the enormous fireplace on rainy June nights.

Most inns do not have television sets in individual bedrooms, but many hide one set in a small public room that is usually less attractive than the other rooms. At The Melrose the "television room" is exceptionally pleasant, with two rows of white-wicker chairs, one behind the other, set up as though this were a tiny theater. During our first visit here, every chair was taken by guests who ignored the bright sunshine and gave up a beautiful day at the beach so they could watch the Senate Watergate hearings televised in 1973.

The dining room has an old-fashioned sense of propriety, with polished silver and white linen napkins that are placed after dinner in paper napkin rings marked with each guest's name. The dinner menu is extensive and varied, with offerings prepared in a simple manner ranging from boiled lobster to prime ribs of beef. Two regular dishes on the menu are clam chowder and baked stuffed quahogs. The quahog (pronounced co-hog) is a clam with a thick, strong shell, and the smallest ones, called littlenecks, have no necks at all and are considered a delicacy by many people. The steamer clam, or soft clam, has a long black neck. You can make clam chowder using the steamer or the quahog clam. Some people say the quahog gives a chowder a zestier flavor, and others insist on discarding the steamer's black neck so the color of the soup will not be marred. No matter which clam is used, a New England clam chowder is made with milk and never includes tomatoes, a primary ingredient in Manhattan chowder. When a New England inn lists "clam chowder" on its menu and does not specify which kind, it invariably means New England chowder.

Directions to the Inn: From New York, take I-95 north to Providence and I-195 to Mass. 25 to U.S. 6 east to exit 8. From Boston, take Route 128 to Route 3 to U.S. 6 east to exit 8. At the end of the end of the ramp, go right onto Route 124 to Harwich Center. Turn left on Main Street and right on Bank Street, continuing for about 1.5 miles. Go left on Main Street in Harwich Port to the Inn.

THE HOLDEN INN

Wellfleet, Massachusetts

There are so many interesting things to do in Wellfleet, about two-thirds of which belongs to the National Seashore, that this town is probably the last place on the Cape we expected to find an inn off the beaten track.

The Holden Inn, while hardly isolated, is between the town and the bay on a road with the unlikely name, Commercial Street. The inn personifies the exact opposite of Commercial Street's connotation. It is small-scale and homey like a guesthouse that also serves breakfast and dinner.

Open from the last week in June through Labor Day, the inn has twenty-four bedrooms, housed in the three-story inn, in a white-clapboard cottage next door, and in a larger house behind the inn, called The Lodge. The prettiest bedrooms are in the inn: some have cheerful wallpaper, others have walls painted yellow with white trim or a warm pink with white trim. One of the public rooms is a delightful sitting room with white wicker furniture and yellow cushions. When the weather is warm, breakfast and dinner are served on the screened-in porch. (The inn does not serve liquor, although guests can bring their own wines and liquor and be served.)

The Environs: Wellfleet, with a year-round population of 1,743, is picturesque without the clutter of shops, stores, and restaurants lined up in a row that characterizes many Cape towns. When you walk along the main street, notice the house in the center of town called Belvernon. This is now a private home, but it once belonged to Captain Lorenzo Dow Baker (1840–1908), who had an eighty-five-ton schooner called *The Telegraph* and was in the shipping trade. He imported bamboo from the West Indies and on one trip he decided to bring a few bananas back to America. The new fruit was received with acclaim, and Captain Baker's decision resulted in the United Fruit Company, which was established in 1899. Captain Baker became the managing director of the firm's Jamaica division.

You will find the headquarters of the National Seashore right off Route 6 in Wellfleet. The stretch of sand near the parking lot is called Marconi Beach in honor of Guglielmo Marconi. North of the parking area you will see an open-air building marking the site of the first transatlantic wireless station. It was from this station that Marconi, who invented the wireless telegraph in 1896, sent the first wireless message in 1903 to King Edward VII of England from President Theodore Roosevelt.

The Wellfleet Bay Wildlife Sanctuary is one of the largest private bird-banding stations in the world. Its 700 acres include nature trails, a salt marsh, and pine woods. The Goose Pond Trail, a self-guiding nature trail, passes the pond over a wooden boardwalk, and if you take the loop trail to the right, you will wind up on Try Island. Twice a year, at the vernal and autumnal equinox, the entire marsh is inundated by the tide except for Try Island. To get to the sanctuary, cross from Eastham to Wellfleet on Route 6, watch for the Audubon Society's sign on the left, turn and follow the signs to the sanctuary. From the parking area, walk to the left to the sign for Goose Pond Trail.

Directions to the Inn: From New York, take I-95 north to Providence and I-195 to Mass. 25 to U.S. 6 east toward Wellfleet, watching for a sign, "Wellfleet Center." At the sign, turn left onto Main St., continuing for one-eighth mile to a rowboat filled with flowers. Go left onto Commercial St., continuing one-eighth mile to the Inn on the right. From Boston, take Route 128 to Route 3 to U.S. 6 and continue as above.

CORNWALL HOUSE

North Truro, Massachusetts

One Sunday when George Beiers was six years old and the family cook had the day off, he tiptoed into the kitchen, peeled and sliced several potatoes, sprinkled them with pepper, and rustled up some French fries for his parents. Mr. Beiers has been cooking ever since, and now you can sample the results of his efforts at La Méditerranée, a restaurant Mr. and Mrs. Beiers run next door to the Cornwall House.

The Cornwall House is where the Beiers welcome guests from June 25 through September 8. There are four suites, each consisting of a sitting room, a bedroom with twin beds, and a private bathroom. In the inn, its brochure says, "The emphasis is on tranquillity and in view of this, Cornwall House is not suitable for children under 12 or pets. Glamour picnics will be made to order by La Méditerranée, and there are facilities for boiling water for tea, soups, etc. A continental breakfast of freshly made croissants or other French pastries, fresh orange juice and coffee or tea is served every morning."

The restaurant, La Méditerranée, has attracted visits from many food critics, among them James Beard and Craig Claiborne. Mr. Claiborne described the duck pâté that Mr. Beiers makes with truffles and cognac in these words: "one of the most memorable dishes at the Méditerranée—and it would be a credit to any restaurant—was a freshly made pâté of duck livers, beautifully seasoned with spices and cognac."

The food here is imaginative and, for an inn, the offerings are extraordinarily varied. They include gigot d'agneau en croûte (baby leg of lamb boned and stuffed with truffles, pâté de foie, veal kidneys, and cognac, baked in a puff pastry crust); mussels Portugaise (mussels cooked in white wine, shallots, and olive oil); and game pie (partridge, pheasant, rabbit, and duck cooked with a wine, herbs, and spices marinade in a puff pastry crust).

Other entrees that are served from time to time include choucroute Alsacienne (a variety of sausages, smoked bacon, and pork loin chops cooked in sauerkraut with white wine and chicken consommé); curried chicken, fish, or meat; and fish stews such as the robust bouillabaisse. If you have room for dessert, your choices will include fresh fruits, chocolate mousse, coupe aux marrons, and Paris-Brest, a hollowed ring filled with crème pâtissière and sprinkled with pralines.

The extensive wine list, offering mostly French wines, ranges from $4.50 for a Spanish Blanco to $125 for a 1945 Latour-Pauillac.

The only meal served in the restaurant is dinner for guests and the public. The decor is imaginative and romantically flamboyant, with wicker furniture, red-and-white striped vinyl tablecloths, some white ice-cream parlor chairs, an intricate carved screen at the main dining room's entrance, and a hot-colored Haitian painting on the French blue wall of the second dining room. The contrast of the interiors with the very plain, clear pastels of the countryside gives the restaurant an exciting atmosphere.

Scenic Drive: To Pilgrims Lake.

Directions to the Inn: From New York, take I-95 north to Providence, and I-195 to Mass. 25 to U.S. 6. Follow U.S. 6 to North Truro Highland Road exit, turn left on Highland Road, and continue 400 yards straight ahead to the Cornwall House and La Méditerranée on your right. From Boston, take Mass. 3 to U.S. 6 and follow New York directions from that point.

Vermont

Let us do all we can to keep up the notion among our city cousins, that to live "away up in Vermont," is the American equivalent for being exiled to Siberia.

ABBY HEMENWAY
The Vermont Historical Gazetteer [1867]

For fourteen years—from 1777 to 1791—Vermont, New England's maverick state, was an independent republic. It maintained a militia, carried on "foreign" trade, regulated weights and measures, and naturalized its own citizens. Vermont's five post offices at Bennington, Brattleboro, Newbury, Rutland, and Windsor connected with the United States postal system at Albany, New York.

Not that Vermonters were united on the issue of independence. They were not. Vermont's complicated boundary dispute with New York and New Hampshire resulted in controversy. Even George Washington got involved. In 1784 he wrote to the president of the Congress that in his opinion Vermont would have to be conquered by force of arms. In the end Vermont joined the United States on March 4, 1791. Of course, a Vermonter might tell you, "The United States joined us." But, then, that is Vermont.

Vermont, bordered by Canada on the north, Massachusetts on the south, New York on the west, and New Hampshire on the east, is New England's only state that does not confront the Atlantic Ocean. People who know both Vermont and New Hampshire well often speak of them as a pair. In 1923 Robert Frost (Vermont's poet laureate since 1961) wrote of New Hampshire, "She's one of the two best states in the Union. Vermont's the

85

other." But a lot of people who have never been here confuse the two. Apparently, the Georgia legislature made that mistake in the 1800s.

Vermont's 1777 constitution was the first in history to prohibit slavery in any form. Vermonters were so outspoken in their opposition to slavery that from 1833 until 1837 alone, there were sixty-eight antislavery organizations formed in the state. In the decade before the Civil War the legislature passed more than fifteen antislavery resolutions. This so infuriated the Georgia legislature that it advised President Franklin Pierce, a New Hampshire native, to "employ a sufficient number of able-bodied Irishmen to proceed to Vermont, and to dig a ditch around the limits of the same, and to float 'the thing' into the Atlantic." It would have been difficult to accomplish, especially because Vermont is bordered on the east by New Hampshire, which separates it from the ocean.

In 1861 Vermonters went so far as to vote overwhelmingly for Abraham Lincoln for president, giving their native son who opposed him, Stephen A. Douglas, only 20 percent of their votes. Not all Vermonters accepted Lincoln's victory. One man, Eleazer Albee, born in Rockingham, moved to Stanstead, Quebec, where he died on August 28, 1864. This is the epitaph on his gravestone: "He went into Voluntary Banishment from his Beloved Native Country, during the Reigning Terror in the Third Year of the Misrule of Abraham the First."

For all its separatism and its proud tradition of articulate dissension, Vermont is a great state to visit. The Green Mountains that divide the state do not have the grandeur of New Hampshire's White Mountains, but what Vermont's landscape lacks in size, it more than makes up for in its disarmingly inviting roads and enchanting little villages and towns. In 1939 the Vermont Association for Billboard Restriction asked Maxfield Parrish, a New Hampshire artist, to design a poster and postcard. He did. The slogan was, "Buy Products Not Advertised On Our Roadside." Now Vermont no longer has billboards, and that alone makes this state a greater delight to visit than any other in New England.

Even the interstate highways in Vermont afford wonderful scenery. You can take Vt. 100 almost the length of the state (it is 157.5 miles as the crow flies from Canada to Massachusetts) for a scenic trip, but be sure to notice the turnoffs to villages such as Hyde Park and Moscow. Moscow is said to have been named when someone at a school meeting in 1839 struck an object against a large saw blade and somebody else thought the sound resembled church bells in Moscow, Russia.

Vermont's villages and towns are the most consistently appealing in New England. Take almost any road, turn a corner, and suddenly you are in a tiny, tidy settlement where the clapboard houses cling to a vintage village green, smoke curls from the chimneys, the general store has a gas pump in front, the frozen laundry flaps from porches in the winter, a small sign announces a church supper, a carved pumpkin smiles from the doorstep of an inn, the American flag marking the post office hangs over the doorway of a barn, as in Peacham, and the way out of town is through a one-lane covered bridge.

Vermont also has the highest standards of innkeeping and the most imaginative inns anywhere in New England. In the past, Vermont also had the most unusual inn—the Windham County Jail in Newfane—where, for nearly one hundred years, prisoners and paying guests ate and slept under the same roof. People called it the Jail-Hotel.

When you go to Newfane now, you cannot miss the Greek Revival courthouse on Vt. 30. Alistair Cooke called this "the most beautiful courthouse in the United States, not excluding the pompous Greek wedding cake of the new United States Supreme Court building." The Windham County Courthouse stands alone on the town green and has a serene, majestic air. After you notice the graceful windows, the four-pillared portico, the decorative modillions, and the capped tower, stand in front of the courthouse and look across Vt. 30. You will see the 2½-story Jail-Hotel set back from the road next to the Newfane Store. It is now occupied by a Vermont state trooper and his family.

The homely white-clapboard jail was built in 1825 at the same time the splendid courthouse was going up on the green. Together, they cost $10,000 to construct. From 1825 until 1853, the jail looked as it does today except for the porch, which was added later. It was in this building that the jail keepers also had their living quarters. Mr. and Mrs. Keith N. Crowell of the Windham County Historical Society traced court records that showed that in 1853 Vermont's General Assembly authorized the building of an addition to both the courthouse and the jail. That was when an L-shaped wing was constructed on the jail. It was on the southern side of the building, the right side as you face it. And that was the beginning of the Jail-Hotel.

"It was built on to accommodate the jury at the court," Mrs. Charles Whitney of Newfane told us in an interview. Mrs. Whitney and her late husband ran the Jail-Hotel from 1934 until 1956, when the hotel addition was taken down and the jail was remodeled. "Back in the days when they had no automobiles or transportation, the witnesses and jurors had to stay through the week, and so they stayed at the hotel. We had a jury room—one large room—upstairs on the third floor, and before women were allowed to serve on juries, the men all stayed up there on cots: thirteen jurors and the officer in charge. That was when the jury had to be sequestered on a murder trial or a serious criminal case. They would stay in the courthouse until it was time to go to bed and then come over to us in a body. They were allowed in the dining room, but there was always a deputy sheriff with them. They weren't allowed to converse with anybody else."

One of the United States presidents who visited Newfane was Rutherford B. Hayes. Hayes's family lived in nearby Dummerston Center until 1817 when they moved to Ohio, where he was born. His grandfather was a Vermont saloon keeper. Hayes became president of the National Prison Association, and in 1889, the year his wife, nicknamed Lemonade Lucy for her temperance activities, died, Hayes traveled to Vermont. On October 10, 1889, he spent the night at the Jail-Hotel. His name appears near the front of the registry book, which starts on September 21, 1889. That book is now owned by Mr. and Mrs. Norman Robinson of Newfane, who lived in the jail keepers' quarters from 1959 until 1970. Apparently, Hayes enjoyed the fall foliage in early October so much that he returned the next year. The entry for October 4, 1890, says, "Rutherford B. Hayes, Fremont, Ohio."

In 1895 the jailers, Charlotte and Charles Underwood, had their daughter's wedding in the front parlor of the hotel. Susan Underwood, twenty-four years old, was married to Walter Wheeler. She wore "a white dotted-swiss wedding dress all trimmed with satin ribbon and puffed sleeves," her daughter, Mrs. Paul Graham of Newfane, recalled. "The wedding was on August 21, 1895, which was my father's twenty-third birthday.

His wedding coat was a dress suit cutaway," Mrs. Graham said.

After President Theodore Roosevelt visited Newfane, his reaction to the Jail-Hotel was widely quoted. Margaret and Walter Hard remembered it in their book *This Is Vermont* (1936) with these words, "Do you remember what Teddy said the time he came here and saw the prisoner inside there? He looked across the peaceful village and said, 'Someday when I've got some reading to do and I need a rest, I'm coming up here and commit some mild crime.'"

Roosevelt was not the only one who thought that staying at the Jail-Hotel would be something to look forward to. According to Mrs. Whitney, "As a rule, the prisoners weren't charged with very serious crimes. Petty larceny, and mostly intoxication. They used to make an effort to come in to stay for the winter. They liked it there and they had no home. They were habitual drinkers—alcoholics, we call them today. And we liked them very much. The ones we knew who'd come each year were allowed on the grounds. They were able to mow the lawn, shovel snow, do various things for the privilege of being out. We didn't have to worry about their running away."

If the prisoners helped defray the cost of overhead and upkeep at the Jail-Hotel, they also took care of the problem of leftovers. We asked Mrs. Whitney if the prisoners and paying guests ate in the same dining room. "Never," Mrs. Whitney said. "They mingled only if the guests talked to the prisoners when they were outside working; otherwise, they were locked up in the jail. In the dining room—it was on the first floor—we had separate tables with white tablecloths and napkins, and one long table we called the jury table. The prisoners' meals were served in the jail, taken in on trays. We had two floors of cells for men, and then there was one big room on the third floor for women with a couple of cots in there. We rarely had a woman but occasionally we'd get one for intoxication."

What did Mrs. Whitney serve? "I tried to offer country cooking, New England style. One specialty was doughnuts. I used to get up every morning and make doughnuts. Of course, in a real busy season I had a cook and I always had to have table girls. This sounds funny but we didn't have to worry about having a lot of food left over from the dining-room table, because it could always be served in the jail—and the same with the doughnuts. The prisoners didn't get fresh doughnuts every morning—but they got doughnuts."

Mrs. Whitney's menus included some traditional New England meals. "On Saturday night we nearly always had baked beans. I liked to serve New England boiled dinner with corned beef, cabbage, johnnycake, and Indian pudding. Of course, on the Fourth of July there was salmon, new potatoes, and green peas. For the jury I ran a special for forty cents. You could do it back in '34. They always expected a cooked meal at noon, so for the forty-cent special, I'd serve meat loaf, corn dried beef, a salmon loaf on fish day, cheaper cuts of meat. I don't remember serving fried salt pork, though. That was an old-fashioned dish, but I never served it to the jury. We used to run special Sunday dinners: roast turkey, roast duck, chicken pie, things like that. Sunday dinner was a dollar fifty."

The Jail-Hotel was popular and had many returning guests, but people who were just driving through often stopped for a meal, too. If you had been among them, you would have stopped your car along Vt. 30, walked toward the Jail-Hotel, and confronted two signs. The sign on the left side of the building said, "Windham County Jail," and the sign above the right-hand door, "Windham County Hotel."

And what were the going rates? "I had boarders staying there for seven dollars a week, including three meals a day. Of course, we had low overhead and the state paid us so much a prisoner. When we went there in '34, it was seventy-five cents per day for a prisoner, and that included the meals. When we left in '56, the state was paying us a dollar fifty a day. I had a few regular people: one woman stayed there for years. She paid seven dollars a week all the time she was there, and she didn't leave until we did."

Did the jail attract overnight guests for the hotel? "Oh, yes, we got guests because of the jail. We had jail literature that was very popular with houseguests. And they liked to come there because they said they stayed in jail. The jail stationery was quite a curiosity. The heading on the letters was 'Windham County Jail.' People thought it was a great joke."

Was the Jail-Hotel a friendly place? "I think so," Mrs. Whitney said. "Yes, I think people would tell you that. They were quite exciting days."

Well, you cannot stop at the Jail-Hotel anymore for doughnuts or baked beans, but Vermont's inns offer a variety of interesting and memorable meals to choose from. Among the state's annual events that attract visitors, here are some well-established festivals that food lovers will enjoy. Vermont towns and churches hold many chicken-pie suppers, turkey suppers, and barbecues, but those listed here are among the more unusual food events. For more information, write to Information Travel Division, Vermont Development Agency, 61 Elm Street, Montpelier, Vt. 05602.

- March 26–27, Maple Sugar Square Dance Festival, Burlington
- April 9–11, State Maple Festival, St. Albans
- June 5–6, State Dairy Festival, Enosburg Falls
- Late June, Strawberry Festivals, Plymouth and Londonderry
- Early July, Sugar-on-Snow Supper, Morgan
- Mid-October, Apple Pie Festival, Dummerston Center
- Late November, Wild Game Supper, Bradford

Tourism is important in Vermont, where more than half the 9,276 square miles of land is now owned by people from out of state. After the Second World War, skiing became big business in Vermont, and land developers flocked here to build vacation homes. Vermonters objected, though, and in 1970 the state legislature passed Act 250 that restricts development.

Ironically, one of Vermont's founders was a land hustler himself. Ira Allen, Ethan Allen's brother, was among the settlers from Connecticut who came north and named Vermont "New Connecticut" for five months in 1777. Ira Allen wrote the preamble to the constitution that declared Vermont "a free and independent state," and he was the republic's first treasurer.

Allen, whose nickname was Stub, once owned a great deal of acreage in what is now Vermont's skiing capital, Stowe, and in the nearby town, Underhill. In 1772 he traveled with his cousin with the memorable name Remember Baker to survey the property he had not seen. This land is highly prized today, but when Allen saw it, he was disgusted. "I was owner of very near one third of the town," he wrote, "and could not discover lands that would make one good farm. This gave Baker an opportunity to pass many hard jokes on me respecting my purchase."

He decided to sell his acreage, but he had to do it in such a way that the prospective purchasers would not know the land had no agricultural value. There was one hitch. In putting the land up for sale, Allen had to describe the boundaries, and that posed a problem. It was, in Allen's words, that "a great proportion of the corners of said lots were made on spruce or fir timber, and if I described them as such, it would show the poorness of the town, and raise many questions that I wished to avoid. I made use of a stratagem that answered my purpose."

Allen's ruse was to refer to the spruce and fir trees as "gumwood." When the prospective buyers from Sharon, Connecticut, wanted to know what "gum-wood" was, Allen told them, "Tall Straight trees that had a gum, much like the gum on cherry trees." Just to cinch the deal, Allen pretended to be interested in buying land nearby. This convinced the unwary purchasers who had not seen the property that the land was valuable and worth owning as farmland.

Allen's deception worked and the land was sold. "Having closed this business satisfactorily to myself, I returned to my brother's and had a hearty laugh with my brothers Heman and Zimri, on informing them respecting the gum-wood." If Ira Allen could see Stowe today, the chances are he would not be laughing.

Stowe is the town that lies in the shadow of Vermont's highest peak, Mount Mansfield, altitude 4,393 feet. With neighboring Spruce Peak, Mount Mansfield makes up one of the largest ski areas east of the Rocky Mountains. By Vermont standards, Stowe is highly developed and commercialized with more than sixty motels, motor inns, and ski lodges, and many gas stations and bars. During a good snow season—from early December through mid-April—you will find Vt. 108 from Stowe to Mount Mansfield lined with cars. Cross-country skiing is increasingly popular in Stowe, but most winter visitors are still downhill skiers, whose plastic, foam-filled boots and fiberglass skis are a far cry from the equipment people first used here.

"Around 1902 to 1905, a few of us took hardwood boards and bent up one end, nailed on a toe strap and thought we were ready to ski," Craig O. Burt, Sr. of Stowe recalled in *Mansfield: The Story of Vermont's Loftiest Mountain,* by Robert L. Hagerman. "The poles were 1″ × 1″ hardwood and quite long—there were no grooves in our skis so control was at a minimum. Our skiing consisted of straight running down a slope. But the spills without the thrills was not really skiing, and all of us lost interest. The infection, however, was there."

The "infection" did not catch on until a simple device, the rope tow, was introduced in the United States. The first rope tow in America was built in Woodstock, Vermont, in 1934 on Clinton Gilbert's farm. It was powered by a Model-T truck engine, and it allowed skiers, holding onto the rope, to be pulled slowly on their skis up a pasture hill.

Three years later the rope tow was installed for commercial use in Stowe. The rope was 1,000 feet long, and the tow was powered by a 1927 Cadillac engine. When it began operating on February 7, 1937, a day ticket cost fifty cents and a season pass was five dollars.

The annals of Vermont hospitality portray even the first governor as an amiable host, whose warm welcome was appreciated by travelers. Three early accounts describe his house as humble. Eben Judd, a Vermont surveyor who visited Thomas Chittenden in 1787, wrote, "Crossed the river to Williston to see his excellency, Governor Chittenden of Vermont. I found him in a small house in the woods."

There is a fascinating story about the effect Chittenden had on the Reverend Nathan Perkins, a West Hartford, Connecticut, minister who traveled by horseback through Vermont in 1789 when it was still a republic. Rev. Perkins describes his first impression of Chittenden: "Thursday 20 of May set out for Williston where governor Chittenden lives. . . . A low poor house—a plain family—low, vulgar man, clownish, excessively parsimonious."

That was Thursday, May 20, 1789. By Saturday, May 22, the minister had practically become a family member. In his diary he writes, "I perform this day 22th Saturday the office of physician & nurse to Mrs. Chittenden who is very sick with a disorder called St. Anthony's fire. Miss Leita Chittenden, the young Lady 16 years old, & I, nurse together. They seem to love me, as a brother, & the Governor as a son. I struck them upon the right key.—Queer is human nature & has a blind side. His Excellency picked me out to understand human nature, at first sight."

It was against the law to travel on Sundays in Vermont, so Rev. Perkins on "Sabbath Evening left his Excellency's & went over Onion River to Jericho. . . . His Excellency at parting with me, in Jericho, where he accompanied me—bid me farewell & shook hands with me, & left a dollar in my hand." The minister's last entry about Chittenden is on June 8. He writes, "Monday morning June 8th set out for home. Met the governor of Vermont on my rode to Shaftsbury. He expressed much love for me. Bid him farewell."

Two years later, after Vermont had joined the United States, John Lincklaen visited Chittenden, who "received us without ceremony, in the country fashion. He is a man of about 60, destitute of all education, but possessing good sense & sound judgment. . . . Born in Connecticut, he still retains the inquisitive character of his compatriots, & overwhelms one with questions to which one can scarcely reply. . . . His house & way of living have nothing to distinguish them from those of any private individual but he offers heartily a glass of grog, potatoes & bacon to anyone who wishes to come and see him."

If you would like to join the "251" Club, named for Vermont's 251 towns and cities, write to Mrs. Lillias M. Bailey, Secretary, 27 Deerfield Drive, Montpelier, Vt. 05602. The "251" Club is an informal group of Vermontophiles whose objective is to visit each town. There are almost four thousand members from thirty-five states, the Canal Zone, the Yukon Territory, and several Canadian provinces. The club has a board of directors, car-identification decals, and a quarterly newsletter, *The Wayfarer*, which says, " 'Visit' means not to 'drive through' but to linger a bit, talk to someone who lives there, visit a store or the post office, take notes for a diary, perhaps stay overnight."

When you visit the Green Mountain State, you will find that Vermont's innkeepers have a lot more than a glass of grog, potatoes, and bacon with which to welcome you. Vermont's best inns for imaginative food are The Four Columns Inn and The Old Newfane Inn in Newfane, The Reluctant Panther Inn in Manchester Village, The Three Clock Inn in South Londonderry, and The Lodge at Smugglers' Notch in Stowe. When you make reservations at them, bear in mind that the atmosphere is free but for everything else they charge.

The furnishings in Vermont inns, on the whole, tend to be more interesting and unusual than elsewhere in New England. The most outstanding furnishings are at The Old Tavern at Grafton, and at The Inn at Sawmill Farm.

It is hard to define what makes an inn all-American to the core, from its menu to its bunk room for skiers, but that is exactly what we think of whenever The Green Mountain Inn in Stowe comes to mind. Throughout New England many inns have motel units adjacent to the main building. The best one we have seen is at The Green Mountain Inn.

Of Vermont's picturesque villages that have inns, our favorites are Brookfield, Grafton, Marlboro, and Newfane. In West Arlington you will find New England's most personal inn, Grandmother's House. You can only get to it by going through a red covered bridge.

Finally, Vermont has the one inn we would rather not tell you about: The Inn on the Common in Craftsbury Common. This inn has the wonderful combination of good food, imaginative furnishings in the public rooms, the bedrooms, and the bathrooms, and a great setting in an alluring village with a view. What is more, the inn is small. If you insist on separate tables in a dining room and a bathroom accessible from your bedroom, this may not become your favorite inn—which is a nice way of saying that we would like to keep this inn all to ourselves.

THE INN AT SAWMILL FARM

West Dover, Vermont

In the early 1800s, anyone could buy the services of a traveling portrait artist for between four and fifteen dollars plus lodging and meals. The artists combed the countryside for customers, carrying brushes, canvases, and palettes with them. Sometimes they brought figures of children already painted except for the face. That meant a child would not have to sit very long, but it also meant that the child's face on the painting looked dislocated from the body.

The Inn at Sawmill Farm has one of these curious primitive portraits of a girl, whose meticulously detailed white dress is typical of the work done by tavern sign painters. You will find the portrait in the dining room. It is only one example of the inn's antiques, folk art, old utensils, and signs that will delight even the most casual lover of Americana.

The Inn at Sawmill Farm, open all year except between about November 15 and December 5, has sixteen outstanding bedrooms in a converted barn and farmhouse. Aside from the distant view of the Mount Snow Ski Area two miles north, the inn's setting in this small, homely, southern Vermont village is not unusual. But inside you will find a bridal suite, several suites with fireplaces, and a bedroom with a large canopied bed. The inn serves two meals daily: breakfast to houseguests and dinner, by reservation only, to guests and the public.

Although many New England inns are run by husband-wife teams and often involve other family members in primary roles, here this happy combination has produced magnificent results. When innkeepers Rodney and Ione Williams converted the old Upton farm in 1967, they merged their respective talents as architect and interior designer.

Rodney Williams retained the wooden beams, posts, braces, and irregular barn siding so that every room is dominated by the timber's strong horizontal and vertical lines. In some first-floor bedrooms, once cow stalls, the wall posts have silky smooth corners where the cows rubbed their necks against the wood. Ione Williams has furnished the inn with fabrics and wallpapers that complement the warm texture of the hand-hewn and rough-sawn wood. The patterns tend toward traditional themes such as baskets, fruits, and flowers; the colors and designs are consistently lively and uplifting.

Together, the Williamses have filled the inn with their collection of antiques started long before they opened the inn. There are copper pots and copper planters, a lavishly handsome English grandfather clock, a wooden egg case from Boston, strings of sleigh bells, a plowman's rake, old signs, and a hay cycle with a beautifully curved handle. A wooden Vermont butter churn sits beside the pay telephone under the eaves.

In the entry there is a sign the Williamses bought at an auction because they thought the decorative filigree would make it attractive for the inn's sign outdoors. When they cleaned it carefully, they found a painted sheep, an apple tree, and flowers beneath the dirt. The sign has stayed indoors ever since.

In the taproom there is one sign that is still a mystery. It says, "We Sell Woods," but no one has been able to figure out what product was being advertised. The Williamses found it under a manure pile near the inn and decided to shade the taproom walls subtly with a matching citron color. Over the copper-topped bar there is an apple-barrel stencil and a pair of American wooden ice skates. The cash register (made of brass and bronze) is ninety years old and only rings up to ten dollars. The taproom also has copper-clad tables, a player piano that works, and an old pot-bellied stove.

When we stayed here, the four-course dinner began with

asparagus tips wrapped in smoked Vermont ham and baked with a little cheese. The soups were crab bisque and cream of walnut (made with chicken stock, curry, cream, and chopped walnuts). We had a rack of baby lamb that was crisp on the outside and deliciously moist and tender inside. It came with barely glazed fresh carrots and a large, baked, fresh mushroom cap filled with cream cheese, egg yolk, onion, and Tabasco sauce. The other entrees were Châteaubriand for two, Icelandic lobster tails, steak au poivre, backfin crab meat au gratin, and chicken breasts cooked with black olives and wine sauce.

The inn's most popular dessert is vanilla ice cream with chocolate butternut sauce. The recipe for the sauce was given to the Williamses when they opened the inn, on the condition that they not reveal it; in spite of many requests, they have kept that promise. The wine list offers domestic and imported wines.

The breakfast menu during our stay offered freshly squeezed orange juice, pancakes rolled with a fresh raspberry purée, poached eggs, shirred eggs, and a version of eggs Benedict called eggs Sawmill. This dish consists of the following: a toasted English muffin topped with a slice of baked tomato, a strip of crisp, dry bacon, a poached egg, a light hot Hollandaise sauce, and a sprinkling of fresh minced parsley.

The inn's bridal suite, once a hayloft, has a tiny dressing room between the beautifully furnished bedroom and the bathroom. All the private bathrooms are attractive; like many, this one has a wash basin recessed in a copper-topped vanity, and it has a wooden medicine chest. In the white-clapboard farmhouse there is another suite with several twin-bedded rooms with patchwork quilts, and a living room with a working fireplace and a small television set. The suite is set up so you can close off one or two bedrooms for separate parties.

Although families come here at Christmas and over the George Washington Birthday weekend, the inn is most popular among couples who go skiing at Mount Snow and Haystack. You can bring your ice skates to use on the inn's two-acre pond, which is cleared in the winter. In the warm months guests play golf at two nearby eighteen-hole courses and swim in the inn's small pool outdoors. The overall atmosphere here is casual. Still, men are asked to wear jackets at dinner and, as the inn puts it, "ladies should wear appropriate après ski wear."

Scenic Drive: To Newfane, Grafton, Weston, and Manchester and back.

Directions to the Inn: From New York, take I-95 and I-91 to Vt. 9 west (exit at Brattleboro) to Wilmington, then Vt. 100 north to West Dover. From Boston, take Mass. 2 west to Greenfield to I-91 north to Vt. 9 to Wilmington to Vt. 100 north to West Dover. In West Dover, watch for the inn's sign on the left as you drive north on Vt. 100.

GRANDMOTHER'S HOUSE

West Arlington, Vermont

"Would you like to get up at 5 A.M. to watch Millard Vaughn milk his cows next door?" Innkeeper Mrs. Walter Finney posed this question to us at dinner. "You've got to be kidding," we replied. But Mrs. Finney was not. "In that case," we said, "we're game."

At 5 A.M. Millard Vaughn's large red barn at Battenkill Farm was ablaze with the only lights in this tiny valley surrounded by pine-covered hills. During the night a mid-November snow flurry had dusted the mailbox in front of the inn, the covered bridge, the Methodist Church, and the dirt road from the inn to the farm. The dark-green spruce trees on the hills were outlined in white, and our breath froze in the air.

Inside the warm barn, Millard was hand feeding four calves less than three days old their two quarts of milk each. "Animals aren't supposed to know anything," he said, "but calves stand up fifteen minutes after they're born, and babies are useless for two years." He did his milking with clockwork efficiency while fifteen cats tagged after him, nuzzled up to our ankles, avoided the twenty-eight Holstein cows, and terrified the calves by even approaching them. "For fourteen years I went to school and put up with being told what to do. Now I work for myself. It's hard work but I love farming." Saying that, Millard Vaughn handed us a ladle of raw milk to try. "I hate pasteurized milk," he said. "When the milk is boiled, the flavor changes and, to me, it tastes funny."

After the milking was finished, we sat down in Mrs. Finney's kitchen to a breakfast of scrambled eggs, bacon, toast, and tea. The kitchen was replete with photographs of her family, a radio to listen to the morning news from Brattleboro, and the customary kitchen utensils acquired in a home over twenty years.

At 7:30 A.M. a bright-yellow school bus stopped on the far side of the valley's 1852 red covered bridge. It spans the Batten Kill River, a celebrated trout stream, and leads the few yards to Grandmother's House. A lone figure in a camel-colored coat, clutching some books, ran past the inn down the road to the bridge. "That's Millard's oldest girl, Sylvia," Mrs. Finney said. "She's a little late for school this morning."

Grandmother's House, a small inn in southwestern Vermont, has four bedrooms and serves dinner and breakfast for guests family style. It is open all year and reservations are required. Norman Rockwell, the artist and illustrator, used to live in this white-clapboard house before he moved to Stockbridge, Massachusetts, selling the house to the Finneys in 1954. After Mr. Finney died, Mrs. Finney opened her home to guests in 1969. Today Grandmother's House is the most personal inn we know of in New England.

When we arrived here, Mrs. Finney came outside to greet us. "Well, hello, hello," she said, introducing herself as "Betsy or Grandmother, whichever you prefer." After showing us to a comfortable bedroom with a four-poster bed, Grandmother said, "I'll have to let you know exactly what time dinner will be. I think I'll see if the young couple who live just down the road can join us. It's always nice for young people to meet."

Dinner with Grandmother and the couple down the road was held at the lace-covered table in the dining room in front of a roaring fire. Candles were lit on the mantelpiece and on the table. The fire's flickering flames and the candles provided enough light to eat by and created a warm, cozy atmosphere conducive to a relaxed chatty evening.

Before dinner, Grandmother said grace. "Thank you, God, for the fun of meeting around the table and for the opportunity to make new friendships and to renew old ones. Bless this food to our use, oh Lord, and us to thy service. Amen."

The meal began with a crabmeat cocktail, followed by the entree, a large sirloin steak with diced onions on top. We helped ourselves to the green beans, creamed corn, baked potatoes, and pink chablis wine. For dessert, Grandmother had made an apple pie with an indescribably light crust and a succulent filling. After dinner, tea was made in a china pot with a crewel cover to keep it warm while the tea was brewing.

The bedrooms are furnished in a homey style, with antiques such as a maple, tiger-striped, four-poster bed, innumerable books, assorted chairs, knickknacks, and many old magazines that Grandmother says "people love to read because they wouldn't do so in their own homes." From the four-poster bed, you can look directly out through second-story windows at the red covered bridge, the blue stream, and the white-spired church against the green hills. It is a lovely view to wake up to, even if it is 5 A.M. and the alarm clock is ringing in your ears.

The Environs: If you are here in the summer, you can take a dip in the "swimming hole" under the covered bridge, fish in the river, and play tennis. In the winter you can drive to Big Bromley, Snow Valley, Stratton Mountain, and Magic Mountain ski areas.

Scenic Drive: Vt. 313 to U.S. 7 north to Skyline Drive (toll road) up Mount Equinox.

Directions to the Inn: From New York, take the Taconic Parkway north to the Mass. Turnpike east to N.Y. 22 north to Vt. 313 east (at Cambridge, New York). Drive twelve miles on Vt. 313 to the inn and the bridge. From Boston, take Mass. 2 west to I-91 north to Vt. 9 west (at Brattleboro) to U.S. 7 north to Vt. 313 west. From the juncture of U.S. 7 and Vt. 313, drive four miles on Vt. 313 to the inn and the bridge. Drive through the bridge. Grandmother's House is straight ahead at the top of the rise.

THE FOUR COLUMNS INN

Newfane, Vermont

As a boy in Épernay, France, innkeeper René Chardain vowed that he would never follow in the footsteps of his restaurateur father. But Monsieur Chardain had a change of heart and now, as a restaurateur in this southeastern Vermont town of 900 people, he has earned quite a reputation for himself.

In spite of its American-sounding name, The Four Columns is more like a French inn than any New England inn we visited. It has a legion of loyal followers who swear by its excellent French cuisine, served in a red-clapboard building behind Newfane's town green.

The Four Columns Inn is open from the end of May through October and from the end of December until April. It is closed on Mondays. The inn serves lunch (in the summer) and dinner (all year) to both guests and the public. Breakfast is available for houseguests only. There are twelve bedrooms here, each with a private bathroom.

In the low-ceilinged dining room we found Madame Chardain hurrying from the kitchen, potholders in hand, as she delivered the piping-hot entrees to the inn's guests. A robust fire crackled in the fireplace, and a large display of wines gleamed by the door. Wesley Chardain, the maître d' in formal attire, scanned the room for a diner's glance as if he were a sentry on duty.

The lavish attention to detail here is what brings people back to The Four Columns Inn. After we had ordered, a pre-appetizer unexpectedly arrived consisting of a bubbly miniature Coquilles St. Jacques with mushrooms, clams, and scallops in a Béchamel sauce, topped with melted Gruyère and Parmesan cheese. A gentleman at a nearby table who ordered the escargots was delighted when the waitress brought a little scoop of lime sherbet in a bowl to take away the taste of the garlic. Leaning toward his companion, he said, "I must say, I'm impressed. Now that's class!"

The appetizers when we were there included pâté du chef, fresh oysters on the half shell, tartar steak, and Nova Scotia home-smoked salmon. The salmon was beautifully presented, with a generous helping of caviar, slices of Spanish onion, capers, and a slice of lemon. A pepper mill and a small can of Filippo Berio olive oil were brought to the table.

The entrees included roast duck Bigarade flambé, filet mignon with Béarnaise sauce, rack of lamb for two, frog's legs Provençale, Châteaubriand, and veal scaloppini Marsala made with dry Florio, the Sicilian wine. The veal came with a perfectly cooked green spaghetti, thinly coated with butter and Parmesan cheese. Hot, chewy French dinner rolls and crispy garlic bread came with the meal.

For dessert, the choices include crêpes Suzette, Cherries Jubilee, peach Melba, coupes aux marrons, pear Hélène, Indian pudding, French caramel custard, French chocolate custard, and ice cream. Strawberries Romanoff are often a weekend feature. After dinner, the inn serves espresso coffee and Irish coffee, along with tea and American coffee.

At the annual New Year's Eve dinner, guests, by reservation only, spend the entire evening at one sitting in the company of "no music, no trinkets, no noisemakers, just good food," as Monsieur Chardain puts it. The menu is set. In past years it has included terrine of pheasant truffée, feuilletée of turbot sauce champagne, roasted partridge forestière, sorbet bourguignon, filet de boeuf en croûte aux deux sauces, assorted cheeses, strawberries Rothschild, and demitasse.

One of the inn's summer specialties is pheasant, which the Chardains raise themselves. They also have several fresh-water trout ponds in back of the inn, and they keep pigs from which they make pâté.

Compared with the food, the inn's bedrooms are relatively unimaginative. Most wallpaper patterns are flowers within stripes, and most chairs have braided seat coverings. One of the sunniest bedrooms is Room 9, a corner room with a hand-hewn horizontal beam underlining the window on one wall. The twin beds have gleaming wooden headboards, white bedspreads, and pale-lavender blankets.

The inn is named for one of its two buildings, a white-clapboard former home with four columns on the front. It was built before the Civil War by General Pardon T. Kimball, who called it Kimball Hall. It is said that General Kimball's wife was unhappy living on Newfane Hill, and that when the village moved to its present location, the good General built this house, a replica of his wife's southern girlhood home. Behind this building is the red-clapboard restaurant. You will find both buildings in back of the Windham County Courthouse on Newfane's green.

Scenic Drive: Vt. 30 and Vt. 100 north to Weston, or Vt. 30 and Vt. 35 north to Vt. 121 north to Grafton.

Directions to the Inn: From New York or Boston, take I-91 north to the Brattleboro exit for Vt. 30. Follow Vt. 30 north twelve miles to Newfane. The inn is one hundred yards off Vt. 30.

THE OLD NEWFANE INN

Newfane, Vermont

After we sat down to dinner at the neighboring Four Columns Inn, Wesley Chardain recalled that he and his parents used to run The Old Newfane Inn. "You know The Old Newfane Inn no longer exists," he said offhandedly. "Oh?" we said. "Yes," he replied, "when we moved here, The Old Newfane Inn moved with us." Well, the fact is that The Old Newfane Inn is alive and healthy on Vt. 30 opposite the Windham County Courthouse—just where it has always been.

This white-clapboard inn has ten charming bedrooms, including one of New England's most romantic ones. It serves excellent, imaginative food, with lunch (in the summer) and dinner (all year) open to the public. Breakfast is served to houseguests only. The inn is open from mid-May through the end of October and from mid-December through the end of March. Walk upstairs to the second floor and you will see the distinctive flat-barrel ceiling and lovely irregular maple floorboards that once were part of a ballroom, measuring about forty by twenty feet. It was the custom in the 1800s to build ballrooms with a moveable partition. The partition could be hooked to the floor, creating two rooms, or it could be raised to the ceiling to make one large room. When a meeting, dance, or other large gathering took place in an inn, the partition was raised. Otherwise, it was lowered so the two rooms could be used as bedrooms. Today the partitions dividing the old ballroom into bedrooms are permanent.

The most romantic bedroom here is Room 20. Some guests refer to it as the "lilac room" because it has lilac-patterned wallpaper. The flat-barrel ceiling gives the room a canopy effect. There is a flower picture in an eight-sided shadow box between the twin beds, a rocking chair, a small desk, and a private bathroom. From the "lilac room," you look out at the handsome courthouse in one direction and across the road at the Newfane Store, a small grocery store, and at the former "Jail-Hotel" (see the introduction to Vermont).

While The Four Columns Inn has its aficionados, so does The Old Newfane. You can stay here for a weekend and try eating at both places or simply choose between the two. We have met some travelers who have asked us, "Well, which of the two do you prefer?" Our most honest answer is, "You really can't go wrong with either one." Newfane is a classic example of a small town with an outstanding green and two inns almost side by side that, by competing, have both achieved a high standard of innkeeping.

At The Old Newfane the fourteen appetizers and soups on our menu included creamed watercress soup, gazpacho Andalluz, French onion soup, and consommé à la maison. Among the appetizers were Fettucine alla Alfredo for two, smoked goose pâté, ragoût fine gratiné, pâté du chef, Nova Scotia salmon, escargots Bourguignon, and prosciutto with melon.

There are usually about two dozen entrees, most involving a lot of preparation. The night we were there these included rack of lamb bouquetière for two, Long Island duckling au Cointreau à l'orange, shrimp scampi à la maison, Châteaubriand for two, tournedos of beef au poivre, Louisiana frog's legs, scaloppini of veal Marsala, and pepper steak flambéd with brandy. Some tasty Lyonnaise potatoes and fresh broccoli came with the entrees.

You will have many choices for dessert. Among the desserts offered us were coupes aux marrons, soufflé glacé Grand Marnier, strawberries Romanoff, pear Hélène, peach Melba, three kinds of parfaits, and frosted banana-cream pie. The inn offers three flaming desserts for two: crêpes Suzette, Cherries Jubilee, and peach bonne auberge. During our visit the inn was also having a five-layer sponge cake with a mocha-buttercream filling between each layer.

The wine list is extensive and mostly French. You can have two special after-dinner drinks here (besides coffee, tea, and milk). "Devil's Milk" is a combination of milk, brandy, and grenadine; "Café Newfane Inn" is a mixture of coffee, Tia Maria, and whipped cream. If you linger too long in the inn's cozy taproom —as we did—you can always go for a walk afterward around Newfane's splendid town green.

Scenic Drive: From Newfane, take Vt. 30 south to West Dummerston, turning through the covered bridge and continuing on the town road to Dummerston Center.

Directions to the Inn: From New York or Boston, take I-91 north to the Brattleboro exit for Vt. 30. Follow Vt. 30 north twelve miles to Newfane. The inn is on Vt. 30.

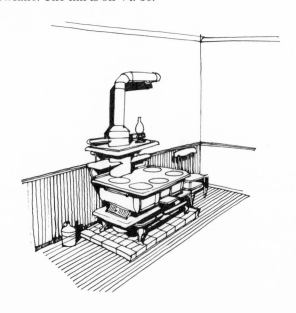

THE RELUCTANT PANTHER INN

Manchester Village, Vermont

The white-marble sidewalks are what you will probably notice first in this southwestern Vermont town where Mrs. Abraham Lincoln spent her summers. When some of these sidewalks, made of sawed marble slabs, deteriorated over the years, they were repaired with concrete. But the terrace in back of The Reluctant Panther Inn is nothing but white marble. Even the floor of the inn's boot room, where you can leave your ski equipment, is marble; so is the short path from West Road to the inn.

The Reluctant Panther Inn is intensely romantic in an unexpected and highly successful way. From the vibrant lavender-clapboard exterior to the smoked salmon à la Moscovite (salmon, whitefish caviar, sour cream, and jellied consommé Madrilène), innkeepers Mr. and Mrs. Stephen Wood Cornell III have carried out a radical departure from the old-fashioned inn. They have done this with consistent boldness and a strong sense of showmanship. The results? A visually exuberant atmosphere, excellent, imaginative food, and unforgettably flamboyant furnishings.

The inn is open from Memorial Day through November 1 and from December 20 through Easter. Dinner is served daily except Tuesdays, and the dining room is open to the public.

Breakfast is available for houseguests only. There are eight bedrooms here, each with a private bathroom. These include four with working fireplaces, one of which is among New England's most romantic bedrooms. The inn does not accept children as guests, but you would not want to bring your children here anyway. The Reluctant Panther is definitely an inn for couples who want to spend time alone.

During dinner in the tiny slate-floored Solarium, the smallest of the inn's two dining rooms, we watched a full moon rise slowly in an ink-blue sky. We suggest you reserve a table in this room, which has a sloping glass roof, carefully pruned hanging plants, and only four tables. The roof, the plants, and the asparagus fern in the window boxes create a greenhouse effect.

We started the four-course dinner with trout à la ora, a tiny whole boneless trout with a mayonnaise and caper sauce. The soups that night were split green pea, minestrone (made with beef broth, carrots, cabbage, zucchini, and kidney beans), and Avgolemono, a Greek soup made with chicken stock, eggs, lemon juice, and rice.

The eight entrees included crêpes filled with minced chicken and veal, crêpes filled with baby shrimp and curried cream sauce, sirloin steak in boneless strips with a Béarnaise or mustard sauce, roast duckling with an orange sauce, and rainbow trout stuffed with shrimp and crabmeat. The inn also offers a fondue for two consisting of filet mignon cut into one-inch cubes and served with a pot of boiling oil and various sauces, relishes, and condiments.

The desserts, presented on an attractive tray, included a maple mousse that was sweet and delectably light.

The wine list is extensive. The taproom is larger than the Solarium and has a bar, tables, and paintings on the walls.

From the double bed in Room D, the most romantic bedroom here, you can look out through the window at Mount Equinox. This room has a working fireplace, a brass headboard, and it is decorated in various shades of lavender. There is a dark-lavender shag rug on the floor, a medium-lavender bedspread, and light-lavender painted on the ceiling, the mantel, and behind the highly decorative headboard to set it off. The wallpaper pattern has large pink, white, and lavender flowers with green leaves. There is nothing old-fashioned about Room D, but it is intimate, interesting, and the color scheme works.

All the bedrooms have wall-to-wall, flecked shag rugs, as thick as unmown grass, on the floors, and built-in window seats.

(In one room the rug even climbs up a wall.) All the wallpapers are large, stylish prints in extroverted colors. Each room is decorated individually and has a television set, a telephone, and oversized, thick towels in the bathroom. If you like buttermilk pancakes, be sure to order them for breakfast. They are cooked thoroughly on one side but only partially on the other, leaving them light and delicious. Ours were brushed with melted butter and came with a pitcher of steaming Vermont maple syrup.

The breakfast menu also offers French toast made with homemade bread, eggs Benedict, boiled eggs, and scrambled eggs with chives. You can have American bacon, hickory-smoked Canadian bacon, or a local brand of sausage. The beverages include a cranberry and orange juice mixture beaten to a froth, fresh ground coffee, milk, and Darjeeling tea. (The inn also serves a Continental breakfast.)

The Environs: Outside, The Reluctant Panther lies in the shadow of Mount Equinox, altitude 3,816 feet, where an automobile road is open from May through October. The Sky Line Drive, a toll road, starts from U.S. 7 (between Manchester and Arlington) and winds past picnic areas where some outdoor fireplaces are made of granite. There are many hiking trails here. From the road you will see one building resembling a factory on this otherwise undeveloped mountain. It is a Carthusian Monastery made of Barre, Vermont, granite blocks set on end in poured concrete. Since it houses an order of cloistered monks, it is off limits to the public.

You can browse in the shops along U.S. 7 in Manchester (population 2,919) any time of year. Manchester includes Manchester Center, the business section, and Manchester Village, which is primarily residential. Manchester Village is a handsome, polished-looking place, with tall elms, many large homes, and attractive plantings around crew-cut lawns. It is in the center of what has been a traditional marble-producing area in Vermont. If you are in the mood during a summer visit here, ask Mr. and Mrs. Cornell for directions to the marble quarry, where you can take a swim.

During the winter, most visitors at the inn are skiers who have nearby Snow Valley, Big Bromley, Magic Mountain, and Stratton Mountain ski areas to choose from.

For summer travelers there are concerts, art shows, and ballet dancing at the Southern Vermont Art Center in Manchester Village. And do not forget your bathing suit. If the marble quarry does not appeal to you, the Cornells will direct you to a mountain waterfall.

Scenic Drive: Sky Line Drive.

Directions to the Inn: From New York, take the Taconic Parkway to the Mass. Turnpike east to U.S. 7 north toward Manchester. Just beyond the Johnny Appleseed Bookshop, bear left on West Road. The inn is the lavender building on your left. Note: if you are driving south on U.S. 7, check your mileage at the juncture of Routes 7, 11, and 30 and continue south on U.S. 7 for 1.15 miles. Just past the buff-brick Mark Skinner Library on your right, turn right on West Road. If you go as far as the Johnny Appleseed Bookshop, turn around. From Boston, take the Mass. Turnpike west to U.S. 7 north and follow directions above.

THE THREE CLOCK INN

South Londonderry, Vermont

People say it is a little hard to find The Three Clock Inn, hidden just off Vt. 100 behind the church in this southern Vermont village. We did not have any trouble at all, but if you do, just remember that your effort will be well rewarded.

The Three Clock Inn serves extraordinary food in two dining rooms that are snug and very romantic. The inn is open from mid-December through early April and from Memorial Day weekend through mid-October. Breakfast is offered only to houseguests and dinner is available for both houseguests and the public daily except Mondays. There are just four bedrooms here, each with a private bathroom. The inn is a flower-bordered, white-clapboard building surrounded by a white-picket fence. The living room is comfortably furnished with sofas and a fireplace. You can sip a drink here before dinner, study the menu and the wine list, and give your order in the presence of three clocks hanging on the walls. We began dinner with eggplant carbonata, a cold mixture of eggplant, tomatoes, celery, olives, capers, and onions, topped with sliced almonds.

The dozen entrees on our menu included duckling à l'orange, frog's legs Provençale, scampi à la maison, veal scaloppini piccata, lamb chops, and cutlet of veal Zingara. The evening's specialty was tournedos with Béarnaise sauce. The plate was beautifully presented, with the sauce resting in a fresh artichoke heart. The meal came with lightly sautéed, thinly sliced zucchini and some crispy fresh French fried potatoes.

The half a dozen desserts offered us included peach Melba, pear Hélène, and a lovely strawberries Romanoff that was made with fresh strawberries despite the fact that the strawberry season was over.

The intimate dining rooms are furnished with red-and-white checked wallpaper, exposed ayzed beams, blue tablecloths, some cheerful braided rugs, and regal pepper grinders on each table. The tables are placed far enough apart for guests to have breathing space without feeling that this is a formal dining room. The coziness is reinforced by the red candles on each table and the cluster of multicolored candles on the fireplace mantel.

Mrs. Heinrich Tschernitz greets you warmly, with a smile that is sure to make you feel at home. During our visit she was reminiscing after dinner with a couple celebrating their sixth wedding anniversary about their wedding reception held at The Three Clock Inn. Mr. Tschernitz kept appearing from the kitchen throughout the evening, lingering in the dining room only long enough to ask guests if the meal had been prepared to their satisfaction. The attitude of goodwill expressed in his eyes suggested that he was accustomed to being answered in the affirmative.

The bedrooms on the second floor are popular among skiers during the winter, even though The Three Clock Inn is better known as a restaurant than a hostelry. One bedroom has a canopy bed. When you arrive, you will notice the evening's menu placed conspicuously by the front door. Take a good look at the prices, if you are interested; the menus presented to guests sipping sherry in the living room do not list the prices—on purpose.

Scenic Drive: Vt. 100.

Directions to the Inn: From New York or Boston, take I-91 north to the Brattleboro exit to exit 30; follow Vt. 30 north to Vt. 100 north to South Londonderry. When you cross the bridge, Vt. 100 makes a sharp left turn. At this point drive straight up the hillock beyond the church and you will see the inn.

THE OLD TAVERN AT GRAFTON

Grafton, Vermont

"When Aunt Pauline died, she left her money to her two nephews, in trust—to Dean Mathey of Princeton, New Jersey, and to me. She left a note saying that she hoped we would find some worthy use for these funds that would be stimulating to both of us and that we could get a great deal of pleasure out of. Needless to say, we both spent many hours trying to figure out what she had in mind." The speaker is the late Mathew Hall, who fell in love with this southeastern Vermont village in 1936. Mr. Hall told his story in the November 1967 issue of *Yankee Magazine*, from which the excerpts quoted here are used by permission.

During a period of almost five years after her death we were unable to decide what to do with the money, and we did have "a little bit o' luck," as the song says, and the funds increased. I was out here at my home one lovely July morning when Dean Mathey came in, fire literally shooting from his eyes. He said, "Matt, I've found the answer to Aunt Pauline's money . . . it's Grafton. There are a number of houses in town that are architecturally perfect but run down and without modern conveniences. Why don't we use these funds to put these houses back in their original condition, except that we'll put in modern kitchens, plumbing and heating? Why isn't this exactly what she had in mind for us to do?"

That was the beginning of the Windham Foundation, formed in 1963. First, the foundation tackled the Village Store, then it restored some old homes, and in 1965 it went to work on The Old Tavern.

Thanks to Pauline Fiske, Dean Mathey, and Mathew Hall, Grafton (population 465) is now a much-photographed, picture-postcard village, dominated by the handsome Old Tavern in the center of town. The first time we drove into Grafton, it was snowing. The village looked like a Grandma Moses painting, with snow dusting the paved road, the two churches, the brick and clapboard houses, the post office, the tree limbs, and the picturesque sign in front of the inn.

The Old Tavern has thirty-six consistently appealing bedrooms, each with a private bathroom. Most of the bedrooms are in several white-clapboard houses across the road from the main inn. The inn is open all year except during April. Three meals are served daily for houseguests and the public, and box lunches are put up on request.

The entire inn is exquisitely furnished in a traditional style, with graceful antiques everywhere, canopied beds in four of New England's most romantic bedrooms, and seven spit-and-polish public rooms tucked away in the attractive buildings. Since there are so many antiques, including more than 450 English nineteenth-century satirical prints, children under eight years old are not accepted as inn guests.

The Old Tavern has an unusual variety of intimate bedrooms. There are two bedrooms with a double bed and a fishnet canopy (Rooms 4 and 33). Room 20 has a double bed with a boxed canopy, and Room 36 has twin beds with fishnet canopies.

In the winter you can leave your skis and equipment in the breezeway between the main inn and a detached barn that houses the inn's taproom. When you walk inside the barn, you will notice the giant crossbeam that dominates the central space.

It is from a dismantled covered bridge in northern Vermont. You will see an enormous gun hanging from the crossbeam. It was made about 1850 as an advertising model for a Boston gunsmith's shop.

In the main inn, the dining-room floors gleam and the simple pine tables are set without placemats or tablecloths, showing off the inn's colorful "Dr. Syntax" plates. These white plates have fanciful English illustrations depicting an imaginary schoolmaster, Dr. Syntax, and his horse, Grizzle. Compared with the inn's setting and the elegant tone of the furnishings, the food is not so special. During our visit there five entrees for dinner: broiled filet of sole amandine, tenderloin of beef en brochette, broiled calf's liver, sirloin steak with fresh mushroom caps, and veal scaloppini Marsala. The veal consisted of veal chunks in a thick brown wine gravy, instead of paper-thin slices.

The wine list offers imported and domestic wines. You can have an after-dinner drink either in the dining room or in one of the comfortable living rooms where guests gather in front of the fireplaces, chatting about the weather and skiing conditions.

Purists sometimes criticize The Old Tavern because it is a reconstructed inn with a newly built interior inside the remnants of an 1801 shell. But the refabrication was sensitively carried out and re-creates an atmosphere that is cozy, relaxed, and informal. There is nothing impersonal about the inn, even though it is a far cry from Grafton's first "hotel," which was homey, to say the least. If you wanted to spend the night in town in the 1780s, you were welcome to stay at Henry Bond's hotel. Mr. Bond ran the hotel and store in his two-room log cabin. According to the *History of Grafton, Vermont, 1754–1971* by Helen M. Pettengill, "One room and one bed were reserved for the Bond family and guests."

The Environs: Walk from the inn along Townshend Road and you will come to The Grafton Village Cheese Co., where you can watch cheddar cheese being made several days a week. It takes from one day to a day and a half for the raw milk to become cheddar cheese. During the process, the milk breaks down into two parts: the curds from which the cheese is made and the whey residue.

The Old Tavern is within an hour's driving distance of several good downhill ski areas. Member passes are available for the semiprivate Timber Ridge Ski Area, just fifteen minutes away. You can cross-country ski on the village's many walking trails, which are open to the public. And the inn has snowshoes, toboggans, and sleds for you to use. Bring your ice skates if you come in the winter; the pond is cleared for skating. In the summer the pond is a lovely swimming pool with water lilies at one end. There is an outdoor tennis court here, too.

Scenic Drive: Vt. 121. Note: from Grafton west almost to North Windham, this is a dirt road through the woods.

Directions to the Inn: From New York, take I-95 and I-91 north. From Boston, take Mass. 2 west to I-91 north. Leave I-91 at exit 5 and take Vt. 121 west to Grafton.

THE NORWICH INN

Norwich, Vermont

When President James Monroe toured New England on horseback in 1817, he came to Norwich on July 22 for a dinner personally prepared by innkeeper Eleazer Curtis. Since then, Curtis' Hotel has been named The Union Hotel (1832), The Norwich Hotel (1889), and The Newton Inn (1905). Now it is The Norwich Inn, but it is still a convenient stopover for travelers in northern New England.

The inn, less than a mile from I-91, is in east-central Vermont across the Connecticut River from Hanover, New Hampshire, the home of Dartmouth College. There are twenty bedrooms in the main inn and seven additional bedrooms in an adjacent motel. The inn is open all year, serving three meals daily to houseguests and the public. Box lunches are put up on request.

The center of Norwich, population 1,966, is stretched out along the town's main street, where you will find The Norwich Inn next to a small gas station and a fairly modern grocery store called Dan and Whit's. The sometimes bustling pace of activity nearby changes completely when you walk through the wide front door of the inn. There is an unhurried feeling in the living room, where guests often have afternoon cocktails, setting their drinks on the marble-topped tables.

When we stayed here in late May, a thunderstorm was splashing rain so hard in front of the inn that it bounced off the pavement. But inside the inn, the atmosphere was tranquil and warm. There were pink apple blossoms spilling out of a blue-and-white china pitcher, reflected in a huge gold-leaf mirror above the living-room fireplace. A stoic portrait of one of innkeeper Bill Dibble's ancestors seemed to be quite at home here, too.

The inn's guestbook lay open on a desk, filled with phrases written in moments of spontaneity with little thought to their permanence. "What an Inn *Should* Be," someone declared in ballpoint pen. "Good mints!!!" somebody else exclaimed. One line in tiny script began, "Mr. and Mrs." and ended, "Having a Terrific Honeymoon." A man from Rye, New York, said, "A tribute to Vermont cooking." And a couple from Rochester, New York, summed up their feelings with "We felt so at home here."

When we entered the dining room, Mrs. Dibble was seating guests. A salad bar at one end consisted of a huge bowl of chicory and iceberg lettuce and numerous small bowls with relishes and salad garnishes such as onion slices and croûtons. For the first course, there was a tomato-vegetable soup made from scratch and a fruitcup of fresh orange, grapefruit, and apple slices with a large spoonful of sherbet on top.

The seven entrees on our menu included baked stuffed chicken breast, filet mignon wrapped in Vermont bacon, beef Stroganoff on buttered egg noodles, and seafood Newburg with rice. During the meal the waitress came by with a basket of sliced oatmeal bread.

The inn offered a lot of desserts: strawberry, rhubarb, and apple pies, strawberry shortcake with whipped cream, maple-nut sundae with Vermont maple syrup, and various parfaits such as ginger brandy, Crème de Menthe, wild cherry brandy, and apricot brandy.

The wine list had about twenty wines, ranging from an Italian Soave to Piper Heidsieck-extra dry. The "Norwich Inn cocktail" was made with rum, Vermont maple syrup, and fresh lime juice. The bedrooms in the inn are furnished with lovely flowered wallpaper, white curtains, and maple bedsteads. Most rooms have one-piece desk and dresser sets (like those often found in motels), along with relatively modern lamps. In this way the furnishings bridge the decors typical of inns, on the one hand, and of motels, on the other.

During our visit the Vermont Chamber of Commerce had a small luncheon meeting in one dining room. Afterward, the men milled about, exchanging greetings and small talk. We found a Dartmouth College professor settled in a deep chair, puffing a pipe, and reminiscing about his adventures as the Honorary Mayor of Norwich.

The professor recounted the day he was formally received by the Lord Mayer in Norwich, England. After the ceremonious introductions, the professor saw the Lord Mayor turn to his aide. The Lord Mayor said politely, "Have we ever heard of Norwich, Vermont?" "Oh, yes," the aide quickly replied, reminding the Lord Mayor, "We have been in correspondence with Norwich, Vermont." "Of course," the Lord Mayor murmured as if he were trying to refresh his memory but had not quite succeeded.

The professor interjected. "Perhaps, sir, you've heard of Norwich, Connecticut?" The Lord Mayor nodded, "Yes, Norwich, Connecticut, is a child of ours." The professor said, "Norwich Vermont, in turn is a child of Norwich, Connecticut." "Ahhh," the Lord Mayor exclaimed, a smile spreading across his brow, "Another grandchild swum into the ken."

After meeting the Lord Mayor, the professor was interviewed by a local reporter who asked, "Where is Norwich, Vermont?" The professor explained, "The Connecticut River divides Vermont and New Hampshire. And Norwich is across the river from Hanover, New Hampshire, where Dartmouth College is. You could say that Norwich is a bedroom town of Hanover." "Bedroom?" the reporter said, frowning, "And what might that be?" The professor replied, "A lot of our people work in Hanover but live in Norwich." "Oh," the reporter said, eyebrows raised: " 'Dormitory town' we call it. So much nicer."

Scenic Drive: I-91 south to I-89 north to U.S. 4 south to Woodstock. Note: the Appalachian Trail passes near The Norwich Inn.

Directions to the Inn: From New York, take I-95 to I-91 north to exit 13. From Boston, take I-93 to I-89 to I-91 north to exit 13. At the end of the ramp, follow signs west to Norwich. The inn is less than a mile from the exit along the main street.

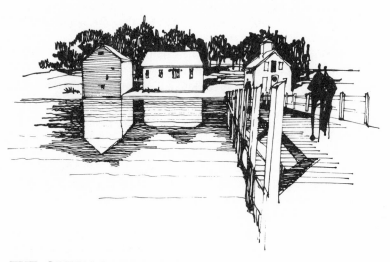

THE GREEN TRAILS INN

Brookfield, Vermont

Of Vermont's inns tucked in snug villages off the beaten track, The Green Trails Inn in central Vermont is unique because it sits beside New England's only floating bridge.

In most New England villages the town center is organized around the green or common, used first as a pasture for grazing animals. But here the village center is shimmering Sunset Lake and the 320-foot wooden-plank bridge that spans it. The buildings belonging to The Green Trails Inn are clustered near the bridge, with The Fork Shop, the inn's restaurant, alongside the lake. In the summer you can sit outside at tables beneath umbrellas, while children swim in the lake and horses and riders cross the wooden planks.

The Green Trails Inn is open from Memorial Day through Thanksgiving and from December 26 through March. There are seven cheerful, old-fashioned bedrooms in the inn and three efficiencies above the Pond Village General Store. (The efficiencies have kitchens, living rooms, and bedrooms, and they are open all year.) Breakfast and dinner are served daily to houseguests; lunch is now available at the store, and dinner is open to the public. The inn puts up box lunches on request.

Since the inn is owned by two families—Chris and Sherrill Williams and Ed and Mary Ellen Taylor—children are welcome here. "We like to think of ourselves as a family place because both of our families have young kids and our kids enjoy playing with the children who stay at the inn," Chris Williams says.

The room furnishings vary, from the efficiencies for families, which have old-fashioned bedrooms and flowered wallpaper, to the exceptional Stencil Room in the Williams' own house. You can spend the night in this twin-bedded room that has interesting furniture, a private bathroom, and walls with beautiful hand stenciling done in the early 1800s. Seven layers of wallpaper covered the stenciling until the wallpaper was removed in the early 1900s, revealing well-preserved designs of wicker baskets and floral sprays in grass-green and a light red-brick color.

The bedrooms in the main inn are furnished with graceful antiques, large headboards, and, during the summer, pitchers of fresh flowers. Some beds have delightful patchwork quilts. The wallpaper patterns have pretty flowers or blue-and-white stripes.

The inn's restaurant is a separate rustic building that used to be a factory producing hand-forged steel pitchforks. That is why it is called The Fork Shop. When you walk inside, you will see the old farm tools, horse-show ribbons, and saddles on the walls. From the player piano you will hear tunes such as "Alexander's Rag Time Band."

There are usually ten entrees at dinner, ranging from chopped beef and fried chicken to the day's specialties (sometimes New England boiled dinner, baked stuffed shrimp, or Maryland crab). The inn has a small wine list.

The Environs: The town's picturesque floating bridge leads past open meadows and thick woods to Allis State Park, where you can take your picnic lunch and look at the lovely view of mountains and valleys from the lookout tower. The bridge is open to traffic all year except when covered by snow. It has white railings, hinged ramps at either end, and a middle section held up by 380 barrels. The original bridge was built in 1812 after a man named Belknap drowned in 1810 while trying to cross the frozen lake. In 1936, when the present bridge was constructed, fifty-gallon wooden barrels were placed beneath it as pontoons. Today as these barrels become waterlogged and sink or drift to shore, they are replaced by steel drums filled with styrofoam.

In his 1968 edition of *Vermont: A Guide to the Green Mountain State*, Ray Bearse wrote, "When the state offered to build a modern overhead bridge here, the citizens of Brookfield rejected the proposal in a characteristic Vermont manner, saying that they had used a floating bridge for 124 years; it had been good enough, and they figured it would continue to be good enough."

Two other proposals rejected by the good citizens of Brookfield involved I-89 and the dirt crossroads by the lake. When I-89 was being built in the 1960s only half a mile from Brookfield, the townspeople voted against construction of an interchange that would have made access to the village fast and easy. Find Brookfield on a Vermont state map and you will see that it looks as though it is next to I-89. But that is only as the crow flies. It will take you about thirty minutes to drive from I-89 to the floating bridge along secondary roads.

Then there was the question of whether the dirt crossroads by the floating bridge should be paved. "I think it was in 1971 that the Highway Department had a hearing on that," Town Clerk Edson Bigelow recalls. "There were quite a lot of letters written to the governor and the Highway Department from people who didn't want it paved. They wanted a rural road."

The village with the floating bridge, the dirt crossroads, and The Green Trails Inn at the center of it all was assured of future protection when, in 1972, it was designated a Vermont Historic District. Now it is listed on the National Register of Historic Places. The population of Brookfield, which includes the village, East Brookfield, and West Brookfield, declined from 762 in 1950 to 597 in 1960. That trend was reversed in the 1960s, though, and the 1970 population was 606.

When you stay at The Green Trails Inn during the summer and fall, you can ride horseback or hike along the nearly one hundred miles of dirt roads and paths in the immediate vicinity. (The stables are next door to the inn and offer basic instruction as well as guided trail rides.) In the winter this is an excellent place to cross-country ski, snow shoe, toboggan, or join one of the sleigh rides on Sunset Lake.

All in all, Green Trails is a well-rounded inn for people of any age. It is an inn for couples as well as families, for horseback riders, for cross-country skiers, for walkers, and for people who want to enjoy the annual Ice Harvest Festival. In the early 1900s there was a large commercial ice operation on Sunset Lake. During the ice-harvest season (New Year's Day through February), horse teams scraped snow off the ice, which ranged from fourteen to twenty-eight inches in thickness. This tradition has been revived as an annual Brookfield event.

In the 1800s Brookfield was on the main stagecoach route between Boston and Montreal. People who come here now do not pass through anymore. Instead, they arrive because Brookfield has become a destination in its own right. When we visited this tiny unspoiled and unpolished village, we had the distinct feeling that we and we alone had discovered what Ray Bearse called "a mountain village with a certain amount of cobwebby atmosphere and off-trail charm." The chances are that you will have the same sensation.

Scenic Drive: Go to Rochester on state roads, about an hour's drive from the inn. Drive by the common for a few yards, at the fork bear left over a small bridge uphill and continue for several miles. This side trip from Rochester will reward you with superior views amid hillside farms. But this drive is only for the adventurous, since the state map does not record these roads.

Directions to the Inn: From New York, take I-95 north to I-91 to I-89 to exit 4. From Boston, take I-93 to I-89 to exit 4. Drive to Randolph Center and follow Vt. 14 north to the turnoff for Brookfield. For a delightful alternative, turn left at the stop sign in Randolph Center and continue straight on this road, ignoring the signs toward Vt. 14. This becomes a dirt road for almost the seven miles to Brookfield, with pleasant views of the mountains to the west. When the dirt road ends, turn left to the inn. Note: if you take public transportation, the innkeepers will meet you if you come to Montpelier Junction by train; to Montpelier by plane; to Barre or Randolph by bus.

THE GREEN MOUNTAIN INN

Stowe, Vermont

If you have ever yearned for the good old days when people traveled by stagecoach and no one had heard of a car, consider what it was like to take a trip in 1833. That was when The Green Mountain Inn was built in the middle of this northern Vermont town as a stagecoach stop.

Stagecoach passengers who spent the night at an inn usually slept in their clothes and rose well before dawn to start the next "stage" of their trip, often on an empty stomach. Even in good weather, they were constantly jolted from their thin-cushioned seats as the horse team hauled the coach (without shock absorbers) over "corduroy" roads made of logs.

When the coach was stuck in mud, the passengers, wading through the mud themselves, got out to lighten the horses' load. When it rained, they often arrived soaking wet at the next stagecoach stop—only to be greeted by a cold supper.

In the 1830s the signs in front of Vermont inns were made to swing back and forth on hinges instead of to stand or hang fixed as they did in neighboring New York State. Those hinged signs are about the only thing that stagecoach stops and inns today have in common.

The Green Mountain Inn has outlived both the stagecoach days and the tourists who arrived in the mid-1800s when it was fashionable to climb Mount Mansfield in the summer. Today this red-clapboard inn is open from Memorial Day to November 1 and from December 15 to April 15. There are sixty-one consistently appealing bedrooms, each with a private bathroom. The inn serves three meals daily to guests and the public. Box lunches are put up on request.

During our visit, the fragrance of blueberry or date muffins baking in the morning in the kitchen filled the inn, whetting the appetites of skiers eager to take that first run on the slopes. Everyone assembled in the inn's living room even before breakfast began, exchanging opinions in still sleepy voices as to whether it would snow later that day (it did).

From the inside, the inn seems smaller than it is because many of the bedrooms are housed in motel additions behind the main building. These red-clapboard structures have been designed in an unusually sensitive way, like a series of stable stalls with carriage lanterns providing the outdoor lighting. You can hardly see them from the main street because they are hidden from view by a timber archway that connects the inn's second floor to the second floor over the general store next door. (The rooms above the store are bedrooms, too.)

The inn's bedrooms, including the motel rooms, are furnished with tastefully chosen reproductions of antiques, cheerful flowered wallpaper, and water colors of Vermont scenes. We were assigned to a room in the motel, and found it as pleasing as the rooms in the inn. The wood-paneled bunk rooms on the inn's second floor are among the nicest we have seen in New England.

In the dining room there are about thirty dissimilar carriage lanterns on the walls. The focal point is an ornate dumb-waiter that the waitresses still use. The Green Mountain Inn is best known for its excellent homemade soups and its wonderful cream pies. On successive evenings we had corn chowder, tomato, cream of mushroom, and vegetable soups. The entrees here included a hot, juicy roast beef, Yankee pot roast, and broiled scallops. The salad was a mixture of greens, with an oil-and-vinegar dressing, presented in a large wooden bowl that was set in the center of the table. There was enough salad for two people each to have two helpings.

The inn's menu is direct and unassuming. As innkeeper Parker Perry puts it, "A word we have never had to use or feel like using is *gourmet*. Today, it is gourmet this and gourmet that. If it is hamburg, why call it chopped sirloin? We don't do this at The Green Mountain Inn."

The desserts range from apple pie and Indian pudding with vanilla ice cream to the memorable cream pies. During our visit these included banana cream, coconut cream, a delectable maple cream and black-bottom pie, a chiffon pie in which the chocolate layer on the bottom is covered with a rum-flavored layer and the top with whipped cream and chocolate shavings.

The inn's no-nonsense attitude is summed up by this statement at the bottom of the wine list, which offers about thirty mostly imported wines. "Wine impresario Alexis Lachine says, 'No basket.' But if you must have a basket, we have baskets."

Downstairs, the wood-paneled taproom has hand-hewn beams, more carriage lamps, a fireplace, and dozens of whips displayed on the walls. The idea behind calling the taproom The Whip is that Mrs. Perry (whose maiden name was Whipple) has been called Whip all her life. The beautiful dried-flower arrangements throughout the inn are her handiwork.

Scenic Drive: Vt. 108 north and the toll road to the top of Mount Mansfield, Vermont's highest peak. Continue on Vt. 108 north through dramatic Smugglers' Notch to Vt. 15 east and Vt. 100 south back to Stowe.

Directions to the Inn: From New York, take I-95 to I-91 to I-89. Leave I-89 at exit 10 and take Vt. 100 north to Stowe. From Boston, take I-93 to I-89, getting off at exit 10. Then take Vt. 100 north to Stowe. To park your car at the inn, drive through the archway into the courtyard by the motel additions.

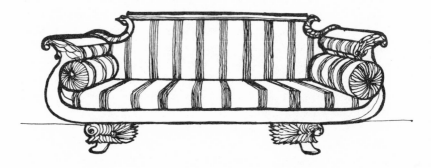

THE LODGE AT SMUGGLERS' NOTCH

Stowe, Vermont

When ski lessons were given outside this white-clapboard farm-house in 1936, the entire ski-school staff consisted of one person. He was a twenty-eight-year-old Austrian who arrived in America on December 10, 1936, to be an instructor for the Mt. Mansfield Ski Club. His name? Sepp Ruschp.

At the 1960 dedication of a double chairlift, twenty-four years to the month after he stepped off the boat, Mr. Ruschp was introduced as "the first Austrian to become a native Vermonter in one generation." Today he is the president and general manager of the Mt. Mansfield Co., Inc., a multi-million-dollar business that controls the ski-area facilities, the Mt. Mansfield Tennis Club, and three lodging places. Of these, The Lodge at Smugglers' Notch most resembles a country inn.

There are almost no other buildings between the inn and the Mt. Mansfield Ski Area a few miles north on Vt. 108. In the winter this is a dead-end road because Vt. 108 through Smugglers' Notch (where some approaches are 15 percent grade) is not plowed. In the warm months the inn is at the gateway to one of New England's most scenic drives. The Notch, at 2,162 feet in altitude, contrasts with the sheer cliffs on either side, which culminate at Mount Mansfield's summit of 4,393 feet, Vermont's highest peak.

The Lodge at Smugglers' Notch is open from mid-June through mid-October and from mid-December through mid-April. It serves excellent, imaginative food at lunch (in the summer) and at dinner and breakfast (all year) both to houseguests and the public. Reservations for meals are required. Box lunches are made on request. There are a total of forty-five bedrooms in the inn and a cottage behind it amid tall pines.

Some people may come here primarily for the activities, but to us the biggest drawing card is the food. The dining room itself is unpretentious, with textured beige wallpaper and blue-painted wainscoting. The table settings are what give this room an elegant air. There are pale-pink tablecloths, candles on each table, and white-china dishes with gold stars. The mood during our visit was lively because a pianist was playing cheerful, light music while a tuxedoed head waiter received guests with soft-spoken courtesy and polish.

The first thing we saw when we walked into this room was the high, three-tiered dessert cart dominated by a beautiful glass bowl of fresh fruit. In addition to the fruit, the inn was having assorted cheeses, a raspberry pie, peach cheesecake, and a crème caramel for dessert. This is the only large inn we have visited in New England where the tea was prepared in the English manner. Two china pots were brought to the table, one containing tea leaves and hot water, the other just steaming-hot water. At breakfast the tea was presented in the same way.

We started our dinner with pâté maison (it had flecks of black truffle through it and was garnished with aspic) and with a fresh, perfectly ripe papaya filled with a thick cranberry sauce. The soups included green pea and turtle soup with sherry.

Among the entrees were broiled filet of beef with a Béarnaise sauce, roast leg of veal Florentine, sautéed frog's legs, roast rack of lamb Pascal, and sautéed calf's liver. We had sautéed English sole with almonds, which was cooked whole, presented at the table, and then swiftly deboned. It came with Lyonnaise potatoes and a vegetable mixture of green peas, green beans, and tiny white onions. The salad was Boston and endive lettuce. The Roquefort dressing contained real Roquefort cheese rather than blue cheese.

Compared with the food, the bedrooms are ordinary. They are furnished functionally, with subdued wallpaper patterns or knotty-pine paneling. (As if anticipating minor problems caused by tumbles on the ski slopes, the inn has placed a matchbook-like packet in each room. Inside are two white buttons, one small safety pin, and six colors of thread. Another packet contains a manicure set.) The cottage behind the inn has a living room with a fireplace, a twin-bedded room, another room with a single bed, and a bathroom.

The Environs: In the winter Stowe is a popular area for cross-country as well as downhill skiing. In the summer you can hike, swim in the heated outdoor pools, or pay extra to play on the Stowe Country Club's eighteen-hole golf course and use the six clay courts at the Mt. Mansfield Tennis Club.

When you drive north on Vt. 108, you will come to the marker at Smugglers' Notch explaining the origin of its name. The marker, placed by the Vermont Board of Historic Sites, says, "Forbidden trade with Canada passed through here, 1808–14. The Notch gained its name after Jefferson's Embargo Acts of 1808 and the War of 1812, when cattle were driven north and Canadian goods were smuggled into New England through this picturesque gap beside majestic Mt. Mansfield remote from revenue officers." According to local historians, the use of the Notch as a thoroughfare for smuggling or as a meeting place for law-breaking smugglers is more legend than fact.

Scenic Drive: Vt. 108 and the toll road to Mount Mansfield's summit.

Directions to the Inn: From New York, take I-95 to I-91 to I-89 north to the exit for Vt. 100 north. From Boston, take I-93 to I-89 north to the exit for Vt. 100 north. Follow Vt. 100 north to Stowe center and take Vt. 108 north to the inn.

THE WINDRIDGE INN

Jeffersonville, Vermont

In the winter the only way you can go from Jeffersonville south to Mount Mansfield, Vermont's highest peak, is to ski across the mountains.

This homely village, named in 1827 for Thomas Jefferson, is the northern terminus of the Smugglers' Notch Road (Vt. 108), which connects Jeffersonville and Stowe. During the winter the dramatic road through the notch is impassable because of heavy snows, closing off Jeffersonville from road access to Mount Mansfield.

Despite its proximity (in the warm months) to Stowe, Jeffersonville is worlds removed; it is as quiet and unpretentious a village as Stowe is a lively, sophisticated, and tourist-minded one. The Windridge Inn is well suited to Jeffersonville's unadorned simplicity. It is a tiny, rustic village inn that describes itself as "a pure Vermont product." It is run by Alden Bryan, a landscape painter who first came here in 1938. He is one of the founders of the Smugglers' Notch Ski Area and also runs the Windridge Dairy Farms and Creamery.

This red-clapboard inn has five bedrooms, each with a private bathroom. It has reasonable rates and is open all year. Lunch and dinner are served daily to guests and the public except on Mondays when the inn is closed for lunch. On Mondays you can have lunch at the Windridge Dairy Kitchen next door. It is a bakery and coffee shop where inn guests (and anyone else) can have breakfast. Both the Dairy Kitchen and the inn are informal eating places, popular with local people. The inn puts up box lunches on request.

The dining room, the small sitting room, and the bedrooms are all furnished with pine tables, chairs, and chests in a variety of honey-toned hues. These utilitarian country pieces, along with the crude pine beams and posts, create an atmosphere of spartan simplicity.

In the bedrooms the twin beds have antique headboards and subdued cotton patchwork quilts (one is the Log Cabin design) that fit in with the sedate braided and hooked rugs on the pine floors. Electrified metal kerosene and candle lamps light up the second-floor landing, the bedrooms, and the bathrooms.

The dinner menu usually offers about ten entrees, such as ragoût of beef with burgundy wine, and breast of chicken in a casserole. The inn has a special dinner menu with pheasant, roast beef, Rock Cornish game hen, roast lamb, cheese soufflé, and escargots. You must order from it in advance. During our visit dinner began with a garlicy cheese spread brought to the table with a basket of inch-square pieces of toast. The Windridge special seafood chowder, made with clams, lobster, potatoes, and milk, was outstanding. It had that subtle tang produced in a chowder by starting it with salt pork.

The Windridge cheesecake (also available at the Dairy Kitchen next door) was an interesting variation on the usual cheesecake. This version, made only with egg whites, had no crust. The full-bodied flavor and the grainy texture of the cake resulted from using Baker's cheese, a cheese similar to cottage cheese but drier. Other desserts included brandied peaches, chocolate angel cake, compote of Mandarin oranges with Cointreau, and ice cream.

The wine list offers a dozen imported red, white, and rosé wines, along with Molsons Canadian Ale and Molsons Lager Beer.

The Environs: In the summer the inn sponsors a tennis camp for over 225 boys and girls. In the winter you can use the Windridge Tennis Camp's indoor courts for an extra fee by making telephone reservations at the Windridge Dairy Kitchen not more than four days in advance.

Jeffersonville (population 382) has its own Smugglers' Notch Ski Area, six miles south of the village, at Madonna, Morse, and Sterling mountains. It attracts skiers willing to make a longer drive in return for a low-density rate on the slopes. And by using a network of trails and lifts, you can ski from Smugglers' Notch Ski Area over to Spruce Peak and Mount Mansfield.

The village of Jeffersonville is part of the town of Cambridge, and Cambridge has three covered bridges. The Cambridge Junction or Poland Bridge, built in 1887, crosses the Lamoille River. In 1968 the Cambridge Teenage Club had a rock dance in the bridge. After about seventy-five people listened to music performed by the Galvanized Toadstool, the club's president, Chris Page, described the bridge's acoustics as "terrific."

The Gates or Little Bridge, built in 1897, crosses the Seymour River. The Grist Mill or Grand Canyon Bridge nearly slumped into the Brewster River in June 1952 when heavy rains raised the river's level and one abutment started to give way. A new concrete abutment was finished later that year, but it cost the town nearly $4,800. Mr. Bryan, whose property is near the bridge, helped to defray the cost by giving the town a substantial donation.

Scenic Drive: Vt. 108 through Smugglers' Notch and the automobile road up Mount Mansfield.

Directions to the Inn: From New York, take I-95 and I-91 north to I-89 to the exit for Vt. 100 north to Vt. 108 to Jeffersonville. From Boston, take I-93 to I-89 to the exit for Vt. 100 north to Vt. 108 to Jeffersonville. Note: in the winter take Vt. 100 north to Morrisville and Vt. 15 west to Jeffersonville.

THE INN ON THE COMMON

Craftsbury Common, Vermont

When we unlatched the white-picket fence in front of The Inn on the Common, it was the height of the foliage season in Vermont's Northeast Kingdom. The vivid yellow maple trees arching over Craftsbury Common's only road stood out against the white-clapboard houses and brown tree trunks. In the inn's ivy-filled yard, the sugar maple (thirteen feet in diameter) was golden. The moment we stepped past the two pumpkins on the doorstep, we felt as if we were guests in a small, friendly, beautifully furnished home.

From the outside, The Inn on the Common fits in perfectly with the village, which, except for the pavement on the road and the few cars that go by, has been untouched by the twentieth century. Inside, Penny and Michael Schmitt have imaginatively bridged the nineteenth and twentieth centuries by furnishing the inn with showpiece antiques, wallpapers and fabrics of traditional designs, and cheerful modern art on the walls. The inn, in contrast with Craftsbury Common's pristine plainness and serene quietude, is alive with the invigorating presence of the twentieth century.

The Inn on the Common is open from early May through mid-November and from Christmas through March 31. There are six charming bedrooms here, including one of New England's most romantic bedrooms. Dinner and breakfast are served to houseguests only. Lunch at the inn and box lunches are available on request.

The Schmitts are cooking and wine buffs and like to present fresh foods on their set dinner menus. Visitors eat dinner here at one large candlelit table in the handsome dining room. When we stayed at the inn, the Schmitts ate dinner with the guests, and the conversational topics ranged from national news to current movies and stock market trends.

Dinner began with a fresh tomato soup made with newly picked tomatoes, spices, and tiny pieces of onion and celery. A large slice of sirloin steak came with a fresh mushroom sauce, tender green beans, and potatoes that had been mashed and then baked with butter, eggs, salt, pepper, tarragon, basil, and chives. For dessert, Mrs. Schmitt had made a mouth-watering pumpkin pie.

Behind the inn there are several vegetable gardens and an asparagus bed. Mrs. Schmitt uses her home-grown produce for salads that vary from tomato aspic to cucumber-and-sour-cream mold. At dinner the salad consisted of apple slices, cooked beets, onion, and celery, all of which had been marinated in dry white wine.

The contemporary oil paintings throughout the inn are by artists living and working in Vermont. A local gallery, The Garden House, uses the inn to display them. Many are abstract paintings with bright colors and refreshing effects. The paintings would be memorable in themselves and so would the Schmitts' antiques, inherited from both families. These include a William and Mary oyster-wood cabinet dated around 1700, a Hepplewhite console table, and an American tavern table, probably from Virginia. But what is most impressive is the rich interaction of the antiques and the modern art. The contrast between the old and the new is interesting and harmonious, like melodies in counterpoint in a song.

The bedrooms are beautifully furnished, with great attention to detail. For families, there is one room with a bunk bed where two children can sleep. Since none of the bedrooms has a private bathroom, the Schmitts have placed two bright-yellow terry-cloth robes in each clothes closet. The shared bathrooms (and the bunk room) are as carefully furnished as the rest of the house, with thick towels and cheerful shower curtains.

The most romantic bedroom here is "the back porch." It is on the second floor and has large windows with a long-range view of Mount Mansfield and a close-up view of the perennial border flower beds behind the inn. This room has a sofa that opens into a double bed, a tape deck, an FM radio, a chess set, an old bar game called skittles, and an attractive collection of duck decoys.

The Environs: Craftsbury Common is an extraordinary hilltop village (vintage nineteenth century) on a steep bypass from Vt. 14. There are not many hilltop villages in New England anyway and fewer still have inns. Walk to the village common or to the back of the inn and you will have a sweeping view of undulating green pastures and Mount Mansfield rising twenty-five miles to the west.

What is there to do in a place like Craftsbury Common? Many people like to hike or bicycle along the roads in and around the village, which afford bucolic views as they climb uphill and down. In the spring you can rent canoes from Horace Strong for use on nearby Black River. During the summer inn guests have privileges at the Windridge Tennis Camp on Big Hosmer Lake, where you can play tennis, swim, canoe, or sail. If you would like to learn how to make gravestone rubbings, the Schmitts will teach you. In the winter you can cross-country ski around Little Hosmer Pond. (The 1975 national cross-country finals were held in Craftsbury Common.) Cross-country ski instruction, guided tours, a waxing clinic, and equipment rental are available, too.

Twice a year Craftsbury literally overflows with visitors: on the last Saturday in July a contest for country fiddlers is held, and on the last Saturday in September banjo players meet here. In 1974 the fiddlers drew an audience of about fifteen thousand people; the banjo players attracted around four thousand. In early July there is an antiques fair. And in August, Old Home Day is an annual event when local women display handmade braided rugs and quilts, homemade breads and jellies, and the firemen barbecue chicken and broil hamburgers. For the children there is a pet contest.

The rest of the year Craftsbury belongs to the 632 people who live here in the town named for its first settler, Col. Ebenezer Crafts. Colonel Crafts, after selling his land in Sturbridge, Massachusetts, moved here in 1788. When he arrived, the town had been named Minden since 1781. But, because Minden sounded so much like nearby Lyndon, the name was changed in 1790.

Today Craftsbury includes Craftsbury Common, Craftsbury Village, and East Craftsbury. Most residents are retired people and dairy farmers. If you go to East Craftsbury, stop at the John

Woodruff Simpson Memorial Library. It is housed in what was once a general store. The counters, shelves, and drawers are filled with books instead of groceries, bolts of cloth, and Lydia E. Pinkham's Vegetable Compound. The magazine room has an impressive array of current magazines and a Ping-Pong table that attracts local young people after church on Sundays. If Miss Jean Simpson, the library's founder, is there, ask her to recite her humorous poem, "The Chant of the Unworthy Ancients."

Scenic Drive: Over the Lowell Mountains to Eden; then past Mount Belvidere to Hazen's Notch Road; from the Notch up past Jay Peak, returning via Vt. 14 through Irasburg and Albany in the Black River Valley. This drive combines spectacular mountain scenery, quiet gravel roads, lush rolling farm land, and small pretty towns.

Directions to the Inn: From New York, take I-91 to I-89 to exit 7; follow Vt. 302 east to Vt. 14 north to well-marked right turn eight miles north of Hardwick to Craftsbury Common. From Boston, take I-93 to Vt. 18 to U.S. 2 west to Vt. 15 north to Vt. 14 north.

THE RABBIT HILL INN

Lower Waterford, Vermont

"Go ahead and light the fire in the fireplace if you want to. Just be sure the damper's open," innkeeper John Carroll called after us as we went upstairs for the night. We thanked him, checked the damper, and lit the newspaper beneath three eight-inch-thick logs. The fire, alternately crackling and glowing for twelve hours, was still flickering the next morning, a comforting sight on a drizzly day.

The Rabbit Hill Inn is only 1½ miles from the New Hampshire border in a small northeastern Vermont village. Lower Waterford, overlooking the reservoir behind Moore Dam on the Connecticut River, is nicknamed White Village because all ten of its post–Revolutionary War houses are painted white. It is a little village, legally part of Waterford, which has 586 residents.

The inn, across the road from the white-spired Congregational Church (1798), overlooks the Connecticut River and the Franconia Range of the White Mountains in New Hampshire. It is open all year, serving breakfast and dinner to houseguests and the public. (The dining room is closed on Tuesdays during the winter and on Christmas Eve and Christmas Day.) There are eight old-fashioned bedrooms and twelve additional bedrooms in an adjacent motel, all with private bathrooms. You can play shuffleboard here in the summer and go cross-country skiing in the winter. The inn puts up box lunches.

In a state that has more than its share of well-polished and sophisticated inns, The Rabbit Hill Inn's appeal is that it is genuinely homey. There are family photographs in the entry, a vast collection of Hummel figurines and Currier and Ives prints. Like the sparsely settled area around it, where passing trucks haul huge logs as often as anything else, this inn is modest and unassuming.

Lower Waterford is ten miles southeast of St. Johnsbury, known to residents as "St. J." The white-clapboard inn was built in 1830 as a manufacturing plant for sleighs and winnow mills, devices that blow the dust out of grain. In 1840 when the Connecticut River was frozen over, a team of oxen dragged four thick pine trees across the river. These were used to support the building's second and third floor piazzas. Over the years the four pillars were shaped by hand in the Doric style. Today The Rabbit Hill Inn's guests use the upstairs porches in warm weather. You can sit out there with a book and gaze at the White Mountains in the distance.

On rainy days you can curl up in a comfortable chair in the inn's reading area. It is on the second floor at the top of the stairs, where the bookcases are brimming with readable novels, the Hardy Boys series, over seventy cookbooks, and volumes of Readers Digest condensed books.

The old-fashioned bedrooms are on the second floor and also above the inn's gift shop, The Briar Patch, next door. There are working fireplaces in two inn bedrooms and in two bedrooms over The Briar Patch. The motley furnishings include wide floorboards painted dark gray and speckled with other colors of paint, wallpaper patterns of Victorian flower prints, white curtains, Hummel figurines, dark-green wing chairs with brass tacks, and one room with a nonworking organ. Two bedrooms have four-poster canopy beds.

The two dining rooms are cheerful and attractive, with bright wallpaper, crisp white trim, working fireplaces, and beautiful silver serving dishes on the mantels. The tables have mustard-yellow cloths with pewterlike salt-and-pepper shakers, sugar dishes, creamers, and service plates.

When we stayed at the inn, there were six entrees: baked stuffed jumbo shrimp, veal cutlet, baked Virginia ham, chicken Teriyaki, pork chops Teriyaki, and broiled sirloin steak. The first-course soups were onion and clam chowder. The inn is best known for its pies made by Mrs. Gladys Whittemore, who lives down the road and whose specialties include pecan pie and New England apple crunch. On Saturday nights the inn's smorgasbord is especially popular with local people.

The wine list has both imported and domestic wines, including Vermont State Apple Wine. We thought this would be a very sweet wine, but it turned out to be so dry it almost made us thirsty to drink it. In the taproom there are small wooden tables, two old school desks, portraits of John and Ruth Carroll, about forty china figurines of rabbits on the mantel, and a collection of chess sets.

Mr. Carroll has been teaching cooking to juniors and seniors at St. Johnsbury Academy since 1970, when twelve students enrolled in his first class, ten of them boys. Now the class is so popular that students raise money for food-oriented trips by selling their baked bread and by giving special dinners from time to time at the inn. Several members of the kitchen staff are former students, now graduated.

The Environs: Before you leave Lower Waterford, walk down the unpaved road by the church to the third-class post office, a clapboard building with the American flag out front and sleighbells on the door. Inside, postmaster Dorothy Morrison and her husband, the Honorable Arthur Morrison, a former state legislator, take delight in showing visitors the wooden miniature buildings on display. There is a replica of Lower Waterford's church, a large doll house, and a miniature covered bridge. The buildings were made by the late W. J. Morrison, who was Lower Waterford's blacksmith. On a chilly day you can warm your hands in front of the wood-burning stove in this cozy, wallpapered, one-room post office.

Scenic Drive: N.H. 135 across the Connecticut River affords lovely views of Lower Waterford as it winds past dairy farms. The unnumbered road connecting Lower Waterford with East Barnet (on Vt. 5) has good views of the Connecticut River. Note: take this road only in good summer weather, since the 10-mile road is unpaved for 2.8 miles, and after a heavy rain or in spring mud season it can become icy or slippery.

Directions to the Inn: From New York, take I-91 to Vt. 5 to Vt. 2 east to Vt. 18 east. From Boston, take I-93 to Vt. 18 west. The inn is just off Vt. 18.

THE TYLER PLACE INN

Highgate Springs, Vermont

Robert Benchley wrote, "In America there are two classes of travel—first class, and with children. Traveling with children corresponds roughly to traveling third class in Bulgaria. They tell me there is nothing lower in the world than third-class Bulgarian travel." Well, to every rule there is an exception, and at The Tyler Place Inn on Lake Champlain, three miles south of Canada, they are doing all kinds of things to prove Benchley wrong.

This is an inn for families with children, and there are not any "but's" to it. You can come to The Tyler Place with a brood of kids from eight days old to eighteen years and nobody will blink an eye. They are used to it. Not only that, they are set up to please parents who are happy to forgo the experience of third-class Bulgarian travel and to satisfy children who do not want to go anywhere first-class.

Here is how they do it. There are daily supervised activities at an unrelenting pace for children from three years old up. If you have children under three years of age, you can hire a "Mother's helper" from the inn's list of available babysitters. You are responsible for your children from 2 to 5 P.M. and after 9 P.M. each day. The rest of the time the children are supervised by staff members. Finally, there are separate dining facilities for children and parents so that adults can eat three meals a day in the exclusive company of other adults.

All this happens in an atmosphere as happy-go-lucky as a summer camp. The inn describes itself as "about as commercialized as a dandelion," and that attitude is reflected in the reasonable rates. These rates vary for children, depending on their age, and are specially reduced for couples in June. The Tyler Place is open from late May through Labor Day weekend. There are twenty-seven cottages and houses (of different sizes) set on 165 acres, including one mile of shoreline on Lake Champlain. Three meals are served daily to guests.

Although couples can and do stay here, The Tyler Place is enormously popular with large families who sign up well in advance for their next vacation. During our visit the largest cottage was occupied by a couple with six children, ranging from ten years to two months old. Often, close to 50 percent of the available lodging space is reserved a full year ahead. (There is room for about fifty couples plus a variety of children.) Most families stay at least a week. The maximum visit for a family is two weeks during one summer.

When you come here for a week's stay, you will probably arrive sometime on Saturday. The Tyler Place is quietest on Saturday evenings, when families who have driven from New York, New Jersey, and Connecticut are bleary-eyed after the long trip. In the dining room most adults usually ask for a table for two. By Wednesday or Thursday, the chances are that you will be requesting a table for six or ten so that you, like your children elsewhere, can eat alongside newly made friends. By Friday, the dining room is no longer subdued but filled with laughter and animated talk.

And that is just the dining room for adults. The children, divided into five groups, meet separately for breakfast, lunch, and dinner. The planned activities vary, depending on the age group. They include boating, swimming, horseback riding, softball games, cookouts, marshmallow roasts, water regattas, hootenannies, and (for the "Senior Teens") bonfires in the evening. There are two weekly talent shows: one given by the children and the other by the staff.

Many staff members are college students, and they are exceptionally friendly and accommodating. As a group, they set the tone of good fellowship that we found everywhere—from the boat dock and the riding ring to the tennis courts and the swimming pool. The Tyler Place does not permit guests to tip individual staff members; instead, there is a reasonable surcharge added to your bill. The inn has had this policy since Mrs. Edward J. Tyler and her late husband started The Tyler Place in 1945.

The rates here include food, lodging, and all activities. There are three things for which you pay extra: bar bills, motor rentals for boats, and Mother's helpers. The Mother's helpers are young babysitters, many of them local girls, with whom you make your own arrangements. (The inn suggests a minimum amount to pay them.) You can employ a Mother's helper for a few hours a day or around-the-clock for live-in babysitting. This allows even couples with very young children to attend evening activities, which include a square dance, an informal dance, bingo games, a "candlelight dance," and a staff talent show. You do not have to go to any of them if you prefer not to.

What is most impressive about The Tyler Place is the wholesome atmosphere of good fun, cheerful people, and the loyalty that even first-time guests feel after their vacation here. Take, for instance, what happened after the 140-year-old red-clapboard inn burned to the ground on September 4 and 5, 1974.

The Tyler Place had closed for the season several days before the inn caught fire. It was three stories high and towered over the little settlement of Highgate Springs. Firemen from ten departments in Vermont, New York, and Quebec could not save the building, but they managed to move out the Victorian furniture, mirrors, and pictures from the first floor and to prevent the fire from spreading to other buildings.

Within days, Mrs. Tyler and her daughter, Pixley Tyler Hill, mailed a newspaper account of the fire to guests, along with a questionnaire soliciting opinions on where the new inn should be sited. One guest who had stayed at The Tyler Place with his family earlier that summer was Bill Collins, an architect from Cleveland, Ohio. He returned in the fall to design a new building at the inn. Construction was begun on October 19, 1974, for the 1975 season.

In a letter to the inn's guests, Pixley Tyler Hill wrote, "When we sent you news of the fire, I didn't realize what an understatement I had made when I said The Tyler Place was really its spirit and not just the old inn. Hundreds upon hundreds of letters and calls and offers to help have come in. What that support and concern did for us cannot be put into words."

Directions to the Inn: From New York, take I-91 to I-89. From Boston I-93 to I-89 north to exit 22. At the end of the ramp, drive south on U.S. 7 for three miles. The Tyler Place is on U.S. 7 across from Highgate Springs' grocery store, a red-roofed church, and a gas station.

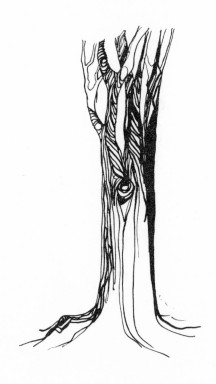

New Hampshire

"I built it for a pastime and to cure the dyspepsia more than anything else."

SYLVESTER MARSH
October 22, 1883

John Gunther wrote that New England is a region of "more mildly crazy people than anywhere in the nation." Take Sylvester Marsh, for instance. They called him "Crazy" Marsh when he asked the New Hampshire legislature in 1858 for a charter to build a railroad up Mount Washington, New England's highest peak at 6,288 feet. The legislators laughed, approved the charter anyway, and suggested an amendment that would give Marsh permission "to continue the railroad to the moon."

Marsh apparently got the idea for the cog railway, the first in the world, from another New Hampshire native, an inventor named Herrick Aiken. In the early 1850s, Aiken approached prominent railroad men with his model of a roadbed and track with a cog rail to build on Mount Washington. They said it was impractical. So in 1854 Aiken turned his attention to inventing the first circular knitting machine that could make a seamless stocking in less than five minutes. He also manufactured latch needles for making hosiery.

If Aiken conceived the cog-railway idea, it was Marsh who would not take no for an answer. He had made and lost one fortune after inventing meat-packing machinery and then recouped his losses in the grain business, retiring in 1855 at the age of fifty-two. When Marsh wrote about the cog railway to the president of the Boston, Concord, and Montreal Railroad, John

141

E. Lyon ignored his letter, thinking it was from "some crazy man." But Marsh persisted anyway.

It took Sylvester Marsh eleven years, but the cog railway was built on the mountain with the reputation for the world's worst weather. Marsh recruited workers from New York and Boston to clear the wilderness. They hauled materials and supplies by ox team from Littleton, twenty-five miles away, and camped in the woods until a log cabin was "rolled up." Then they built the railway.

Except for the first quarter-mile, the railway was built as a trestle, ranging from two feet high to about thirty feet at Jacob's Ladder. The average grade of the tracks is 25 percent, and the steepest grade (at Jacob's Ladder) is 37.41 percent. The first locomotive, christened Hero, was quickly nicknamed Old Peppersass. On July 3, 1869, the first train chugged up the mountain, where two hotels, The Summit House and The Tip Top House, had already been built at the top.

From the 1860s until about 1930 the most dangerous (and thrilling) way to get down Mount Washington was by slide-board. The slideboard, about a foot wide and three-feet long, had two friction-brake handles and fit over the central rail. It was made of wood and reinforced steel. When workmen at the summit heard the five o'clock whistle blow at the base of the railway, they would get on their slideboards and start the descent as if they were on toboggans. When you take the cog railway down the mountain, you will savor the sensational view of the broad Ammonoosuc River Valley and the panorama of mountain peaks for seventy minutes. It usually took a workman on a slideboard about ten minutes to descend the 3¼ miles from the alpine flower region above treeline to the balsam-fir and red-spruce forest at the base. The record was two minutes and forty-five seconds.

Besides the railway, hotels, and slideboards, Mount Washington had a daily newspaper printed on the summit every summer from 1877 until 1908. The paper was called *Among the Clouds*. It recorded the names of people who poked their heads inside the printing office after ascending by the conventional routes—the railway and the carriage road. The newspaper also kept track of the mildly crazy people who came up Mount Washington to set records by walking barefoot, bicycling, or running all the way.

Once a year *Among the Clouds* printed a special edition the day after the Coaching Parade in Bethlehem or North Conway. The reporters who covered the parade wrote their copy as they rode the train and then the cog railway up the mountain. As soon as they reached the printing office, the type was set and the papers were printed, hand-folded, and bundled during the night. At about 3 A.M. the railway men got on the slideboards. With bundles of newspapers between their knees, they descended in the moonlight. At the base of the mountain a wagon with a team of fast horses took the papers to Bethlehem or to the first train going down to North Conway. And that was how *Among the Clouds* competed with "city" newspapers.

If you lived in Boston in the late 1800s, you could board a train, ride to the base of the cog railway, take the railway to the summit, and stay at a hotel. But on August 30, 1899, the automobile age came to Mount Washington when Mr. and Mrs. Freelan O. Stanley drove up the carriage road in the steam Locomobile Mr. Stanley and his twin brother, Francis, invented in 1896. The first car race was held here in 1904. It was called "Climb to the Clouds." The winner was Harry Harkness of New York, who drove up the carriage road to the top in 24 minutes, 37.6 seconds. His car was a sixty-horsepower Mercedes, stripped to one seat on the chassis.

When the second "Climb to the Clouds" race was held in 1905, the contestants included a Stanley Steamer, an Olds, a Reo, a Maxwell, a Pope, a Pierce-Arrow, a White Steamer, and a Columbia. Newspapers throughout America carried reports about these races, sponsored by the Glidden Tour. The Tour also attracted attention and some sharp words from *The Manchester Union Leader*. A 1905 editorial said, "The whole thing is an unmitigated nuisance. The lives and property of perfectly helpless people have been menaced for no reason than to provide amusement for total strangers. Automobiles are a good thing; some drivers can be trusted, most cannot. Take the record of their run from Concord to Manchester: 18 miles in 40 minutes. Have they any right to do such a thing? If these people think of coming up another year, let 'em stay in jail a couple of days and everyone will be the better for it."

Maybe it is because Mount Washington is the highest mountain east of the Mississippi River and north of Mount

Mitchell in North Carolina. Or maybe it is because Mount Washington's weather is the most severe in the world outside of polar regions. Whatever the reason, Mount Washington has been the scene of a lot of records, some natural and some man-made. Here are a few people who challenged this peak and won:

• The principal of Phillips Exeter Academy set an example for his students by running up the eight-mile carriage road in one hour and fifty-seven minutes. His name? Harlan P. Amen. The year? 1875.

• Albert Farrington of Lowell, Massachusetts, and Mrs. Frances Cogan, a widow from Fryeburg, Maine, celebrated their June wedding on the summit. The date? June 2, 1877.

• The only person to drive a sled dog-team to the summit without assistance was a woman, Mrs. Florence Murray Clark. The lead dog? An Eskimo huskie named Clarkso. A recent event? Not exactly. It happened on April 3, 1932.

• In the 1930s Carl Weiss of New York, a blind man led by a seeing-eye dog, climbed from the base station to the summit on the Jewell trail. His time? Five hours, including a stop for lunch.

• On August 6, 1932, R. E. Welch, a one-legged station agent of the Boston and Maine Railroad, walked to the summit with a crutch alongside the cog railway track. His time? Three hours and eleven minutes. His age? Thirty-eight.

Mount Washington is notorious for high winds, low temperatures, rime-forming clouds, and sudden storms. The Mount Washington Observatory, a weather station staffed all year, is chained to the ground. In the winter the building is coated with rime, ice particles caused by supercooled water droplets that freeze on contact with an object. When the wind screeches and howls, the rime creates frost feathers that look like flags of layered ice jutting into the wind.

Since the first recorded fatality on Mount Washington in 1849, more than fifty people have died in these mountains from exposure and exhaustion and from falls, ski accidents, and drowning. Perhaps none is better remembered than Lizzie Greene Bourne, who was twenty-three when she died on September 14, 1855, of exhaustion and exposure only yards from the summit. When you visit the mountain, you will see the Lizzie Bourne monument, now a landmark, near the railway tracks.

Mount Washington still holds the world's record for the highest wind velocity ever recorded. It was 231 miles an hour on April 12, 1934. Observers have said that the wind has probably been higher than that on Mount Washington's peak. But before 1934, when wind velocities approached 150 miles an hour, the anemometers had a tendency to blow away.

During the Second World War this was a test site for equipment performance under severe winter conditions. The U.S. Navy tested searchlight penetration of fog here; the Goodyear Tire and Rubber Company tested synthetic tires; the Naval Research Laboratory tested phosphorescent paints; B. F. Goodrich Company and Northwest Airlines did de-icing research for airplanes; and the General Electric Company tested electric blankets, electric flying suits, boots, gloves, goggles, and sunlamps. When the U.S. Army sent a group of scientists to test a Swedish primus stove for carbon-monoxide fumes, the stove worked fine on the summit but the tent blew down in a hurricane.

The average annual temperature is 27.1 degrees, and winters for the weather observatory crew are cold. There is at least one fringe benefit, though: making ice cream. This is how *The Manchester Union Leader* described the process in 1947: "All that is necessary is a good swift kick. At a low temperature a slight jar will cause freezing water to crystallize—and presto! ice cream. The crew whip up a batch of cream, place it in the outer entry or in the observation tower to cool. Then the next man who goes by to make an observation just kicks the pan or jar. And the stuff freezes nicely. Tastes good, too."

Most visitors come to the White Mountains from May through October. You can ascend Mount Washington by these methods:

• Take the cog railway off U.S. 302. It operates weekends only from Memorial Day through mid-June and from the week after Labor Day through Columbus Day; daily the rest of the summer.

• Drive up the carriage road in your car or ride up in a four-wheel drive "stage" operated by the Glen and Mt. Washington Stage Company. The road is open from mid-May through late October.

· Hike up or bicycle. These are the only ways to reach the summit without paying a fee. Two good trails up are the Tuckerman Ravine Trail (4.1 miles to summit; approximate hiking time 4½ hours; it starts from the Pinkham Notch Camp on N.H. 16) and the Ammonoosuc Ravine Trail (3.86 miles to summit; approximate hiking time 4½ hours; it starts from the cog railway, joining with the Crawford Path to the summit).

If you hike up Mount Washington during the winter, be sure to sign in at Pinkham Notch Camp, the headquarters for hiking in the White Mountains, before and after your hike. Even during the summer you should wear sturdy boots, and if you encounter a storm, turn back.

No matter how you get to the summit, you will be rewarded on a clear day with a breath-taking, spectacular view that extends one hundred miles in all directions over sections of five states and the Province of Quebec. To the east you will see a silver thread on the horizon. That is the Atlantic Ocean off the coast of Maine. Look carefully and you will spot Maine's Camden Hills (see The Whitehall Inn in Maine), Sebago Lake (see Migis Lodge in Maine), nearby Tuckerman Ravine in the foreground (see Pinkham Notch Camp), Mount Chocorua in the distance (see Stafford's-in-the-Field), and the Appalachian Mountain Club hut in the foreground by the Lakes of the Clouds. Turning from south to west, you may be able to see Vermont's highest peak, Mount Mansfield (see The Lodge at Smugglers' Notch and The Green Mountain Inn in Vermont). Finally, to the north, Mount Megantic in Quebec Province (see The Glen) juts up behind Mount Sam Adams and Mount Adams.

Other highlights in the White Mountains include:

· The Old Man of the Mountains, a forty-foot-high natural rock formation that looks like a sculptured human face. Drive on U.S. 3 north toward Franconia and you will see it in Franconia Notch on a sheer cliff 1,200 feet above Profile Lake. It gave Nathaniel Hawthorne the theme for his story "The Great Stone Face" and prompted Daniel Webster to write, "Men hang out their signs indicative of their respective trades: shoemakers hang out a gigantic shoe; jewelers, a monster watch; and the dentist hangs out a gold tooth; but up in the mountains of New Hampshire, God Almighty has hung out a sign to show that there He makes men."

• The Flume, an 800-foot-long natural gorge with fractured granite walls 20 feet apart. It is on U.S. 3 not far from the Old Man of the Mountains. You can walk through the chasm on boardwalks above the waterfalls. It is open from late May to mid-October.

• The Lost River Reservation, N.H. 112 in Kinsman Notch. It has rustic ladders through glacial caverns and boulder caves following the river's course as it disappears underground and then reappears, forming Paradise Falls. It is open from mid-May to late October.

• The Kancamagus Highway, 34½ miles of unspoiled scenery with picnic areas, extraordinary views, feeder trails to waterfalls, and campsites. This is a west-east road (N.H. 112) from Lincoln to Conway that cuts through the heart of the White Mountain National Forest. The forest comprises 728,516 acres, including 45,944 acres in western Maine.

If you want to drive through the White Mountains during the foliage season (usually the last week in September and the first week in October), you should go with realistic expectations. The chances are ninety-nine to one that if you stick to the main roads and go on the weekend, you will not have a relaxing time. Your best bet is to go during the week, and if you cannot do that, skip the White Mountains and go elsewhere. One weekend when we found people honking their horns in the bumper-to-bumper traffic in Conway, there was almost nobody in northern Vermont, where the foliage colors were glorious, and that is not to mention the Connecticut Lake region in northern New Hampshire.

In this region, the least well-known section of New Hampshire, the rugged terrain is extensively forested with balsam fir, red spruce, and white spruce. There are four Connecticut lakes— and they are beautiful—in an area largely owned by timber companies. Vast woodlands of spruce and fir, as well as hardwoods, supply pulp for northern New England's paper industry. The rough, remote environment here is unspoiled, undeveloped, and often overlooked, with logging roads and foot trails leading to streams, ponds, lakes, and waterfalls.

In extreme contrast to the Connecticut Lakes region is New Hampshire's southeastern corner, which is becoming a suburb of Boston and an industrial center, with firms moving here in full force. The seacoast is so popular that if you find yourself in the late Sunday afternoon traffic on I-95 when everyone is leaving the beaches for home, you will never forget it. This area is highly commercialized, with treeless parking lots outside one "steak pit" after another, interspersed with ugly gas stations and many buildings with neon lights. We once saw the broad, sandy beaches from an airplane on the way to Portland, Maine. From that distance they looked very appealing. But of the many areas in New England we plan to visit again, New Hampshire's seacoast is not among them.

Our inns in New Hampshire are almost as varied as the state's terrain, which ranges from sea level to mile-high Mount Washington. The one thing most of them have in common is an outstanding view of the mountains. Otherwise, New Hampshire's inns are rustic and sophisticated; homey and elegant; down to earth and up in the clouds. One is a large, formal resort: The Spalding Inn Club. At the other extreme is the Rockhouse Mountain Farm Inn, a casual place with horses in the barn. Then there is the Pinkham Notch Camp and Lodge, which does not have beds at all: it has bunk beds and mountain huts.

The best New Hampshire inns for imaginative food are Hide-Away Lodge in New London and Wells Wood in Plainfield. The most beautifully furnished inns are The Lyme Inn in Lyme and The Colby Hill Inn in Henniker. New Hampshire's most romantic bedrooms are Room 8 at The Lyme Inn and the bedroom suite at Wells Wood. An outstanding room with wall murals is Room 14 at The John Hancock Inn in Hancock. New Hampshire's best all-around inns are Wells Wood and The Homestead in Sugar Hill.

THE JOHN HANCOCK INN

Hancock, New Hampshire

When people in this southern New Hampshire town head for the town hall on Election Day, they have the opportunity both to pray for guidance and to cast their votes in a double-duty church. It is the white-steepled First Congregational Church of Hancock. When you go inside, you can climb a winding staircase to the second-story church or walk four steps down to the town hall below.

Only a handful of houses away sits The John Hancock Inn, which dominates this village of 909 people. The inn is open all year except for one week in the late spring and a week in the early fall. It is also closed on Christmas Day. The inn serves three meals daily, all open to the public. Box lunches are made on request. There are ten bedrooms here, including one of New England's most romantic bedrooms, the Mural Room.

Most of the wallpaper patterns throughout the inn are of small designs with eagles, scrolls, ships, and bells. The bedrooms are furnished unpretentiously, with simple maple headboards, white curtains, solid-colored bedspreads, and painted floorboards. The Mural Room is an exception. When you wake up here in the cannon-ball double bed, you are surrounded by the murals of trees, hills, a river, a few small buildings, and expansive sky painted by Rufus Porter (or one of his apprentices) in about 1825. The colors are mostly greens and blues, and they contrast with the crisp-white wainscoting, mantel, and trim around the door. The Mural Room has a private bathroom.

Pink geraniums were in full bloom at The John Hancock Inn when we stayed there, and a steady stream of customers was arriving for dinner on a Saturday night. The inn's sixteen entrees included prime ribs of beef, broiled scallops, pan fried baby-beef liver, chopped sirloin steak with mushroom sauce, broiled lamb chops, and rainbow trout amandine. The prime ribs of beef was tender and moist. Mashed potatoes came with the entree, along with baby carrots and peas. The appetizers included a thick clam chowder, fruitcup, shrimp cocktail, onion soup, and eggs à la Russe.

At the table next to ours a young woman interrupted an involved conversation about a local drama group called the Peterborough Players long enough to order the prime ribs herself. "I would like it rare, just as rare as you can get it," she told the waitress. Soon after the beef arrived, the chef appeared. "Is it rare enough? I have a piece that's just a little rarer than that one," he said. "This is perfect," the young woman said. "Oh, good," the chef replied as he disappeared around the corner.

The John Hancock, built in 1789, is the oldest operating inn in New Hampshire. The inn honors John Hancock because he once owned much of the town. Hancock, a signer of the Declaration of Independence, made his name synonymous with "signature" because he signed so boldly, in lavish, large script. He was also a Boston land speculator. He left no records to show that he ever visited his 1,800 acres of property in Hancock.

The Environs: As a general rule, the villages in Vermont are more consistently picturesque than in New Hampshire, but Hancock is a notable exception. It is in what the travel brochures call "the Currier and Ives corner" of New Hampshire, because this is where you find the little villages that exude charm. In Hancock the clapboard homes along Main Street are lined up at slight angles to the street, with a dirt path meandering along instead of a sidewalk. One house had a pine-cone Christmas wreath hanging on the door —in July. It was in perfect condition. It is true that in New England the Christmas wreath is a decoration for the entire winter snow season, and you will find wreaths on front doors well into February and March. But July, even for a pine-cone wreath, would seem to set a record.

In the summer you can check the town bulletin board near the inn for dates and times of this area's auctions and cultural activities. The Peterborough Players perform nearby, the Monadnock Musicians move from town to town giving concerts in July and August, there are weekly square dances in Fitzwilliam, and hiking up Mount Monadnock is very popular (you can also drive up). In the winter there is skiing at several ski areas, including Onset and Crotched mountains.

During the day you can wander along Main Street and have a look inside the double-duty church. It is closed in the evenings except when the annual town meeting or special town meetings are held. Nursery and kindergarten classes meet here in the winter, and sometimes school plays are staged downstairs. In December, when town organizations have the annual Christmas party for schoolchildren, Santa Claus makes his appearance in the town hall while the upstairs church is being decorated for Christmas services.

Scenic Drive: Here is a circular drive that will take you past Lake Skatutakee, through Harrisville, a nineteenth-century town with brick houses, and through the tiny village of Nelson. From the inn, take N.H. 137 south to the unnumbered road (to the right) marked Harrisville, continue on the unnumbered road marked Nelson, and follow the signs to N.H. 9 north to N.H. 123 south to the inn.

Directions to the Inn: From New York, take I-91 north to the Brattleboro, Vermont, exit for N.H. 9 to Keene. Take N.H. 9 to N.H. 123 south to Hancock. From Boston, take U.S. 3 north to N.H. 101A to N.H. 101 to U.S. 202 north to N.H. 123 to Hancock.

THE COLBY HILL INN

Henniker, New Hampshire

Meet Mrs. Elizabeth Gilbert, an innkeeper whose smile is as warm as the first sunlight on a cold, crisp day. You will find her at The Colby Hill Inn, set on a side street in this southern New Hampshire college town.

From the outside, this white-clapboard inn with green shutters is not unusually alluring. But Mrs. Gilbert has a way of bringing out the best in things, and her attitude is reflected inside the inn. She has furnished the inn beautifully with antiques, American primitive portraits, dried flower bouquets, and Woodbury Pewter reproductions in the dining room. The Colby Hill Inn exudes a hard-to-define but very definite feeling of tranquillity and sincere welcome.

The inn is open all year except for two weeks in November and two weeks in April. Breakfast is served daily to houseguests only; dinner is served for guests and the public every day except Monday. There is a well-concealed swimming pool behind the barn in back. The inn has eight lovely old-fashioned bedrooms. Some have private bathrooms; two have double beds. The rates are very reasonable.

When Mrs. Gilbert bought the inn in 1971, her oldest child had already gone to New England College here in Henniker, a four-year coeducational college with about as many students as Henniker has townspeople—1,200. For a widow with two more children to put through college, finding this inn was a stroke of good luck. Instead of sending her children away to college, Mrs.

Gilbert went to college with them: she packed the family belongings and moved to Henniker.

There were some uncanny similarities between the inn, as Mrs. Gilbert found it, and her former New York State home. The inn's living room was decorated in blue and white, as her own had been. The dining-room wallpaper was highlighted with a bittersweet orange, the same shade Mrs. Gilbert had used in her corner cupboard at home. Her furnishings, including pieces collected when she ran a Westchester County antique shop, fit in perfectly with the inn's decor. The Gilberts arrived in Henniker, unpacked, and opened the inn in less than two weeks.

Mrs. Gilbert, an excellent cook, usually serves several entrees for dinner, such as breast of chicken, broiled scampi, and sirloin steak. The half a dozen desserts on our menu included chocolate mousse, pecan pie, Indian pudding, English lemon curd, and ice cream. You can choose among ten reasonably priced imported and domestic (Almaden) wines.

From the breakfast nook there is a delightful view out back at what Mrs. Gilbert calls "my Andrew Wyeth." This is what you see: a weathered barn, an old plow, a wooden gate, a birdhouse, a stone wall, and field grasses.

Many guests like to stay here when the foliage season is at its height, around October 12, but some people who have been won over by the inn's serene atmosphere did not plan to stop here at all. A couple from Southbury, Connecticut, spent the night because their car broke down. They liked the inn so much they stayed for several days. Then there was a group of motorcyclists who were stranded in Henniker one rainy night when all the nearby motels were full. Mrs. Gilbert took them in. At first, their manner of speaking was rough and they draped their wet socks on the living-room furniture. Mrs. Gilbert gave them a receptive greeting anyway, made enough coffee for her twelve new guests, and sat down to chat with them in front of a roaring fire. Before long, they were transformed into quiet, courteous conversationalists, and the socks were removed from the furniture.

Mrs. Gilbert apparently has the same effect on animals. When a former guest gave her a forty-one-year-old green parrot named Polly, the parrot became sick on the way to the inn. Mrs. Gilbert ignored a veterinarian's advice that the bird be put to sleep and nursed it back to health. Today Polly is in the nook near the living room, telling you good-by when you arrive and hello when you leave.

The Environs: In the early spring you can watch ox teams gather maple sap at the Crane Farm, where the sap is also boiled down in the sugar house. During warm months you can canoe on the nearby Contoocook River (it flows north to Concord, where it joins the Merrimac), ride horseback near the inn, rent bicycles in town, or use the college tennis courts. In winter there are cross-country ski trails in Henniker (and skis for rent in town). Pat's Peak, a downhill ski area, is three miles away.

Scenic Drive: For a short drive, take N.H. 114 to New London; for a longer drive, take I-93 north to N.H. 112 east (Kancamagus Highway).

Directions to the Inn: From New York, take I-91 to Brattleboro, Vermont, and N.H. 9 east to Henniker. From Boston, take I-93 north to I-89 to U.S. 202 west to Henniker. At the intersection of U.S. 202 and N.H. 9 in Henniker, drive west on the Hillsboro-Henniker Road for half a mile and watch for the inn on the right.

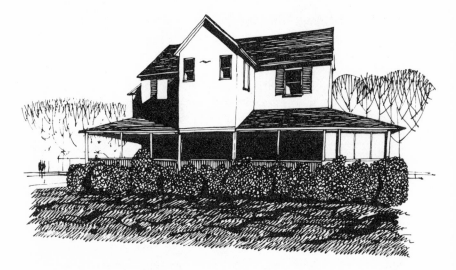

HIDE-AWAY LODGE

New London, New Hampshire

The telephone rang on a Saturday evening in this secluded back road not far from Little Lake Sunapee in southern New Hampshire. Innkeeper-chef Wolf Heinberg, standing just inside the front door, picked up the telephone on the little reception desk beside him. "I'm sorry," he said politely, "but our reservations are full this evening." He hung up the telephone, smiled, and said to a guest, "And we've been full for tonight since early last week."

Wolf and Lilli Heinberg have been building up a faithful clientele at Hide-Away Lodge since 1967, when they bought this large, white-clapboard former home. Now they have regular guests from as far as Saint Thomas in the Virgin Islands and Washington State, who come here to enjoy the imaginative meals, working off the calories by walking in the woods during the day and by swimming in the lake.

Hide-Away Lodge is open from mid-May through mid-October, serving dinner for both guests and the public and breakfast for houseguests only. It is closed on Tuesdays except during July and August. There are eight simply furnished bedrooms, half in the main building and half in a separate building across the driveway. The inn puts up box lunches on request.

If you are vacationing elsewhere in New Hampshire and you want a real treat, come to Hide-Away Lodge for dinner. You have to make reservations ahead, especially on Saturday evenings. When Dartmouth College in Hanover has football games or other popular activities on weekends, the best advice is to call for dinner reservations at Hide-Away Lodge several days in advance.

Mr. Heinberg changes his menu four times a year so that his returning guests can have variety. You may find Paella Valenciana on the menu, rack of lamb Bretonne, veal Marsala, filet of sole in shrimp sauce, duckling with peach glaze, spring chicken Dijonnaise with mustard fruits, and pan-fried calf's liver.

The appetizers here are unusual even for a country inn that is highly food-oriented. They include marinated artichoke hearts with ham mousse, poached egg in tarragon aspic, chilled cream of chicken Senegalese, ramequin of kidney beans with tender ham, and Andalusian gazpacho, a chilled vegetable soup with a tray of diced cucumber, green pepper, and toasted croûtons. There are also escargots Bourguignon, onion soup, and quiche Lorraine. The inn offers several salads, such as Caesar salad or spinach greens with a creamy egg dressing.

If, by dessert, you think you cannot consume another bite, the chances are excellent that you will change your mind when you are reminded of what the inn is having. For example, a nutmeg ice cream meringue with a ginger topping, crêpes pralines, camembert cheese with toasted crackers, French cream Napoleon, chocolate walnut mousse. The mousse is an interesting variation on this much-discussed concoction. Here, it consists of thick frozen slices of a rich chocolate combined with walnuts.

The wine list offers an extensive variety of imported and domestic wines. It is charmingly presented and makes excellent reading even if your palate is not calling for a bottle of wine.

For us, perhaps the most surprising aspect of dinner was the sensitive way in which guests were seated in an efficient but seemingly unhurried manner in the five small dining rooms with attractive prints of fruit on the walls. Lilli Heinberg kept a careful eye on the seating of the seventy people the inn can accommodate. But if we had not known the inn was totally reserved for dinner, we would not have guessed it. In spite of a full house, the Heinbergs both found time to receive and check up on their guests personally, saying good-by as cordially as they had said hello.

For breakfast the morning specialty was a pastry shell containing a layer of ham mousse, two poached eggs topped with Hollandaise sauce. It was splendid. "We have people who come for breakfast and then we don't see them all day. We send them off with a picnic lunch. They're in the woods painting or composing or something," Mr. Heinberg said.

The bedrooms, like the dining rooms, have Oregon fir-paneled walls. They are furnished unpretentiously. For maximum privacy, ask for a room in the building across the road.

The Environs: Mr. Heinberg has spent his life in the hotel business, starting in Switzerland in 1936 where he moved from his native Germany. In a way the town of New London has its beginnings in Germany, too. The lakes, rivers, and mountains in and around New London are said to resemble those of Heidelberg, Germany. So in 1753 this town was named Heidelberg in honor of King George II's visit to his German possessions at that time. It was renamed Alexandria Addition in 1773, and then in 1779 it was incorporated as New Londonderry. The "derry" was soon dropped and it has been New London ever since.

The inn is on the edge of a large woodland tract with miles of well-marked trails. In the summer inn guests can row, canoe, sail, and swim on Little Lake Sunapee a few minutes' walk away. There are tennis courts and a nine-hole golf course there, too.

Scenic Drive: I-89 north to U.S. 4 east to N.H. 11 to New London.

Directions to the Inn: From New York, take I-91 north to exit 7 (at Springfield, Vermont) and N.H. 11 north and east to New London. From Boston, take I-93 and I-89 north to New London.

In New London just north of the town center, Main Street and Newport Road intersect with Little Sunapee Road. Go out Little Sunapee Road toward Twin Lake Village. Hide-Away Lodge is at the end of the road past Twin Lake Village.

WELLS WOOD

Plainfield, New Hampshire

The fourteen-foot-high Palladian windows in the Wells Wood dining room prove that you do not need to know who Maxfield Parrish was to appreciate his sense of design. Parrish built this house overlooking the Connecticut River Valley, starting in the spring of 1898, and he left his mark everywhere. He designed those huge, elegant dining-room windows, for instance, so that when you open them, they slide into the wall. Most of the other windows at Wells Wood do, too.

There are just four bedrooms at Wells Wood. The inn is open all year except for a few weeks in the spring-mud season. It is closed on Mondays. Dinner is served to inn guests and the public. There is a Continental breakfast for guests only, and box lunches are put up on request.

This fifty-acre estate, with a magnificent sweeping view, was Parrish's home and studio from 1898 until he died in 1966. This is where he developed his painting technique with glazes and where he illustrated books, magazine covers, advertisements, posters, calendars, greeting cards, bookplates, and murals. But it is not necessary for you to know that Maxfield Parrish's name was a household word in America from 1900 to about 1930 or that his work has recently attracted a revival of interest. All you have to be is handy with tools around your house to look with some awe at what he did in this clapboard building.

Look in the main dining room, the Oak Room, and you will see the door latches and hinges near the fireplace. They are brass. Parrish made them himself in his fully equipped machine shop (now an antique store) behind the house. The Oak Room is the most exciting dining room we have seen in a New England inn. A 1907 magazine article in *Architectural Record* described the room as "noble." The sense of proportion is what makes it still dramatic today.

The beamed ceiling is almost twenty feet high (the room measures about twenty by forty feet), and there is a stage at one end with a baby grand piano, an easel, and a medieval-looking chair. Innkeeper Thomas Wells, an interior designer, has placed tables and chairs in the room that are massive enough to fit the space but are not pretentious or overbearing. The room and the furnishings are exceptionally well matched. And that is not to mention the food.

The food at Wells Wood, under the direction of Rosalind Wells, is excellent. This is one of the few New England inns that have attracted food critics from urban newspapers. In 1975 *The Boston Globe* gave the Wells Wood restaurant a four-star rating.

Mrs. Wells alternates between two menus, each with half a dozen entrees plus daily specialties. These include crab mornay, chicken amandine, capon cordon bleu, baked stuffed shrimp, and brochette de boeuf. We had a bubbly hot ragoût made with braised beef, red wine, pearl onions, small potatoes, Belgium carrots and peas, presented in an attractive crock with a delectably light pastry shell on top. For an appetizer you can choose among quiche Lorraine, escargots, a shrimp cocktail, and Coquilles St. Jacques. There are numerous desserts, including the inn's chocolate mousse cake of which people speak highly. After dinner, you can order espresso, cappuccino, or Irish coffee. The inn has a varied wine list, and there is a taproom with a splendid view.

As you sit in the Oak Room, picture this scene: it is the first quarter of the twentieth century and you are in Parrish's music room, where singers, pianists, and string quartets give recitals on the stage. Edwin Arlington Robinson (1869–1935), the Maine native who won the Pulitzer Prize three times, read his poetry at least once in this room. Among the guests who came here over the years were President Woodrow Wilson, Judge Learned Hand, Supreme Court Justice Felix Frankfurter, the poet William Vaughn Moody, the writer Walter Lippmann, and the actress Ethel Barrymore, for whom Parrish designed a bookplate. It said, "Ethel Barrymore—Her Book."

If you have been to the St. Regis Hotel in New York City, you have undoubtedly seen the Old King Cole mural that has hung in the King Cole Room since 1935. Parrish painted it here in his Plainfield house in 1906 on a commission for the old Knickerbocker Hotel. When the eight-by-thirty-foot mural was finished, Parrish crated it, and a local driver carried the painting by horse and wagon to the Windsor, Vermont, train depot five miles away.

The astonishing view here of the broad Connecticut River Valley dividing New Hampshire and Vermont is nearly panoramic. From the inn you look past open pastures to rolling hills and woodlands in the distance, with Vermont's Mount Ascutney dominating the river valley. Parrish painted many landscapes of this area, using his glazes that made his blue skies and purple shadows look so real they seem unreal. He and his wife raised their four children here (they called their home The Oaks), and Parrish made toys and games for them, including a parcheesi board said to be as meticulously painted as any of his landscapes.

You can see this twenty-five-mile view from the inn's taproom, the grounds, and the bedroom suite that features a king-size bed, many readable books, a sitting room, and a large, well-organized bathroom. The suite is not furnished in an old-fashioned style, but its spaciousness and the view from the bed make it one of New England's most romantic bedrooms anyway. (The suite can sleep six; we recommend it for two.)

The Environs: In the winter you can cross-country ski here or downhill ski at nearby slopes. In the summer this area, not far from Dartmouth College in Hanover, has art shows, concerts, movies, plays, craft fairs, church suppers, and ponds where you can take a dip after hiking up Mount Ascutney or the Appalachian Trail, which crosses the New Hampshire-Vermont line near Hanover.

The Saint-Gaudens National Historic Site, just off N.H. 12A south of the inn, may bore children, but we thought it was really interesting. Augustus Saint-Gaudens (1848–1907), the sculptor credited with starting the Cornish art colony, had his home (an old stagecoach inn), gardens, and studios here. They are open to the public from the last weekend in May through mid-October.

Wells Wood is easy to get to both from I-91 and I-89, making this an excellent stop for a night on a New England tour. Of course, once you get here, the turnpikes seem far away. Between the inn's alluring setting and the good food, you may decide you would like to stay longer. In 1913 when Maxfield Parrish was asked to become the head of Yale University's Art Department, he was so reluctant to leave this place he turned the offer down.

Scenic Drive: N.H. 12A between Plainfield and Windsor has three covered bridges (two are off 12A), all built by James Tasker, a rural construction genius who could neither read nor write. The Cornish-Windsor Bridge over the Connecticut River is the longest span (460 feet) in New England.

Directions to the Inn: From New York, take I-91 north to the Windsor-Ascutney exit, cross the Connecticut River (through the covered bridge) to N.H. 12A north for eight miles. From Boston, take I-89 north to exit 20 to N.H. 12A south for nine miles.

THE LYME INN

Lyme, New Hampshire

So you want to fall asleep in a four-poster canopy bed in one of New England's most romantic bedrooms? Write to The Lyme Inn and ask for Room 8. If Room 8 is not available, take any room. You will not be disappointed.

Lyme, eleven miles north of Hanover (the home of Dartmouth College), is not the prettiest village you ever saw. But it has twenty-seven outstanding red carriage sheds next to the Congregational Church, and it has The Lyme Inn just across the common. For the inn and the carriage sheds alone, you should put Lyme on your itinerary.

The inn is exquisitely furnished, from the sparkling white-wicker chairs on the porch to the handsome chest of drawers and oblong antique pin cushion with lacy edges in Room 8. It is hard to imagine, but in the summer of 1973 an elderly woman, making a nostalgic visit to the inn, recalled roller skating in the third-floor ballroom as a child. Well, they do not roller skate at The Lyme Inn anymore. The third-floor ballroom consists of bedrooms today.

There are fifteen bedrooms, some with private bathrooms and some with shared bathrooms. The inn is open all year except for the last three weeks in March and the first three weeks in December. Dinner is served daily except Tuesdays. Both breakfast and dinner are open to the public, and the inn puts up box lunches on request.

As a general rule, the most beautifully furnished inns discourage bringing young children as guests. The Lyme Inn's position is this: "Small children do not understand that adults appreciate peace and quiet. Their normal, healthy enthusiasm can be most upsetting to our guests who have planned a quiet holiday—in many instances, from their own children. Therefore, we ask that you not request reservations if children under 8 years old are in your party; please make reservations for older children only if their behavior will permit other guests to enjoy the quiet atmosphere of our dining room and our bedrooms."

If you just strolled through the inn, you would not be conscious that most of the inn's belongings are for sale. There are no price tags on anything. Mrs. Ray Bergendoff, the innkeeper's wife, is an antiques dealer with exceptionally good taste. The colorful patchwork quilts in the second-floor hallway are displayed artistically, and the antiques here have style. Every healthy plant and dried flower arrangement has been carefully placed in one odd corner or another. The bathrooms have been as thoughtfully considered as the other rooms, with many water pitcher sets, nicely lettered signs, and enough marble-topped sinks to make you lose count.

The dining room is memorable for its simple, lovely tables and chairs and for the interesting alphabet samplers on the walls. (The tables are Shaker reproductions made from kits.) The food is not so unusual. When we stayed at the inn, there were seven entrees: country smoked ham, beer-batter shrimp or oysters, Wienerschnitzel, broiled Boston scrod, broiled bluefish, and sirloin steak with mushrooms. The inn's desserts were apple pie and cheese, black Russian pie, cheesecake parfait, and cordial parfaits. Admittedly, the inn's kitchen may be strongest on desserts, but we were too full to eat dessert. The inn has a wine list, and the taproom is open each evening except Tuesdays.

The Environs: Those red carriage stalls across the common were built to provide shelter for parishioners' horses during the Congregational Church services. They were put up at the same time this white church was being erected in 1812. The church construction was financed by selling pew numbers at auction. Dr. Cyrus Hamilton bought No. 1 for $212, and the first six pews altogether netted $914 in bids. Today this is a double-duty church with the church on the second floor and a nursery school and kindergarten on the first floor. For both religion and education, the Congregational Church serves Lyme's 1,112 residents.

The church's original bell, cast by Revere and Sons, contained fifty silver dollars melted down, which Deacon Jonathan Franklin donated so the tone would be sweet. That bell cracked and was recast in 1847 by Hoople and Son, successor to the Reveres. When you spend the night at The Lyme Inn, you will hear the church's bell serenely ringing on the hour.

Within ten miles of the inn there are facilities for skiing, golf, tennis, hiking, and cultural offerings—movies, concerts, plays—at Dartmouth College. You can swim at a lake with a sand beach a mile away.

Scenic Drive: N.H. 10 and N.H. 135 along the Connecticut River.

Directions to the Inn: From New York, take I-95 to I-91 north to exit 14 at Thetford, Vermont. From Boston, take I-93 north to I-89 north to I-91 north to exit 14 at Thetford, Vermont. After you exit from I-91, drive east on N.H. 113A for two miles to Lyme.

ROCKHOUSE MOUNTAIN FARM INN

Eaton Center, New Hampshire

During the winter this farmlike inn about five miles from Conway receives daily morning reports from the major ski areas nearby. But on Friday afternoons, John R. Edge gets in his car, drives down the hill to the paved state road, and starts his own inspection tour of the ski slopes. When weekend skiers arrive on Friday evenings, Mr. Edge is ready with a firsthand report of slope conditions.

This kind of personal attention is typical of the friendly Edge family, John and Libby Edge and their children, Johnny, Jr. and Betsi. They have been running this homey inn since 1946, when they drove up from Montclair, New Jersey, in a 1936 Ford convertible and spent their first winter heating the beds with hot bricks.

Now the Rockhouse Mountain Farm is an unpretentious, family-style inn. It is set on a hillside with a splendid view of the mountains from the clapboard inn, the rambling barn, and the 350 acres of fields and woods. Eaton Center is a hamlet of 221 people just off the beaten track on the southeastern side of the White Mountain National Forest. The road through Eaton Center, N.H. 153, winds around Crystal Lake, where the inn has a private beach with canoes, rowboats, and sailboats. Turn up the road between the post office and the little white church and you come to the inn on the left side.

The inn is open from mid-June through mid-October and from mid-December through April 1. There are seventeen bedrooms, including bunk rooms, and they are furnished functionally. The inn serves breakfast and dinner for houseguests and puts up box lunches. Dinner is available to the public by reservation only.

This inn is especially popular with families because it is a casual place where children can ride horseback during the summer and fall and where in winter beginning skiers can learn how to snowplow on a hill behind the inn. The rates are modest here, with special ones for children based on age. In winter the rate includes use of a rope tow. The inn rents ski equipment and charges reasonable rates for the horseback riding.

During our visit several families were returning guests at Rockhouse Mountain Farm. The children immediately asked Johnny, Jr., who is in charge of the riding, how their favorite horses were doing. While their parents gazed at the scenery and drank in the mountain air, the children ran off to the hay-filled barn to look at the horses and to pat the dogs and cats.

The menu for dinner is set. When we were here, the meal began with a tasty fresh corn chowder garnished with minced fresh parsley. The entree was charcoal-broiled steak with green beans, a broiled tomato topped with bread crumbs, and macaroni and cheese. The slices of homemade whole-wheat bread were full-bodied and fresh. For dessert there was an excellent peach shortcake with home-canned peaches and real whipped cream on top.

Dinner is served at one dining-room table when there are relatively few guests and also at the separate tables in the breakfast room when there is a full house. As we started upstairs for the night, Betsi, who bakes the breads and makes the desserts here, stopped us. "Would you like a glass of milk in the kitchen before you go to bed?" she asked. "That would be very nice," we said.

The Environs: The trails through the woods invite walks in the fall when the foliage is turning, and you can cross-country ski on them in the winter. The ski areas within a twenty-five-mile radius include Cranmore, Wildcat, Mount Attitash, King Pine, Mount Whittier, Black, and Tyrol.

Scenic Drive: Kancamagus Highway.

Directions to the Inn: From New York or Boston, take I-95 to Spaulding Turnpike to N.H. 16 north to Center Ossipee. At Center Ossipee take N.H. 25 east to Effingham Falls and N.H. 153 to Eaton Center. As you approach Eaton Center, watch for the little white church on the right and take the first road on the left after that uphill to the inn.

STAFFORD'S-IN-THE-FIELD

Chocorua, New Hampshire

When Mr. and Mrs. Fred Stafford and their three children moved into this sprawling house in April 1965, the windows were broken, chipmunks were living in the walls, and there was no heat except wood-burning fireplaces. The house, overlooking undulating fields on the southeastern edge of the White Mountains, had been unoccupied for eight years.

It is hard to imagine that in this cozy, old-fashioned inn the Staffords had to stoke the fireplace fires every three hours just to keep the water pipes from freezing. With dogged determination and hard work, the Stafford family transformed the run-down house where they swept a space in the library to bed down that first night. Now it is a delightful, informal inn.

Stafford's-in-the-Field is open from Memorial Day weekend through October and from December 26 through March. The inn serves dinner and breakfast for houseguests and puts up box lunches on request. Meals are not open to the public except to guests of guests and special parties. There are twenty-two simple but pleasant bedrooms, including nine in separate cottages often assigned to families.

Mrs. Stafford oversees the kitchen and sometimes serves Mexican food for dinner. During our visit, the meal began with a fresh minestrone soup with pasta and melted cheese. The thick slices of dill bread made in the inn's kitchen were delicious. The entree was roast beef sliced very thin, crispy roast potatoes, and green peas. The green bean and kidney bean salad was presented on a lettuce leaf with slices of hard-boiled egg and onion. The menu here is set except for dessert, where there were numerous choices, including a light raspberry torte and a Brazilian orange cake. The inn does not serve liquor, but setups are available.

Guests eat at dining-room tables covered with green-and-white-checked oilcloth and lit by old kerosene lamps (the kind with glass handles). It is a quaint room with a player piano, a wood-burning stove, a decorative painted tin ceiling, and wallpaper Mr. Stafford applied himself. The pattern is repeated baskets and flowers. There are old butter churns standing by the entrance and a collection of butter molds above the fireplace.

When we stayed at the inn, Mr. Stafford seated the twenty or so guests at two long tables for dinner. When everybody finished eating, he announced it was his daughter Ramona's twenty-first birthday. All of us broke into a spontaneous round of "Happy Birthday" while Ramona, the waitress here, smiled. Then Mr. Stafford introduced his two teen-age sons, Fritz and Hansel, and said that the three children would sing several songs.

Ramona, Fritz, and Hansel assembled at one end of the room while Mrs. Stafford, wearing an apron, stood near the kitchen door. They sang half a dozen songs. These included two Hungarian folk songs and two folk songs by Johannes Brahms. We all responded with "oohs" and "ahhs" and clapped enthusiastically, and someone said, "It's just how an old-fashioned inn should be."

When you come to Stafford's-in-the-Field, you may not find Ramona and Fritz, who were about to leave as college freshmen soon after we were there. But if you visit during the summer, you will hear the music of the inn's weekly square dances held in the barn. It is a magnificent barn. From the top floor of it the Staffords can see Mount Chocorua when the leaves are off the trees. The 3,475-foot mountain is behind the inn past woods, hills, and ponds.

The Environs: About five minutes through the woods there is a swimming hole where you can take a dip on a hot day. In the winter visitors cross-country ski on the miles of fairly flat dirt roads and paths directly in back of the inn. The Appalachian Mountain Club's map of hiking trails in the Chocorua region is on sale at the inn.

No matter what the season or the weather, you must not leave this area without going to Chocorua Lake, where the birch trees frame Mount Chocorua and its reflection in the peaceful water perfectly. You can walk to the lake on a long winding dirt road from the inn or drive up N.H. 16 north from Chocorua village and take the first road on the left for a matter of yards. It is a picture-postcard view of what Henry James called "the admirable high-perched cone of Chocorua, which rears itself, all granite, over a huge interposing shoulder, quite with the allure of a minor Matterhorn. . . ."

Scenic Drive: Kancamagus Highway.

Directions to the Inn: From New York, take I-95 to I-495 and follow either of the two routes from Boston: (1) Take I-95 north to Spaulding Turnpike to N.H. 16 north to N.H. 113 west to Chocorua village. Go west on 113 for one mile and watch for the inn's sign. (2) Take I-93 north to N.H. 104 east to N.H. 25 north to N.H. 113 to Tamworth. (Do not take 113 to N. Sandwich.) From Tamworth village go east on 113 for two miles and watch for the inn's sign on the left.

THE HOMESTEAD

Sugar Hill, New Hampshire

In New Hampshire's youngest town, you will find New Hampshire's most old-fashioned inn perched on a hilltop with a glorious view of the White Mountains. The setting alone rivals anything you would travel to Europe to see.

We will never forget the panoramic view of the Presidential Range that confronted us on October 4 at the fall-foliage peak. The leaves were bright scarlet and orange, the spruce trees were deep green, and the mountain peaks were snow capped. Clusters of people gathered along the road by The Homestead, staring at this awesome view for as long as half an hour. It was the kind of day that made you stop, look, and really take notice of nature.

You can stop at The Homestead anytime except during April and May. Sometimes this warm, cozy inn is closed between the fall-foliage season and the ski season, but it is always open for Christmas. If you asked us which New England inn we would travel to for Christmas, we would not hesitate to say "The Homestead." Not that we have spent Christmas there; we have not. We spend Christmas at home. But if we were going to spend Christmas at an inn, we would make reservations today at this extraordinarily sentimental inn. There are seventeen bedrooms at the Homestead, including rooms in the inn, the Chalet, and a guesthouse across the road, from which there is a superlative view. The inn serves breakfast and dinner to houseguests daily and to the public by reservation only.

Concerning children, the inn says, "In fairness to parents who should not spend their vacation 'hushing' the children, to children who wake up at dawn and to fellow guests who have come here to rest, we do not encourage families with very young children. Well-behaved youngsters are a joy; some of our dearest guests are families numbering 5 or 6. For these the Chalet is perfect: The fun and laughter that should be part of a family vacation cannot disturb anyone else." The Chalet is a separate building with two levels. Each level has bedrooms, a kitchen, bathroom, and a fireplace.

The Homestead has been welcoming guests since 1881 when Mr. and Mrs. Elder arrived with their baggage from Boston. That in itself is not so unusual. A lot of New England inns have been welcoming guests since long before 1881. What is striking about The Homestead, though, is that the people who run it today are descended from the people who built this house in 1802.

Since the inn has not left the family in all those years, it is filled with a heritage of antiques and interesting objects. Usually we are not crazy about clutter, but in this case we have to make an exception. There are elaborate kerosene lamps converted to electricity, old bells, old chairs, framed photographs, a china collection in the dining room, candy dishes filled with wrapped hard candies, patchwork quilts. Behind one entrance door there hangs a ring draped with brass keys plus one hand-painted key.

Some of The Homestead's possessions are useful, such as the silver napkin rings and the nostalgic sachet bags in the wallpapered closets. And some are decorative hand-me-downs, such as the shadow box in one of the two living rooms where you can study the hand-painted egg shells delicately balanced inside. But whether the furniture and the accessories are heirlooms or recent acquisitions, they have all been placed in the inn thoughtfully and as though each one is a treasure.

The care with which The Homestead is run shows up at dinner as well. Usually there is a set menu for the evening meal, but the inn maintains the tradition of serving a meat entree and a fish entree on Fridays. The Friday we stayed there the inn was having small butterfly shrimp and Salisbury steak with mushroom sauce. There were two appetizers: a robust seafood chowder and a lime-lemon drink decorated with one fresh petunia and presented on a china plate. The entrees came with broccoli, waxed beans, and French fried potatoes. The tables were candlelit, the crackers were unwrapped, and the warm dinner rolls melted in our mouths.

There is something about the mountain air that whets the appetite, and it is a good thing, too, because The Homestead offers a lot of desserts. They range from "Best Ever Pie" (made with raisins and topped with meringue) to a ginger parfait (tiny pieces of candied ginger blended into vanilla ice cream). After dinner, the waitress brought warm fingerbowls with one hydrangea blossom floating on top.

We missed the Harvest Breakfast. Each year the inn celebrates the height of foliage season by serving an old-fashioned breakfast on the October Sunday when the color is at its peak. The breakfast buffet includes fruit compote, chipped-beef-in-cream, baked beans, scrambled eggs, fried potatoes, and apple pie. That list sums up The Homestead's attitude toward food: "We are not interested in pre-portioned or ready-to-serve food. We still run an old-fashioned kitchen. Our menus may not be gussied up with names you cannot pronounce, but the heritage of homemade cooking makes dining with us something special."

The Homestead is special all around. It has cheerful bedrooms, simple food, a great view, patina, and an interesting address. Sugar Hill, once part of Lisbon, was declared a separate town in 1962 by the New Hampshire Supreme Court. The 1970 Census counted 336 people in this mountain hamlet. The name,

Sugar Hill, is said to derive from the large grove of sugar-maple trees in the village.

As we said, we have not been to The Homestead for Christmas. But if we went, we would go with a mental picture of a Christmas tree in the inn's living room, and with the fervent hope that as soon as we arrived on Christmas Eve, twelve feet of snow would suddenly fall, making it impossible for us to leave.

Scenic Drive: Kancamagus Highway.

Directions to the Inn: From New York, take I-95 north to I-91 north to U.S. 302 north to N.H. 117 east to Sugar Hill. From Boston, take I-93 north to U.S. 3 north to I-93 north to Franconia village to N.H. 117 west for two miles. The inn is on N.H. 117.

LOVETT'S INN BY LAFAYETTE BROOK

Franconia, New Hampshire

A sudden hush fell over the dining room decorated with pumpkins at Lovett's Inn. "It's snowing!" someone said. Everyone turned toward the windows where you could see the large snowflakes falling slowly. After a moment of silence, the guests resumed eating and talking, mostly about the weather.

Had it been winter, this news would have whetted the appetites of skiers anticipating fresh powder at nearby Cannon and Mittersill ski areas. But it was early October, and this was the first sign of winter. The scarlet, orange, yellow, and russet leaves had only begun to fall from the sugar-maple trees, blanketing the mountains behind Lovett's Inn. In the reception room a man clutched his jacket around his neck, stamped the snow off his feet and said, "I don't see how people can enjoy the foliage in the snow." A waitress reassured him, "Don't worry. It'll be gone by morning."

Lovett's Inn is a compound of buildings that seems cozy and snug because it is dwarfed by the surrounding mountain peaks. The white-clapboard inn, the yellow-clapboard barn, and the thirteen motel units are the closest buildings to Cannon Mountain. The inn is open from mid-June to mid-October and from Christmas to April 1. It serves breakfast and dinner to guests, and to the public by reservation only. At Lovett's they are "delighted" to put up box lunches; you can make your request to your waitress at dinner the night before.

There is a wide variety of accommodations here, from a cottage called Stony Hill, accommodating four to eight persons, to the inn's best buys in the yellow barn. The old-fashioned bedrooms are those in the inn. There are seven of them, with simple furnishings and cheerful wallpaper. Two of the bedrooms have private bathrooms, and one, the Antique Room, has a triple exposure as well. The other bedrooms share bathrooms. In the yellow barn the seven twin-bedded rooms are furnished dormitory style and share two bathrooms. There are also thirteen motel units, eleven of them with working fireplaces. These units include living rooms with views of the mountains, television sets, sun terraces, and private bathrooms.

The dinner menu offers about fifteen entrees, ranging from broiled bluefish and broiled Boston scrod to curried lamb and calf's liver. The inn serves Harrington's baked ham, an excellent product from Harrington's in Richmond, Vermont (a firm that smokes its own ham, pheasant, pork loin, bacon, and turkey, and does an extensive mail-order business). The entrees came with fresh squash, potatoes baked in a white sauce with melted cheese, and a salad of cucumber and beet slices.

About twenty tempting desserts were listed in white chalk on a blackboard above the dining-room fireplace. These included hot blueberry pie, pumpkin pie, and "Mud Pie" (chocolate and coffee ice cream frozen in a graham cracker crust).

The inn has a wine list and an attractive taproom where you can have cocktails while you gaze at the distant ski trails of Cannon and Mittersill.

You will be well fortified for any hike or a full day of skiing after breakfast at the inn. The menu includes Charles J. Lovett, Jr.'s excellent omelets, wild-rice or blueberry pancakes, shirred eggs with chervil, roast beef hash with a poached egg, and fried corn-meal mush with maple syrup. We had a delicious sour cream and cheddar cheese omelet while we watched the snow melt outside.

During the summer you can swim in the inn's heated pool or in the mountain pond. The bulletin board in the reception room is covered with notices of things to do, such as what movies are playing in Littleton and Bethlehem, where the auctions are, when church services are held, and where to go to play golf. During the winter ski reports are posted at 8:15 A.M. The enclosed sun porch is a game room filled with pinball machines, and it is very popular with children.

The Environs: Franconia's most popular attraction is the Old Man of the Mountains on U.S. 3. There are usually many cars parked along the road while people photograph the impressive natural profile. If you would like to take a short rewarding hike near Lovett's Inn, go to the parking lot across from the Cannon Mountain Ski Area. Take the trail (it starts on the edge of the woods) to Artist's Bluff for a splendid panoramic view.

You can reach the foot of Cannon Mountain by driving several miles along N.H. 18. In the summer and fall the Cannon Mountain Aerial Tramway takes you to the 4,121 foot summit, where the views are spectacular.

Scenic Drive: For an exceptional circular drive, take N.H. 18 south to U.S. 3 south to N.H. 112 east (Kancamagus Highway) to N.H. 16 north to U.S. 302 north to U.S. 3 south to N.H. 141 south to the inn.

Directions to the Inn: From New York, take I-95 to I-495 to I-93 and follow Boston directions. From Boston, take I-93 north to U.S. 3 north to N.H. 18 north. The inn is at the juncture of N.H. 18 and N.H. 141.

PINKHAM NOTCH CAMP AND LODGE

Gorham, New Hampshire

The Pinkham Notch Camp is not an inn at all. It is just one of our favorite places anywhere in the world, and if you do not know about the mountain huts, accessible only by foot, in New Hampshire's White Mountains, we thought you would enjoy hearing about them.

The Pinkham Notch Camp Lodge is the hiking center in "the Whites," as they are called. It is run by the nonprofit Appalachian Mountain Club (AMC), the oldest mountaineering club in the United States. The lodge is dormitory style, serving dinner and breakfast (for guests and the public), and accommodating hikers 365 days a year. It is also the base camp for the eight full-service mountain huts that the club operates from mid-June to Labor Day.

Although most people who stay here are AMC hikers of all ages, you do not have to be an AMC member to stay either at Pinkham Notch Lodge or in the huts. If you want amenities and service, this is not the place to come. But if what you want is shelter, blankets, hot food, the company of hikers, and an exceptionally good buy, this is an excellent place to stay.

Unique at least to New England, if not to the United States, the Pinkham Notch Camp is located in several buildings on U.S. 16 between the town centers of Gorham, eleven miles to the north, and Jackson, eleven miles to the south. The majestic peak of Mount Washington, New England's highest summit, rises above the camp. Between the camp and the mountaintop is the glacial cirque or bowl called Tuckerman Ravine, where thousands of skiers come each year in March, April, May, and June.

The camp's brown-clapboard Joe Dodge Center (named for the former manager of thirty-seven years) has 105 comfortable bunk beds in rooms accommodating two, three, and four persons. There are large, immaculate community bathrooms with terrific showers on both floors. The attractive library is full of books, and the living room'has a large fireplace.

The dining room is in the main building or lodge, where supper is served family style. The menu is set, the food is hot, there is lots of it, and it will not give you indigestion. When we were last there, dinner consisted of a packaged beef-noodle soup, roast beef, creamed potatoes, peas, and a cold baked Alaska for dessert. At breakfast we had hot cereal, scrambled eggs on the dry side, and popovers. You can order trail lunches for a modest charge.

When you walk into the lodge, the chances are that everyone you see—old and young—will be wearing boots or sneakers with wool socks, long pants, sweaters, and flannel shirts. People sit at the six large round tables, spread out their trail maps, and compare notes about routes to take. You can write postcards in the lodge, read the morning Boston and Manchester, New Hampshire, newspapers, and help yourself to coffee and tea from 7 A.M. to 10 P.M.

If you are planning to hike up Mount Washington, the lodge is the place to come to get a weather report and forecast. You do not need to stay here to come for advice about trail routes and weather conditions. (You can buy maps and guidebooks here, too, including *The White Mountain Guide Book*, published by the AMC, which is also available at the trail huts.) Even when the weather on U.S. 16 is fair, it is often raining, snowing, dangerously windy, or just plain cold on the upper reaches of the Presidential Range. The most dangerous condition under which to attempt the climb is the combination of rain and wind. Every year there are near fatalities, and sometimes fatalities, in the Whites. These accidents are usually preventable. So, if an AMC staff member tells you not to climb Mount Washington that day and you have driven hundreds of miles to get here and want to go anyhow, forget it and read a book. If the weather clears up soon enough, you will still accomplish your climb, and if it does not, at least you will go back home safe and sound. When you do hike in the Whites, remember: stay on the marked trails. If you should have an accident, it is much harder for rescuers to find you if you are not on the trail.

The AMC, founded in 1876, started operating the first of its eight huts in the Whites on Mount Madison in 1888. Today the huts extend from Carter Notch in the east to Lonesome Lake in the west. Most huts have a central room that functions as the dining room, living room, and reception area. There are usually two bunk rooms, one for women and the other for men.

The huts do not have electricity or hot running water, but they do have cold running water, bunks, mattresses, pillows, and blankets. You are expected to bring your own towel, flashlight, sheets, and pillowcase (unless you want to buy paper sheets and pillowcases at the huts). The huts also provide dinner at 6 P.M., breakfast at 7 A.M., and trail lunches.

At the beginning of the season, helicopters bring in bottled propane gas tanks to each hut. After that, two crew members walk down from their hut each day to a supply station near a road. They load up to eighty-five pounds of food and supplies on special wooden frames that they carry on their backs to the huts.

The largest hut is Lakes of the Clouds Hut, which, at 5,000 feet, is 1½ miles from the Mount Washington summit and has room for ninety people. The smallest is Zealand Falls Hut at 2,700 feet, which accommodates thirty-six. The huts are about 7 miles or a day's journey apart on the Appalachian Trail, the continuous footpath from Maine to Georgia. They are connected by many miles of scenic trails. The shortest distance between any two is the 4½ miles between Lakes of the Clouds Hut and Mizpah Springs Hut.

Here is a way to stay at two huts without hiking uphill: take the cog railway up Mount Washington, walk the 1½ miles downhill to Lakes of the Clouds Hut, and spend the first night there. The next day, walk the 4½ miles downhill to Mizpah Springs Hut, spend the night, and then walk the 2½ miles down to the road at Crawford Notch.

The lodge at Pinkham Notch Camp does provide sheets, pillowcases, and towels, but if you like a large fluffy towel, bring your own. One thing you will not need to pack is an alarm clock. About fifteen minutes before breakfast at the lodge, a crew member walks through the halls ringing a bell. It is not an unpleasant sound, but we guarantee you will not sleep through it.

Directions to the Inn: From New York or Boston, take I-95 north to Spaulding Turnpike to N.H. 16 north to the lodge, eleven miles north of Jackson. Note: Continental Trailways has bus service twice a day from Boston with a flagstop at Pinkham Notch. The bus stops in front of the AMC lodge.

THE SPALDING INN CLUB

Whitefield, New Hampshire

"I've looked at those mountains since I was a boy but I never get tired of them. Between the shadows and the light, they're never twice the same." Saying that, Randall E. Spalding gestured toward the sixty White Mountain peaks encircling this inn and smiled wistfully.

Mr. and Mrs. Spalding started this inn in 1926. "Back then, if you wanted to live here, you either farmed or you took in summer boarders. Since my parents were already farmers, we decided to take in the boarders," Mr. Spalding said. Then he pointed at the main building here. "Of course, in those days that was only a little old bungalow."

The Spaldings' "bungalow" is now a large brown-shingled inn, one of a compound of eighteen buildings spread out on 300 acres. This complex might seem large if it were set anywhere other than in the White Mountains. But the four mountain ranges surrounding the inn and the grandeur of the peaks make The Spalding Inn Club seem much smaller than it is.

This is the most formal of our inns in the White Mountains, and it is also the largest. There are sixty-five attractive bedrooms, each with a private bathroom. The inn is open from June through October 15 and has three cottages with kitchens that are available through the winter. The Spalding Inn Club operates on the full American plan, serving three meals daily for both guests and the public. The inn puts up box lunches for guests on request. If you are staying elsewhere in the White Mountains and you want a pleasant outing for lunch, we suggest you telephone the inn in the morning. You will be rewarded with plain but tasty American food and a scenic drive as well.

Many of the returning guests, most of whom are retired

people, make reservations as far as a year in advance for stays of a week or longer. They enjoy the resort atmosphere, the quick and friendly service, and the mountain air.

For its guests, the inn offers a variety of activities on the grounds. First among them is lawn bowling. The perfectly level and perfectly manicured bowling green looks like a 120-foot square billiard table with grass instead of felt. There is a Lawn Bowling Sports House with dressing rooms, showers, lockers, and a sign that says, "Old golfers never die; they just take up lawn bowling." The American version of lawn bowling, popular in colonial New England, is similar to the French boules and Italian boccie, but it is not the same game. The first United States Lawn Bowling Singles Championship in 1957 was sponsored by the inn.

During the summer the inn employs a full-time instructor in lawn bowling and a tennis pro. There are three all-weather tennis courts and a heated swimming pool, around which cookouts are held each day at lunch, weather permitting. When it rains, you can sit on the comfortable sofas by the living room's fieldstone fireplace and read books or magazines. As you stand in the living room in front of the picture window, you will see a row of tall pines. Count from the left to the right until you come to the fifth pine tree. Look directly above that tree and you will be gazing at the summit of Mount Washington.

The inn's menus are presented on stiff white rectangular cards typical of resorts. There are usually half a dozen entrees for dinner, such as broiled halibut, boneless breast of chicken, roast ribs of beef, braised smoked ox tongue with Yorkshire pudding, and a plain or ham omelet. When we visited the inn, the appetizers and soups included marinated herring, fresh fruitcup, onion soup, vichyssoise, and consommé. The desserts ranged from apple pie and strawberry meringue glacé to Edam cheese and toasted crackers.

The inn has a wine list with domestic and imported wines, and there is a taproom downstairs in the main building.

For breakfast you can have hot clam bouillon, codfish drops, and popovers—in addition to fruit, hot cereal, and eggs any style with ham or bacon. The portions at all the meals are small, so you can eat every course and still feel hungry by the next meal. After dinner, you will find that your bed has been turned down and any towels you used have been replaced.

The lampshades throughout the inn are handmade at the Oxbow Antique Shop in Newbury, Vermont. They are made of rice paper and decorated with cutouts of flowers, mostly from old English prints.

The wallpaper patterns are unusually pretty here. We overheard seven women comment separately on the exquisite pattern in the nicely proportioned dining room, with its Bentwood Thornet chairs. The wallpaper has a continuous green branch on a white background, with rose-and-yellow pears, flowers, grapes, and pineapples, the symbol of hospitality. If you use the pay telephone in the white-wooden booth near the front door, you will find the wallpaper inside has antique stopwatches on it.

Scenic Drive: From the inn to the cog railway base: take U.S. 3 to Lancaster, U.S. 2 to Riverton, secondary road from Riverton to Jefferson Notch Road south to Mt. Clinton Road (at the cog railway base) to Crawford Notch.

Directions to the Inn: From New York, take I-91 to N.H. 10 (at Woodsville, New Hampshire) to N.H. 116 to U.S. 3 north. From Boston, take I-93 north and U.S. 3 north. In Whitefield take U.S. 3 north and watch for Mountain View Road on the right side. The inn is on Mountain View Road, which connects U.S. 3 and N.H. 116.

THE GLEN

Pittsburg, New Hampshire

Look on a New Hampshire state map and you will find The Glen thirteen miles from the Canadian border. It is named on the map just off U.S. 3 on the west side of the First Connecticut Lake. You do not need to go farther than the shoreline here for one of New England's most spectacular views. The First Connecticut Lake (called "the First Lake") is 3,125 acres in size, with an undeveloped shoreline of 19.4 miles, dominated by stands of spruce and fir. The lake is teeming with fish and wildlife along its shore. From The Glen you face east toward Magalloway Mountain and the mountains in western Maine, which stretch in the distance.

Most accommodations to be found in Pittsburg are housekeeping cottages with a shabby appearance. The Glen is considered the nicest place to stay in this area. It is a traditional sporting camp with six simply furnished bedrooms that are clean and warm in a large rustic lodge, and nine cottages along the lake. The cottages, furnished functionally, have from one to three bedrooms. Each lodge bedroom and cottage has twin beds and a private bathroom. The Glen is open from mid-May through mid-October. It serves three plain hot meals daily, puts up box lunches "with pleasure," and charges reasonable rates. All meals are open to the public by reservation only.

Mrs. Betty H. Falton's cheerful smile and outgoing personality create a friendly atmosphere in this down-to-earth lodge.

After dinner, guests gather in the living room around the huge fieldstone fireplace, and beneath stuffed game animals on the walls, to talk about the fish they did or did not catch and the wildlife they did or did not observe. A woman said, "I saw two bull moose today but I think they're so boring. They're just plain ugly." A professor from Princeton University who stayed at The Glen for six days went back to New Jersey with lists of the eighty-four species of birds he had seen.

The Environs: The Connecticut Lakes region, the northern tip of New Hampshire, is often overlooked by travelers who concentrate on the White Mountains. But it is just as exciting as the mountains. The scenery is beautiful, with lakes, dense forests, streams, old hauling roads, and trails. This area is part of a remote wilderness corridor, mostly owned by timber companies, that extends north along the Canadian border into western and northern Maine.

Of the three paved roads that cross this rugged back country into Canada, two are in Maine (see Sky Lodge) and the third and most southern route is U.S. 3 in northern New Hampshire. U.S. 3 is the only paved road within 189,952 acres comprising the town of Pittsburg. The four Connecticut Lakes, headwaters of the Connecticut River, are all in Pittsburg, New Hampshire's largest town. In 1970 there were 726 year round residents and the population density was 2.4 people per square mile.

There are about two hundred miles of fishable streams in the Connecticut Lakes region. People who fish from mid-May through September catch land-locked salmon, lake trout (togue), brook trout (squaretail), brown and rainbow trout, chain pickerel, cusk, and smelt. In 1964 a twenty-six-pound trout was caught in the First Lake.

Sight-seeing is almost as popular as fishing in the region, and for good reason, too. The sights to be seen are all natural. In the lodge you can buy a detailed roads and trails map that shows the many lakes, ponds, streams, waterfalls, trails, and logging roads, with mileages clearly marked. Here are some names you will find on a detailed map of the isolated Connecticut Lakes region: Hellgate Falls, Magalloway Mountain, Norton Pool, Black Cat Spur, Unknown Pond, Hedgehog Nubble, Teapot Brook, Spooner Hill, Tabor Notch, Coon Brook Bog, Boundary Pond, Ben Young Hill, Boardpile Brook, and the Dead Diamond River.

There are two mountains with lookout towers on their

summits: Magalloway (east of the First Lake) and Deer (not far from the Third Lake). The most panoramic view is from the top of Magalloway (3,360 feet), where the upper portion of the trail is rough and rocky, similar to some trails in the White Mountains. From the summit you look west at the First Lake, north toward the international boundary with Canada, and east toward the mountains and water bodies of western Maine.

The Deer Mountain trail is about 2½ miles long, gradual, and less difficult than the hike up Magalloway. It follows a picturesque brook and passes a pure, cold spring just below the summit ridge. The lookout tower at 3,005 feet is on a subsidiary peak. The true summit is 3,168 feet. From the lookout tower you can see clearly the ridges, hills, and mountains that separate the United States and Canada. These are called "the highlands."

The most remote large pond in this area is Mountain Pond in the northeastern corner of the state. It has been called Boundary Pond for so long that it is even marked Boundary Pond on the detailed map. You have to drive about twelve miles on hard-top and gravel roads before getting out of your vehicle and walking a mile to the pond. It is 120 acres in area, about eight feet deep, and known for its pristine beauty.

East of Magalloway Mountain, an old hauling road leads close to Garfield Falls on the east branch of the Dead Diamond River. The falls, about eightyfeet high, cascade through a small gorge for half a mile above the falls.

Scenic Drive: There is just the one road through Pittsburg, but, from it, you will see Lake Francis, the First, Second, and Third Connecticut Lakes, Magalloway Mountain, and the highlands along the border. The United States-Canadian border affords not one but two sensational views. Both customs offices are on the crest of a hill. From the United States customs buildings there is a breathtaking view to the south of the Third Lake, forests, hills, and mountains. When you cross the border into Canada, you see a completely different spectacle to the north of Quebec's open farmlands and Mount Megantic looming over the flat countryside. You simply cannot go as far north in New England as The Glen and miss these two views. (It is 22.5 miles from the junction of U.S. 3 and N.H. 145 in Pittsburg to the Canadian border.)

When you head south to leave the Connecticut Lakes, take N.H. 145 from Pittsburg to Colebrook. (It is especially pretty from north to south.) When we took this route, it was a drizzly misty day and we still thought the scenery was exceptional. There is a very fine view from Ben Young Hill. The views at the peak of the foliage (around October 1) were superlative, with scarlet maple trees, velvet-green pastures, and distant mountains that reverberated in shades of blue. The open fields and scattered farmhouses contrast with the dense woodlands and beautiful lakes to be seen from U.S. 3 north of Pittsburg village.

Directions to the Inn: From New York or Boston, take I-91 north to U.S. 5, U.S. 302, N.H. 116, and U.S. 3, or take I-93 north to U.S. 3. North of Pittsburg village signs on U.S. 3 will direct you to the private road (a mile long) to The Glen.

Maine

⊷

As Maine goes, so goes the nation.

AMERICAN POLITICAL MAXIM
circa 1888

That anonymous statement, widely quoted every four years on national television, harks back to the days when Maine had its gubernatorial election in September, two months before any other state. Political pundits watched those state elections carefully to see what the trends were in Maine in a presidential-election year.

Maine has its elections for governor in November now. But this state, almost as large in area as the other five New England states put together, still maintains a regional tradition of stanch independence in other ways. This is New England's last frontier, the only state left with vast undeveloped lands. If you explore inland Maine even on a map, you will find that most of Aroostook, Piscataquis, and Somerset counties are accessible only by waterway or lumbering roads. (These are owned by huge paper companies and they are marked, "Private Road. Open to the Public.")

Maine is the final outpost for urban New Englanders who dream of a rural lifestyle "downeast" and sometimes forget that winters here are harsh. Mailboxes are often hung by chains from posts so they can be lowered and raised during winter storms and snowdrifts. Nevertheless, in 1975 the census reported that Maine was the fifth-fastest-growing state in the nation.

In the summer Maine is popular, especially along the coast, where many people from Boston and New York City have summer homes. One evening in Castine, a favorite coastal town of ours, we overheard a fourteen-year-old boy ask his younger

183

brother, "What do you want to hang around with Frank for?" The younger brother replied, "Gee, I think Frank's nice." The older boy said, "But Frank's from New York. He's a city person. I don't see why you can't hang around with Danny. After all, he lives here all year."

Maine has towns named Norway, Paris, Denmark, Sorrento, Poland, Mexico, Peru, China, and Sweden. New Sweden, in Aroostook County, was settled in 1870 after William W. Thomas, Jr., Maine's commissioner of immigration, went to Sweden, recruited fifty-one men, women, and children, and returned with them to the township. Maine was offering free farms at the time. More Swedish emigrants followed, and by 1872 there were about six hundred Swedes living in New Sweden. The last of those original emigrants, Mrs. Agnes M. Anderson, died on March 1, 1949.

Maine is where the natives say "a-yuh" instead of "yes" and where the sound "or" is pronounced with the mouth open instead of with pursed lips. It has the world's greatest tides (an extreme range of 53.5 feet) in the Bay of Fundy, which separates Nova Scotia from Maine. The Appalachian Trail ends here at the top of the state's highest peak, Mount Katahdin, 5,268 feet, in Baxter State Park. The Maine section of this trail (275 miles) was the last and most difficult part to complete because it goes through wilderness. The entire trail extends over two thousand miles to Georgia.

Maine's nickname is the Pine Tree State, but its dual personality is summed up much better in the state seal, which shows a farmer and a seaman. Most farmland is in sparsely populated Aroostook County, famous for potatoes. The children here start school in August and then have a recess in late September and early October to help their parents with the potato harvest.

When we think of Maine, we always picture both a pine tree and a lobster. If you flew along the Maine coast, you would find the shoreline only 228 miles long. But if you planned to meander along the many indentations in a boat, your trip would be 3,478 miles. These coves inspired one of Maine's authors, Sarah Orne Jewett (1849–1909), to write, "A harbor, even if it is a little harbor, is a good thing, since adventurers come into it as well as go out, and the life in it grows strong, because it takes something from the world and has something to give in return."

These harbors are dotted with multicolored buoys marking the lobster traps or "pots," as they are also called, on the bottom. Maine's lobstermen are individualists whose frustrations in living close to the sea provide the nation with 75 percent of its annual lobster catch. Lobsters were once so plentiful in the Bay of Fundy that farmers used them as fertilizer.

Rural roads near the coast often have piles of lobster traps in front of even the smallest homes. If you look at one closely, you will see there are two compartments: the outer one has a funnel of nylon netting and the inner section contains the bait. Once the lobster has crawled into the inner "room," it rarely gets back out, because it cannot figure out how to do it.

Travelers have sometimes asked us about lobsters in Maine. We suggest that you stop at a roadside stand for the best buy in lobsters. These lobster pounds often serve nothing but lobster, clams, and beverages. The rule seems to be this: the shabbier the lobster pound, the lower the price. Even at that, lobsters do not come cheap. But since there are only two ways to boil lobster (in fresh water and in sea water), we recommend the pounds unless you want a full dinner.

If you decide to buy live lobsters to take home just before you leave Maine and you have never boiled a lobster, do not feel squeamish about it. The lobster is a cruel animal who eats almost anything, including smaller lobsters, who are devoured by slowly removing eyes, legs, antennae, and claws while the victim is alive. Male lobsters do not eat smaller females with whom they have mated. But, all in all, the delicious meat belies the fact that the lobster is God's garbage collector on the sea floor. The simplest way to cook lobster is to plunge it head first into rapidly boiling water. That way, it is killed quickly.

One Maine institution that is almost as highly renowned as the lobster is L. L. Bean, Inc. in Freeport. L. L. Bean, established in 1912, is a sports-goods supplier that does most of its business by mail. It now sends almost 1.5 million seasonal catalogues to customers in fifty states and seventy foreign countries. The Freeport store, a rambling building in the center of town, is open twenty-four hours a day, 365 days of the year. In the past five years the wool shirts have become partly synthetic (a salesman explained that they wear longer), the deerskin clutter bags are now made of cowhide, and one corner of the store has sprouted a suspicious-looking group of knickknack souvenirs. But most items are as reliable as ever. Among them are the beautiful, all-wool Hudson's Bay Point blankets, the sleeping bags, and the Bean's Maine Hunting Shoe. The store displays some merchandise not in the catalogue, including (in the fall) women's all-wool skirts, fully-lined, in conservative styles. L. L. Bean is still known for good value and a stubborn resistance to change.

Some of our inns in Maine are known for the same thing. At The Rock Gardens Inn, for instance, you can have boiled lobster three nights a week, an exceptional view, and a happy atmosphere—all at a modest charge. You will find that a surprising number of Maine inns have working fireplaces in bedrooms or cottages. The prospect of a cheery fireplace is reassuring in Maine, where summer evenings almost always call for a heavy sweater.

Since the 1870s brought the tourist trade to Maine, many large resort hotels have sprung up, especially along the coast. While they have their attractions, we have tried to single out the smaller inns that retain intimacy and a highly personal appeal. So we have chosen more guesthouses (bed-and-breakfast inns) in Maine than in any other state. These are located near restaurants that offer you a choice for the evening meal.

All our inns but three are on or near the coast. When you plan a trip to Maine, remember that this is New England's largest state and driving distances are much longer here than in the other five states. (This is not apparent on most regional maps.) When you drive from Route 1 to the tip of almost any peninsula, you can count on being in the car for about half an hour.

Unlike inland Maine, most of the coast south of Ellsworth is highly developed along Route 1. During the summer you may find the traffic stretching for miles, particularly on weekends. Between the New Hampshire border and Brunswick, Maine, Route 1 is extremely commercialized, ugly, and very tiring in traffic. We suggest you avoid Route 1 south of Bath unless you are going to a resort like Ogunquit, York, or Kennebunkport. North of Bath the rockbound coast begins, continuing to the Canadian border.

One welcome exception along the crowded coast is the Eastern Penobscot Bay region, the peninsula just south of Mount Desert Island. Even when there are lots of people at Acadia

National Park in the summer, this thoroughly unspoiled peninsula seems to have relatively few visitors. Blue Hill is a charming, quiet town, famous for its pottery. Castine and Stonington both represent our idea of Maine character at its best in their architecture, their boats, and their self-reliant settings on the sea. They are much more interesting to visit than the self-conscious fishing villages farther south, such as Boothbay Harbor.

Our inns on the Eastern Penobscot peninsula are The Blue Hill Inn and David's Folly. You can also visit this area as a side trip if you stay on Mount Desert Island. (At Stonington, on Eastern Penobscot, a ferry goes to the Isle Au Haut section of Acadia National Park.)

Our three inland inns are Migis Lodge (southwestern Maine), The Bethel Inn (west-central Maine), and Sky Lodge (only twelve miles from the Canadian border). Three more inns on Maine islands are described in the islands section.

Maine's most impressively furnished inns are The Island House in Ogunquit, The Squire Tarbox House in Westport, and The Bethel Inn in Bethel. Our favorite inn on Mount Desert Island (Acadia National Park) is the intimate Cranberry Lodge. For sheer peacefulness, our first choice is Migis Lodge in South Casco, nestled beneath towering pines on beautiful Sebago Lake. And if you have never been to northern Maine, Sky Lodge in Moose River is well worth the trip.

THE ISLAND HOUSE

Ogunquit, Maine

Ogunquit reminds us of Rockport, Massachusetts, because it is a fishing village turned art colony turned tourist haunt that still supports some fishermen and artists.

Ogunquit is very popular during the summer, when flocks of visitors come to its three-mile stretch of beach and to the professional summer playhouse just south of town on U.S. 1. Often, people stay here for several weeks or the entire summer, so there are many restaurants, motels, and guesthouses to accommodate them.

But the intimate Island House occupies the choicest site, a point of land at the end of picturesque Perkins Cove, where closely grouped shops and restaurants attract pedestrians in large numbers. The inn's location affords privacy and panoramic views of the sea, the ragged rocks, and the boats moored in the cove.

The Island House has six bedrooms, all tastefully furnished. The inn is open from June 1 to October 1. A Continental breakfast is served to inn guests only each morning except Sundays. (The cost is included in the overnight rate.) The Island House does not accept children under age twelve or pets.

The living room has a lovely combination of antiques, plants, mirrors, primitive paintings, a marble-topped table, a copper teapot with fresh flowers, and a fireplace. A wooden bowl contains stones of various shapes and colors, glistening from the one coat of quick-drying lacquer applied to them.

The most romantic bedroom here is a double-bedded "honeymoon room," with a magnificent four-poster bed, an arched ceiling, and a private bathroom. The bed is almost 3 feet high, and the posts rise 8½ feet off the floor. Except for one room with a single bed, the other bedrooms have twin beds. Two second-floor rooms share a small balcony overlooking the cove and a much-photographed foot drawbridge.

Ogunquit has so many restaurants that it would take a week plus an iron resolve to diet after sampling them. They range from nearby lobster pounds with moderately priced lobster dinners to expensive restaurants offering French dishes. Innkeepers Paul and Marge Laurent, who opened The Island House in 1946, have a wide variety of menus for guests to study, along with well-considered advice for those pondering the plethora of choices.

The Environs: Marginal Way, a wide, mile-long footpath that winds above the edge of the sea with uninterrupted views, starts behind the public parking lot at Perkins Cove. The path has benches placed intermittently, and a short feeder path leads from Marginal Way to the center of town.

At Perkins Cove you can arrange to join a group for fishing, sailing, or a "scenic lobster cruise" during which a lobsterman empties his traps for the day. As a guest at The Island House, you can swim off the rocks; the public beach is about a mile away.

In July and August Ogunquit seems as crowded as Cape Cod. But in June it is less hectic and in September "the water is warm, the skies are clear, some shops do close, but the summer crowds are gone," Mrs. Laurent said.

Ogunquit is part of Wells, and a word of warning is in order for those who have never driven on U.S. 1 through Wells at the height of the tourist season. In 1653, there were so few roads here that the townspeople in Wells, Saco, and Cape Porpoise were ordered to "make sufficient roads within their towns from house to house, and clear and fit them for foot and cart travel, before the next county court under penalty of 10 pounds for every town's defect in this particular."

Today there are so many cars, hamburger stands, gas stations, and tourist shops that the prospect of traveling through Wells is as discouraging now as it must have been for different reasons in 1653. Once you get to The Island House, though, you will conclude that the drive was worthwhile.

Scenic Drive: U.S. 1A to York Village (south) or Me. 9 to Kennebunkport (north).

Directions to the Inn: From New York or Boston, take I-95 to the exit for York, take U.S. 1 north to Ogunquit, and Shore Road to Perkins Cove. At Perkins Cove drive past the shops and the foot-bridge to the farthest point. The Island House, announced by a small sign beside a dirt driveway, is the last house in Perkins Cove.

ROCK GARDENS INN AND COTTAGES

Sebasco Estates, Maine

"I think we're the only resort in Maine crazy enough to serve boiled lobsters three nights a week and fresh orange juice every morning," innkeeper Gene Winslow said as he paused at our table to welcome us as new guests here.

We were just finishing our boiled lobsters on a Tuesday evening when Mr. Winslow joined us, followed by the waitress who said, "Are you ready for your second lobsters?" There was a moment of complete silence; then we said, "Did you say, 'Sec-onds'?" Mr. Winslow laughed at our astonishment. "Everyone gets seconds on lobsters here," he said. "Today I bought seventy lobsters. I thought that would be enough." We scanned the din-ing room and counted about thirty-five people. "Does everybody order seconds?" we asked. "Usually about 3 percent don't eat lobster at all, and tonight they're having beef pie. People who love lobster look forward to the seconds though." With that, we ordered seconds and Mr. Winslow moved on to the next table, where two generations of one family had already started on their second lobsters.

Named for the flourishing rock gardens outside, this happy inn occupies a promontory of land jutting into Upper Casco Bay. Open from mid-June to late September, it operates on the American plan and serves meals to houseguests only. The inn puts up excellent box lunches on request. There are four bedrooms in the main inn, and there are nine gray-and-white shingled cottages with a variety of accommodations clustered along the promontory.

Rock Gardens Inn has both the most desirable attributes of an inn and the advantage of being located within easy walking distance of a larger, impersonal resort. Inn guests are allowed to use the resort's facilities, which include an Olympic-size salt-water pool, a nine-hole golf course, deep-sea fishing trips, evening entertainment, tennis, shuffleboard, boat trips, and lawn bowling.

At the same time, Rock Gardens, owned and run by Gene and Dot Winslow since 1942, has the highly personal flavor of an inn and an informal atmosphere. Although many retired people return as guests year after year, there is absolutely no reason why younger people would not be perfectly content here, too. There is plenty to do and as much opportunity for privacy as anyone might want.

In the spotless dining room guests are assigned specific tables for the duration of their stay. (In July and August the minimum stay is one week.) The dining room has red-and-white checked tablecloths, the chairs are painted a cheerful blue, and there is matching solid-blue china. After our dinner (which ended with fresh apple pie and vanilla ice cream), the guests gathered in the living room to chat and read back copies of *Yankee Magazine.*

The setting of the cottages is exceptionally appealing, because they command a view of the tufted islands offshore and the inlets (on either side of the promontory) where small boats are anchored. At the tip of the promontory there is a weathered dock on pilings and large stacks of lobster traps.

The inn's bedrooms are furnished simply and are pleasant and comfortable. The cottages offer a variety of accommodations. Each has a working fireplace in a living room and many have screened or glassed-in porches. When two or three generations of one family vacation here, they ask for one of the larger cottages.

Although the inn does not serve liquor, you are welcome to bring your own. You can get ice in a small cottage on the grounds.

The huge rocks separating the inn's lawn from the water are stained by the eleven-foot tide that seems to billow and swell as it comes in. Since the tides here are affected only by lunar pull, they can be predicted accurately. This natural phenomenon helped make nearby Bath the leading shipbuilding city in America from 1841 to 1857. They still make a few ships in Bath, where builders can state five years in advance when the tide will be high on launching day.

The Environs: For a short side trip, go to Popham Beach State Park, where you can swim, picnic, or fish. Fort Popham is a granite-and-brick structure built in 1861 but never completed.

Directions to the Inn: From New York or Boston, take I-95 to exit 9 on the Maine Turnpike and continue on the east branch of I-95 north to Bath. Follow U.S. 1 north to Me. 209 south to the junction of Me. 209 and Me. 217. Drive about a mile south on Me. 217 to the turnoff to the inn.

THE SQUIRE TARBOX HOUSE

Westport Island, Maine

The Squire Tarbox House is a small, perfectly delightful inn about ten miles from Wiscasset on what used to be called Jeremy-Squam Island. It is Westport Island now, but the bridge over the Sheepscot River connecting it to the mainland makes this island seem more like a peninsula than a separate entity.

There is just one paved road, Me. 144, that extends the length of the 8.6 square-mile island. Follow it far enough and you will come to The Squire Tarbox House, a tidy white-clapboard inn with the black shutters that typify Maine. The inn consists of a house and a carriage house linked by a third structure. This is an example of the northern New England tradition of "joined" buildings. There is a well-proportioned lawn here, and in a corner next to the woods, you will find one of the many family graveyards in this area.

The inn is open from May 1 through November 1, serving three meals daily to guests, and to the public by reservation only.

There are seven bedrooms altogether. The menus here are set. Box lunches are put up on request.

There are not many houses (and some are mobile homes) in this town of 228 people, but The Squire Tarbox House is among the most attractive. The furnishings in the sitting rooms, dining room, and bedrooms in the main house include lovely antiques, pretty flowered wallpaper patterns, twin beds, and fireplaces in the public rooms. The bedrooms in the carriage house are furnished in a more modern style, but they are very pleasant and cheerful.

In the morning the aroma of blueberry muffins and bacon fills the inn, luring you to breakfast in the dining room, where guests eat meals together at one table facing a fireplace. The inn is run by Mrs. Eleanor H. Smith and her sister, Mrs. Mary Wright, who takes charge of the kitchen. If you are ready for breakfast before everyone else, Mrs. Wright will invite you to sit at the counter in her kitchen for a first cup of coffee or a meal. Besides the muffins and bacon for breakfast, we had French toast made with Mrs. Wright's bread. For dinner she made a robust meat pie, served with fresh corn on the cob and delicious homemade rolls. The dessert was Mrs. Wright's pound cake and lemon sherbet.

The Environs: The Westport Community Church and the town hall are just down the road from the inn, and before we left, Mrs. Smith asked us if we would like a tour of Westport's town center. Of course we said we would. As we walked along the quiet road, Mrs. Smith recalled the day in 1955 when the Westport Community Church had to be reshingled. There were only fifteen or so families living on this island then. Mrs. Smith hosted a "shingling tea party" for her neighbors here, and the job got done in a day. Everyone who contributed had his or her name printed on the inside of a shingle now gracing the church roof.

Scenic Drive: Me. 144 and U.S. 1 to Wiscasset, which has many well-preserved buildings and numerous ice cream shops. Two of the last schooners in use along the Atlantic coast, the *Hesper* and the *Luther Little*, are much-photographed attractions in the Sheepscot River here.

Directions to the Inn: From New York or Boston, take I-95 north to the Maine Turnpike. Leave the Maine Turnpike at exit 9 and take I-95 and U.S. 1 north to Me. 144 north of Woolwich. (Me. 144 makes several sharp turns. If you wind up at the Maine Yankee Atomic Plant, you have missed one of the turns. Retrace your steps and watch for signs to Me. 144.) The inn is on Me. 144.

THE NEWCASTLE INN

Newcastle, Maine

"Guests Welcomed, Pets Too," the signboard says in front of this comfortable inn only half a mile from U.S. 1.

Since Newcastle is between Wiscasset (to the south) and Waldoboro (to the north), The Newcastle Inn is a convenient destination if you are exploring the Maine coast or taking the long route to Acadia National Park.

The inn, open all year, serves a buffet breakfast for guests only but no other meals. If you want to eat dinner on the road anyway, this inn is a good buy. And if you want to stay awhile, innkeeper Mrs. Carolyn Mercer will tell you about nearby restaurants. The inn has sixteen bedrooms furnished with nostalgic flowered wallpaper, maple furniture, and small desks. Several rooms have private bathrooms, others have connecting bathrooms, and the rest share bathrooms. A motel unit alongside the inn contains seven more bedrooms, each with a private bathroom. The inn's best buys are the third-floor bedrooms with shared bathrooms.

In the living room there are books and magazines you can read. At one end of the room there are five breakfast tables with pale-pink tablecloths, where you can help yourself to juice, milk, coffee, tea, cold cereals, toast, and buns.

In the basement, Mrs. Mercer and her mother, Mrs. Jane Pomeroy, have a collection of several hundred dolls. These include corn-cob dolls, rag dolls, dolls with china faces, costumed dolls from other countries, and highly formal dolls, many of them antiques.

The Environs: Newcastle (population 1,076), set on the bank of the Damariscotta River, is probably best known for St. Patrick's Roman Catholic Church. Built between 1803 and 1808, the church was dedicated by Father Jean de Cheverus, New England's first Roman Catholic bishop. Lincoln Academy, a private school, is also located here.

Scenic Drive: Me. 129 and Me. 130 to Pemaquid Point.

Directions to the Inn: From New York or Boston, take I-95 to exit 9 on the Maine Turnpike and continue on the east branch of I-95 to Bath. Follow U.S. 1 north. After you have gone through Wiscasset, you will see billboards on the right side of U.S. 1 advertising establishments in Damariscotta. Get in the right lane and watch for a sign that says "Newcastle Inn." The sign is very small; it is beside a sharp turnoff to the right. This road, River Road, leads to the inn about half a mile away.

MIGIS LODGE

South Casco, Maine

To many people, Maine brings to mind the inland lakes and forests more than the Atlantic shoreline. If you take an airplane from Boston to Portland or stand on the summit of New Hampshire's Mount Washington on a clear day, the huge, blue, iridescent stretch of water that you see northwest of Portland is Sebago Lake. Up close, it is just as beautiful.

At Migis Lodge (pronounced My-gis) you can spend the night on Sebago Lake, in one of six bedrooms in the lodge or in a cabin by yourself with a wood-burning fireplace. There are twenty-five cabins with a variety of accommodations. All have fieldstone fireplaces. The lodge is open from the end of May through mid-October, serving three meals daily to guests, and lunch and dinner to the public by reservation only. Box lunches are made on request.

As you drive down the narrow, winding road toward Migis Lodge, you too will be enveloped by the intense pine scent for which inland Maine is known. Once you have parked your car beneath the 140-foot pine trees, the chances are that you will want to move into one of those cabins for a good stay. Many people spend their entire vacations here.

Innkeepers Gene and Grace Porta have maintained an overall atmosphere here of civilized informality. On the one hand, you can do what you like—from staying in your cabin on a rainy day to walking on the pine-needle trails through the lodge's one hundred acres of woods. On the other hand, the lodge operates on the American plan, so there are at least two times a day when you will be inside eating.

There is a lovely feeling to the main living room, which we can only describe as purposefully rustic, with cheerful, large braided rugs. In the knotty-pine-paneled dining room, there are linen tablecloths and small vases of fresh flowers on each table. Men are asked to wear jackets to dinner.

During our visit the lodge was serving roast lamb, sautéed lobster with a Newburg sauce, cold roast beef with potato salad, fried sea scallops, and plain or chopped ham omelet. There was chilled tomato juice, cold fresh fruit cocktail, or iced sweet cider for the first course, and a chicken broth with rice or vichyssoise for the soup course. For dessert, the lodge was offering a delicious chocolate cream pie, toasted crackers with Gruyère cheese, gingerbread with whipped cream, chilled melon, mocha parfait, and jello with whipped cream. The lodge serves cocktails and offers a carafe of red or white wine at dinner. Each week there is a buffet dinner, a Sunday morning breakfast cookout, usually featuring blueberry pancakes, and a steak roast on Millstone Island.

Millstone is one of the tiny, tufted, uninhabited islands in Sebago Lake. As you sit in the dining room you will look out at these islands with names such as Honeymoon, Inner Green, and Outer Spectacle. In 1910, when the lodge was built, its site was the town landing, and people coming to what was called National Camps passed those islands on steamships that docked here, unloading passengers and freight. Captain Goodrich, who built Migis Lodge, had a good reason for putting it at the town landing. It was a question of attracting business, since Captain Goodrich also owned the steamship line. In those days the main building at Migis was called the White House, and the cottages were named for different states.

Many activities at Migis Lodge are water-oriented because the lodge has 1,400 feet of lake frontage. There is a small sandy beach for swimming. You can use the sailboats, canoes, and water skis, or bring your rackets and play tennis on the three courts. The recreation hall is popular, especially with children, who enjoy the games, the pool table, the Ping-Pong, and the movies shown during the summer. All the lodge's activities are included in the rates except for motor-boat rentals.

The Environs: Absolutely no one who loves to come to Migis to fish would agree with a fifteen-year-old boy we know who described his first fishing expedition as "about as exciting as waiting for a bus." In May, June, and September the sought-after prize is landlocked salmon, a pinkish and more delicate variety than Atlantic or Pacific Ocean salmon. In July and August the lake yields bass, and it is well-stocked with trout. As the lodge's brochure puts it, "Guide services may be arranged through us. Many people, of course, prefer to rent a boat and motor and go out on their own. The guide fees are $50 to $60 a day with large power boats accommodating up to four people."

Sebago Lake is a reservoir under the jurisdiction of the Portland Water District, and development along its shores is severely restricted. It is no longer connected by canals to the Atlantic Ocean as it was in the early nineteenth century, but the waterway is thirty-two miles long. Sebago Lake opens up into the Songo River (through the hand-operated Songo Locks), Brandy Pond, and Long Lake. The serpentine Songo River makes 26 U-turns.

Directions to the Inn: From New York or Boston, take I-95 and the Maine Turnpike north to exit 8. Take U.S. 302 north to tiny South Casco. It is about eighteen miles on U.S. 302 from exit 8 to the well-marked turnoff on the left side of the road to the lodge.

THE BETHEL INN

Bethel, Maine

When The Bethel Inn was being re-wallpapered in 1971, some of its most faithful guests were asked what color they would like for "their" rooms. That is why some bedrooms are pastel yellow or pale blue. One bedroom, regularly occupied by a retired New Jersey judge, has wallpaper dotted with drums and eagles.

The considerate attitude implied by this gesture permeates The Bethel Inn, a large and elegant resort set in west-central Maine near the White Mountain National Forest. Although inns often become impersonal as they grow larger, this spit-and-polish inn demonstrates that size and personal attention can go hand in hand.

Every niche and corner is beautifully furnished—from the creaseless white-damask tablecloths to the wooden racks that hug the daily *Christian Science Monitor* and *The Wall Street Journal* in the formal reading room. The housekeeping staff has a high standard of cleanliness and is doing an exceptional job.

Located twenty-three miles east of Gorham, New Hampshire, the inn occupies six sunny yellow-clapboard buildings. They are clustered around Bethel's common, a patch of lawn in the center of town. The inn is open from late May through late October, serving three meals a day for both houseguests and the public. Box lunches are put up on request. There are sixty-five bedrooms, sixteen with working fireplaces. All have private bathrooms and room telephones.

One delightful bedroom for a single traveler is Room 14, which the inn calls Aunt Molly's Room. Named for the late Molly Greenway, a regular guest for many years, this bedroom is much more pleasant than some cramped rooms in other inns assigned to single guests. The furniture in all the bedrooms is from The

Hitchcock Chair Company of Riverton, Connecticut, the factory that makes reproductions of Hitchcock's painted and stenciled nineteenth-century pieces. Bethel is where the wooden seats for Hitchcock chairs are made today.

The inn is owned by the Gould Academy, a private, co-educational day and boarding school. Most of the guests are elderly, and many like to stay for weeks at a time. You will find here at least two characteristics typical of inns catering to older people: incredibly comfortable beds (which you will find turned down after dinner) and small portions of food. Men are expected to wear jackets and ties to dinner; the women on an autumn week night when we visited were dressed in light-wool tailored suits. Some were wearing long skirts.

The dining room is elegant, with exquisite silver, spotless glasses, small clay pots of pink begonias, service plates with a colorful poppy design, and candles. Overnight guests are greeted by name and seated at nicely separated tables. The dining-room windows face toward the White Mountains.

During our stay, the dinner menu offered five hot entrees: broiled lamb chops, sautéed jumbo shrimp, a three-egg mushroom omelet, grilled Virginia ham steak, and baked stuffed spring chicken. The two salads were iceberg lettuce hearts and tomato slices with cottage cheese. The thirteen desserts ranged from apple pie and homemade cookies to Casaba melon wedge, blue cheese, cherry jello, and a whole Temple orange. We had a memorable chocolate Vienna torte filled with layers of freshly whipped cream.

The wine list is extensive, and there is a cozy, wood-paneled taproom downstairs.

The breakfast menu included a baked apple, kippered herring, finan haddie, and hash-browned potatoes, as well as eggs any style and pancakes. On Sunday mornings the inn serves codfish cakes and baked beans.

As at other service-oriented inns, the waitresses make it their business to memorize likes and dislikes of the people they serve. At breakfast we overheard a waitress ask a gentleman seated near us: "Do you want just the half cup of coffee again this morning, Mr. O'Grady?" "That would be fine, thank you," Mr. O'Grady replied.

For all its formality, the inn is a friendly place. When we were seated at dinner, no one said hello because we were new. But when we came down for breakfast, a dozen people nodded and smiled, said cheerful "good mornings," and made polite inquiries as to how long we were staying.

The inn's facilities include a popular nine-hole golf course, a heated swimming pool, a tennis court, and a beach club at Songo Pond, where you can canoe, swim, and picnic.

Guests who vent their frustrations on the golf course will be interested to know that the inn's first golf course was built by business executives suffering from nervous breakdowns. They were patients of Dr. George Gehring, who had a clinic in his home on Broad Street. At first, patients lived at the Gehrings' home and ate meals together there. But as the doctor's practice grew, the patients began staying at the Prospect House down the street. When that burned in 1912, creating a housing shortage, four wealthy patients financed construction of the inn. It was built in 1913 and dedicated to Dr. Gehring.

The Environs: This town of 2,200 people has a diverse economic base, with several timber mills and the Gould Academy. Tourists use the town as a center from which to see the Maine lakes in the summer. When you drive or walk down Bethel's main street, you will see that new grocery stores and banks are being built between the nineteenth-century commercial structures. It could be an exciting combination of the old and the new but it is not. The handsome old buildings make the new ones look pitiful.

Scenic Drive: For an excellent circular drive (seventy-eight miles), take U.S. 2 west, Me. 113 south through the White Mountain National Forest, and then Me. 5 north past Kezar Lake to Bethel.

Directions to the Inn: From New York or Boston, take I-95 and the Maine Turnpike to the exit for Me. 26 at the Gray interchange. Continue on Me. 26 north to Bethel.

THE WHITEHALL INN

Camden, Maine

In August 1912 Edna St. Vincent Millay swung around on the piano stool at The Whitehall Inn and recited her poem "Renascence" for the inn's guests. She began, "All I could see from where I stood / Was three long mountains and a wood." One listener, Miss Caroline B. Dow, was so impressed by the twenty-year-old poet that she later arranged a scholarship to Vassar College for her.

Today the inn's music room is a memorial to "Vincent," as her family called her. Her gold-framed diploma from Camden High School, class of 1909, hangs on the wall. There are photographs of her here, and two early poems are displayed: a handwritten one about the Housatonic River titled "From a Train Window," and a poem she wrote at age sixteen in light verse called "Friends."

The inn is open from about June 1 through November 1. The dates may vary depending on the weather. There are thirty-eight bedrooms here, many of them furnished with white bedspreads, white curtains, bamboo chairs with cushions, small desks, old-fashioned black room telephones, and candles in glass candleholders. Several have four-poster canopy beds. The inn serves breakfast and dinner daily to houseguests and the public. During July and August, lunch is available for houseguests only and dinner on Friday nights is a buffet. Box lunches are put up on request.

Since it is so close to the ocean, The Whitehall specializes in seafood such as scallops, shrimp, filet of sole, scrod, haddock, halibut, and bluefish. Men are asked to wear packets and ties in the dining room with "ladies dressed accordingly." The inn has a wine list and an inviting taproom with wood-paneled walls and small tables.

On request, the kitchen will clean, cook, and serve you whatever you have caught on fishing trips. You can ask at the front desk about salt-water fishing parties and about fresh-water fishing licenses. Innkeepers Jean and Ed Dewing have a motor launch called *Little Toot* on which they take guests for rides, and there is a sailboat here for inn guests to use.

The Whitehall Inn, north of Camden village, is an excellent place to stay for a weekend or a night, but it is also equipped to keep guests amused for a week or longer.

If it rains during your visit, there are many appealing corners in the meandering living room. You can write postcards home at two huge writing desks, read one of the inn's hundreds of books in front of a fireplace, or play chess beneath a Tiffany lamp. Two of the inn's interesting clocks were made by Connecticut clockmakers. There is a Silas Hoadley grandfather clock in the living room, and as you register, you will hear the delightful little ticking sound made by the secondary mechanism of the Seth Thomas wall clock above the desk.

In August you may be treated to a staff show, the same occasion that prompted Edna St. Vincent Millay to visit The Whitehall Inn in 1912. Her sister, Norma, who worked as a summer waitress at the inn, asked her to come to a masquerade party. Vincent, dressed as Pierrette, won the prize for best costume, while Norma earned first prize for a waltz. It was after the party that Vincent played several of her piano compositions and then recited the poem that started her career as a poet. In 1923 she was awarded the Pulitzer Prize in American poetry.

The Environs: Large, rambling, and well kept, The Whitehall Inn hugs U.S. 1 half a mile from Camden village, where a waterfall spills into the harbor and windjammers moor between week-long pleasure trips through nearby waterways. During the summer, especially on weekends, Camden (population 4,115) is popular among visitors who enjoy browsing in the inviting shops in town, where flowerpots hang from the lampposts. Walk north along the main street (it coincides with U.S. 1) and you will come to a small park on a hillock overlooking the harbor. It is a lovely place from which to watch the boats, listen to the seagulls, and breathe in the briny air.

You can play golf at the nine-hole Goose River Golf Course in Camden or at the eighteen-hole Rockland Golf Club in nearby Rockland. And if you like to hike, you can hike to the summit of Mount Battie (altitude 800 feet) at no charge. There are walking trails throughout Camden Hills State Park. Maps are available at the park office.

Scenic Drive: The turnoff to Camden Hills State Park is about a mile north of the inn on U.S. 1. The paved toll road here winds to the top of Mount Battie, where, when the fog is not rolling in, you will have an excellent view of Camden Harbor, the islands in Penobscot Bay, and the lower Camden Hills.

Directions to the Inn: From New York or Boston, take I-95 north to exit 9 and continue on the east branch of I-95 to Bath. Follow U.S. 1 north to Camden. The inn is on U.S. 1 half a mile north of Camden village.

DAVID'S FOLLY

West Brooksville, Maine

David Wasson's relatives and neighbors laughed in 1819 when he built a farm, not on a hill, but on Eastern Penobscot's broad meadows. They said that drainage would swamp the farm, and they called it "David's Folly." But David Wasson had the last laugh. He constructed the buildings on ledgerock so that water would drain around them. More than 150 years later, his house and barn are still standing, and they are in fine shape.

Wasson's house and one-hundred-foot-long barn are joined. This "chain" effect is typical of northern New England farms, especially in Maine and New Hampshire, where the climate is coldest. Elsewhere in New England, farm buildings are usually clustered but not connected. Where the winters are most severe, though, the farmer wanted to do his chores without going outside through heavy snow. It was an efficient way to do things.

Today this 300-acre salt-water farm is a small, congenial inn where casually dressed guests, ranging in age from twenty to eighty, come to relax in pastoral seclusion. Innkeeper Minerva E. Cutler bought this property in 1939 and has run it as an inn since the 1940s. The inn's bucolic meadows roll down to a pebbly beach at Wasson's Cove, where you can catch a glimpse across East Penobscot Bay of the Maine Maritime Academy's training ship docked at Castine. This unusual combination of a farm and the sea is symbolized when lunch and dinner are announced both by the ringing of a ship's bell outside and a cow bell inside.

David's Folly is open from mid-June to early October and operates on the American plan. There are thirteen bedrooms, furnished simply, some in the farmhouse and some in the barn. Most have painted furniture, various colored bedspreads, and white curtains. One bedroom has a private bathroom. The rest share bathrooms. All have twin beds. There is a small separate cabin in back with a bedroom, a bathroom, and a wood-burning stove in a little living room. Children under twelve are not accepted as guests; well-trained dogs are permitted only in the barn rooms and cabin. Reservations are essential, but the rates are reasonable. Lunch and dinner are open to the public by reservation only. Box lunches are put up on request.

Guests at David's Folly eat meals together at one sitting and sometimes volunteer to help Miss Cutler pick tomatoes, zucchini, green beans, and lettuce from the vegetable gardens. Miss Cutler, whose delightful smile sets the friendly tone here, introduces guests to each other right away.

All the tableware in the dining room is glazed pottery of various colors made in neighboring Blue Hill. Guests seat themselves in this room, where the art of gentle conversation is practiced by strangers eating at the same gleaming pine tables.

Since the menu is set, the waitresses bring the already filled plates to the tables. For dinner we had baked haddock, fresh green beans, a small buttered baked potato, and stewed tomatoes made with bread crumbs and mushrooms. Dessert was a freshly made lemon meringue pie. (Alcoholic beverages are not served at the inn.)

Friday is "lobster night" at David's Folly. On Sundays lobster stew is often served, and the fish chowder here is made from scratch. The inn carries on the New England custom of serving baked beans and brown bread on Saturdays. They are cooked on the kitchen's wood-burning stove, now converted to kerosene. We have found several of these stoves in Maine kitchens. Those who use them say they are wonderful for cooking dishes that require hours of simmering.

There are many readable books and piles of magazines in the barn's living room, called The Tie Up. This low-ceilinged room is furnished with director chairs, several lounge chairs, and a Ping-Pong table. The farmhouse has two less casual sitting rooms.

The Environs: At dinner you can request a box lunch for the following day if you are planning a picnic or a side trip to Blue Hill's pottery shops, Stonington's fishing village, Deer Isle, Castine, or Acadia National Park. West Brooksville is part of Brooksville (population 673), where you can picnic or hike at the Holbrook Island Sanctuary. Since this inn's location is remote, the happiest people here are those who are self-motivated, ready to search for a quiet place in which to walk through the fields or eager to read a thick book that had been gathering dust at home.

Scenic Drive: Me. 175 south of Blue Hill has outstanding views of Blue Hill Bay for nearly ten miles; Caterpillar Hill on Me. 15 in Sedgwick has a small picnic area with an excellent view of Penobscot Bay; take Me. 15 across the Deer Isle Bridge to Sunset for dramatic views of the Camden Hills.

Directions to the Inn: From New York or Boston, take I-95 north and the Maine Turnpike to Me. 3 east to U.S. 1 north to Me. 175 to North Brooksville. At North Brooksville turn right on Me. 176 and go four miles to David's Folly.

THE BLUE HILL INN

Blue Hill, Maine

You will find The Blue Hill Inn, with smoke curling out of the chimneys on a late summer afternoon and the American flag flying from a white flagpole, just off the main street of Eastern Penobscot's prettiest town. Blue Hill is an excellent home base for exploring Eastern Penobscot, the peninsula south of Mount Desert Island, and you can drive to Acadia National Park from here. It is about an hour's ride away.

For many years, this trim, white-clapboard inn with three chimneys jutting through the roof was a guesthouse, serving breakfast only. Since our visit here, the inn has changed hands, and it is now open all year, serving three meals a day to guests and the public except on Sunday, when the dining room is closed. Box lunches are put up on request. There are eight bedrooms here; two are suites with small sitting rooms. Innkeepers Marion and Richard Yerkes have placed queen-size beds in most of the rooms and a king-size bed in the largest. One room has a canopy bed.

"We have one set menu for dinner which changes each night. We serve boiled lobster, leg of lamb, duck, roast beef, and Coho Salmon, a West Coast salmon they're raising here now. We like to have eggs Benedict for breakfast or blueberry pancakes, as well as eggs any style," Mr. Yerkes said.

If you are here on a Sunday evening, you can have dinner at The Seagull, a casual restaurant just down the street. Your other choices include Eaton's Lobster Pool on Little Deer Isle, about thirty minutes away. At Eaton's the lobster dinner comes with the potato chips customarily served with boiled lobster in Maine and a tiny container of melted margarine. Since we are not crazy about the flavor of margarine, especially with boiled lobster, we ate the lobster plain. It was the most delicious lobster we have ever eaten. Caught that day in the waters off Little Deer Isle, it was very tender and had the fresh bouquet of the salt water.

The Environs: Blue Hill, known first as "No. 5" and then as East Boston, was named for the 940-foot hill north of the village that appears blue from a distance. You can walk to the summit, which affords a view. The white-clapboard buildings on the main street have a polished look for this section of Maine, partly because of the signs. The signs on the post office and stores, even on the grocery store, are black with gold lettering. The winter population of 1,367 more than doubles in the summer, since many people have summer homes here.

In Blue Hill there are two pottery-making establishments: Rowantrees Pottery (named for the European mountain ash, the rowan tree) is almost next door to The Blue Hill Inn; Rackliffe Pottery is about a mile away on Me. 172 north. There is a marked difference between the two: the colors of the pottery at Rowantrees have a more metallic quality than those at Rackliffe. Most people are partial to one style or the other.

During the summer, chamber music concerts are given at Kneisel Hall, a summer music school founded in 1902. Every Labor Day weekend The Blue Hill Fair attracts many visitors. A nine-hole golf course at The Blue Hill Country Club is open to the public.

And now a word of warning about the road-numbering system on Eastern Penobscot. It is complicated. When it comes to reading maps, we consider ourselves accomplished, but the state routes on Eastern Penobscot are something else. The roads meander in a maze-like pattern, and the numbering system defies comprehension. To give you an idea, this is what you will find on one sign south of Blue Hill village: the sign points in one direction and says, "North 15, North 172, South 175, East 176."

Scenic Drive: To Deer Isle.

Directions to the Inn: From New York or Boston, take I-95 north and the Maine Turnpike to Me. 3 east to U.S. 1 north to Me. 15 (three miles north of Bucksport) to Blue Hill. (From U.S. 1, you can also take Me. 172 or Me. 176 to Blue Hill.) The inn is on Me. 177 up a short incline from the main street in the center of town.

ACADIA NATIONAL PARK

The first time we visited New England's only national park, it rained for five straight days. We gave up waiting for the sun to come out, went hiking anyway, and slogged along in perpetually damp clothing. On the sixth morning the clouds cleared, the sky was blue, and we concluded that all the enthusiastic statements we had heard about this park's beauty were true. The dramatic views were worth waiting five rainy days for.

By New England standards, the mountains in Acadia National Park are not high (the tallest, Cadillac Mountain, is only 1,532 feet). But these mountains rise from sea level, and many are steep, making them seem much higher than they are. The effect is stunning, with panoramic views from almost every summit.

The park consists of less than half of Mount Desert Island, Schoodic Peninsula tip (50 miles by car from Mount Desert), part of offshore Isle Au Haut, and several smaller islands. The main part of the park is Mount Desert Island, 105.4 square miles in area. It is accessible by a causeway from Trenton, a few miles from Ellsworth. The park has the only true fiord in the eastern United States, Somes Sound. There are about 120 miles of hiking trails and 45 miles of carriage roads suitable for hiking or horseback riding but not for cars.

If you happen to arrive on a clear day, drive or hike up Cadillac Mountain immediately for an unforgettable view of dense spruce and fir stands, the sea, offshore islands, and the sailboats that ply these waters in the summer. The weather often changes rapidly, and although fog can be beautiful, you may be disappointed if you find yourself on the summit unable to see the view. (Here fifty to sixty days a year are foggy.)

Although Cadillac Mountain is the only mountain you can drive up (the auto road is not a toll road), other summits offer equally rewarding views. Of the mountain trails, the most exciting and dramatic is the Precipice Trail up Champlain Mountain. It is considered the most difficult hike in the park. We do not recommend it for very young children or for people with a fear of heights. The trail is like a Junglegym for adults, and it is strictly one-way up. It climbs an almost vertical face by means of steel ladders in the rock. More steel bars form railings beside the narrowest ledges. The views above tree line are superlative. If you go, take a canteen or thermos of water. The long trail down affords sweeping views and winds back to the road a distance from the starting point.

Less frequented trails like the St. Saveur Trail also offer excellent views and some have more Junglegym surprises. There are wooden ladders here and there on the Pemetic Trail, steel ladders near the summit of the Bee Hive Trail, and steel rungs in the rock at the start of the Goat Trail. From the Bee Hive, you will overlook Sandy Beach, which is blanketed not only with sand but also with pulverized sea shells. The water is extremely cold, even on a hot summer day, because of the Labrador current that comes down from the north.

Over in the western mountains you will find the Perpendicular Trail, the perpendicular part of which consists of hundreds of stone steps in the middle of the woods. These were built in the thirties during the Depression by the Civilian Conservation Corps.

For a flat but pleasant walk, take the trail around Jordan Pond. It offers no views but the constant sight of a peaceful pond. It starts from the delightful Jordan Pond House, open from mid-June to around October 1, where it is a tradition to have pop-overs, homemade ice cream, and tea on the lawn.

For visitors who prefer to drive around the park, Ocean Drive offers many stopping points. Among them are Thunder Hole and Otter Point. The National Park Service has naturalist-conducted walks, mountain hikes, and boat trips to the offshore islands. The park booth just across the causeway has maps and information. More complete information and a film of the island can be found at the Park Visitors Center at Hulls Cove.

Mount Desert Island has two park-run camping grounds (they are very popular) and many private camping grounds, motels, and motor inns.

If you are going to Yarmouth, Nova Scotia, you can take a ten-hour car ferry from Portland (see The Inn on Peaks in the Islands section) or a six-hour car ferry from Bar Harbor, the main town on Mount Desert Island. The Bar Harbor ferries (run by Canadian National Railways) have day cabins, duty free shops, a casino, a cafeteria, and a bar. For schedules, write to Terminal Supervisor, Canadian National, Bar Harbor, Me. 04609.

Directions to Mount Desert Island: From New York or Boston, take I-95 and the Maine Turnpike north to Me. 3 east across the causeway from Ellsworth to Acadia National Park.

McKAY COTTAGES

Bar Harbor, Maine

McKay Cottages are two large yellow buildings on Main Street in bustling Bar Harbor, the primary town on Mount Desert Island. They were named around 1920 when "cottages" were what we would describe as large, spacious houses today.

In the late fall many hostelries on Mount Desert Island, if not most of them, close down completely for the winter. But you can stay at McKay Cottages any time of year. From October through April George and Barbara McKay have twelve of their rooms available for guests. This is strictly a guesthouse: no meals are served at all, there are no living rooms or sitting rooms, and the setting verges on the unattractive. But at McKay Cottages you can spend the night in a charming bedroom at a bargain price. There are thirty bedrooms in both buildings, some with private bathrooms.

George and Barbara McKay are the second generation of the family to welcome guests here. The bright, spotless bedrooms seem to have been well kept over the years in the way you would care for your own home. A few have patchwork quilts, and those that share bathrooms have gleaming sinks in little niches with the kind of old-fashioned faucets that say "Hot" and "Cold." People of all ages stay here, many of them returning guests who buy picnic lunches at Bar Harbor restaurants, spend the day exploring Acadia Park, and enjoy steamed clams and a boiled lobster in the evening at a lobster pound.

If you come during the summer, you will have a wide choice of restaurants on Mount Desert Island. The McKays keep a current collection of menus in the entry hall for you to study. Among the better restaurants in Bar Harbor is Testa's, known for its fresh strawberry, raspberry, and peach pies. (The strawberry pie consists of whole fresh strawberries in a gelatin, topped with heavy cream whipped with confectioners' sugar.) A salad here may have any combination of about fifteen greens, including roquet, a thin-leafed green with a piquant taste. The cheese dressing is made with Gorganzola cheese.

The first time we stayed at McKay Cottages we were awakened about 4 A.M. by flashing red lights, shouts in the street, and the sound of approaching sirens. We turned on the light, threw on our coats, stepped into our shoes, and joined the other guests who were hurrying down the stairs to see what all the commotion was about. Not far down the street an uninhabited building was in flames. People came out of their houses, shivering in their pajamas and trench coats, and watched the firemen hook up their hoses and spray the fire with water. After about twenty minutes, when the fire seemed to be contained, everyone left the sidewalk and returned to bed. That was many years ago. The last time we stayed at McKay Cottages all we heard as we fell asleep was the town clock peacefully ringing eleven.

Bar Harbor was once as fashionable a place in Maine to spend the entire summer as Newport was in Rhode Island. There were sumptuous mansions and extravagant parties in the late 1800s when *The Harvard Lampoon* wrote that this was where "nice Philadelphia girls taught slow-going Bostonians how to flirt." Those were the days when Mount Desert, not yet a national park, was just a beautiful island made famous by the very rich, and Bar Harbor was named Eden. The name was changed in 1918.

Directions to the Inn: From New York or Boston, take I-95 and the Maine Turnpike north to Me. 3 east to Bar Harbor. The inn is at 243 Main Street.

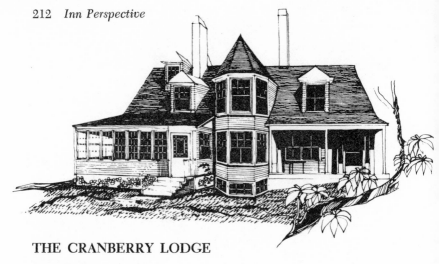

THE CRANBERRY LODGE

Northeast Harbor, Maine

At this intimate retreat, you can strap your cross-country skis on right outside the door, set off on the three-mile trail that starts beside the inn, and ski to Jordan Pond on Mount Desert Island. All told, you can cross-country ski on about fifty-five miles of carriage roads built by John D. Rockefeller in what is now Acadia National Park.

During the summer, Cranberry Lodge houses the manager and top staff of The Asticou Inn, which owns it. But when the larger inn is closed, this relaxed, easygoing place is opened to guests, a happy event that coincides with the off-season solitude of Acadia. We came here in early November when Indian summer had set in, and on a warm Saturday there were only twenty cars driving up Cadillac Mountain. The sunset at 4:23 over the western lakes and hills looked like an egg yolk broken on a purple plate.

There are nine bedrooms here, eight with working fireplaces. Spacious twin-bedded Room 8 not only has a fireplace but also has bay windows, an eastern exposure, and a peek-a-boo view of Northeast Harbor. Mrs. Blanche Megas, the innkeeper, serves breakfast and dinner to houseguests, and to the public by reservation only. If you bring your thermoses, Mrs. Megas will fill them with coffee or hot soup and make you a box lunch. The inn is open from September through May. Reservations here are required.

At breakfast, Mrs. Megas asks guests to agree on a menu for dinner that night. The price depends on what the guests decide to have. "You'd be surprised how easy it is to get people to agree. They often like leg of lamb. Sometimes they choose lobster or steak instead," Mrs. Megas said. The dining room usually has separate tables, but during our visit it was reserved for a private dinner for twelve. Mrs. Megas solved the logistical problem of feeding both the inn guests and the private party by moving all her belongings out of her "office," as she called it.

The office was a tiny room rearranged with one table set for four in front of a crackling fire. The cranberry-colored candles on the table sparkled in an inviting way. "I hope you won't mind eating with our other guests tonight," Mrs. Megas said.

The set dinner menu that night started with a freshly made fish chowder. The haddock (dipped in an egg batter, cooked lightly in a pan, and then broiled) was bought that afternoon at a Southwest Harbor lobster pound. We had deviled baked potatoes and peas with the haddock, ending the meal with vanilla ice cream and Pepperidge Farm Bordeaux cookies.

Mrs. Megas asks guests if they would like a carafe of red or white Almaden wine with their dinner. The inn does not have a liquor license (although it can offer the wine), and if you bring your own alcoholic beverages, Mrs. Megas will provide ice, tonic, and soda water.

While Mrs. Megas emphasizes personal attention, the inn is still large enough to give you all the privacy you want. If it rains during your stay here, you can curl up with a book you have brought in the cozy living room on the first floor. The inn's one television set is hidden away on the second floor in a functional sitting room.

During the summer Acadia is enormously popular, but the rest of the year it belongs to the relatively few who realize that it is open all year. This is a perfectly lovely place to visit for the fall foliage, which usually peaks around October 5. While other travelers are admiring the brilliant splashes of color on New England's deciduous trees in New Hampshire's White Mountains and the Massachusetts Berkshires, you will have Acadia's hiking trails, carriage roads, Ocean Drive, and the sensational view from Cadillac Mountain virtually to yourself.

And if you stay at The Cranberry Lodge, you will leave with memories of a cheerful, friendly inn, whether you spend your evening alone or talking with other guests. Last but not least, you will probably long remember where you paid your bill. The next morning after breakfast, we settled our bill in the kitchen. "I often ask guests," Mrs. Megas said, "if they've ever written a check before on an ironing board."

Directions to the Inn: From New York or Boston, take I-95 and the Maine Turnpike north to Me. 3 east to Me. 198 toward Northeast Harbor. At the junction of Me. 198 and Me. 3, turn onto Me. 3. The inn (just beyond The Asticou Inn) is on the left side of the road.

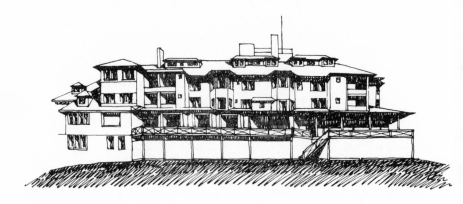

THE ASTICOU INN

Northeast Harbor, Maine

"My dear, it is a perfectly horrid day," the white-haired woman said in a Boston accent. Her companion on the sofa in The Asticou Inn's lounge put her knitting down, gazed at the overcast sky above Northeast Harbor, and agreed: "Yes, it is a horrible day."

It was only the third week of August but already the air had the chill of fall. A couple in their thirties settled down for a sherry at noon in the lounge. "There's no point in going for a walk if we can't see the view," the man said.

This is a formal inn with first-rate service overlooking the private sailboats anchored in Northeast Harbor. Nicknamed Philadelphia on the Rocks because so many summer residents come from Philadelphia, Northeast Harbor is an exclusive summer resort where people sail, play tennis on the town's courts, and hike in Acadia National Park.

Open from late June through mid-September, the inn has fifty-four old-fashioned bedrooms, serves three resort-style meals a day, and enjoys a high rate of returning guests. Meals are served in your room on request or in the inn's formal dining room with lovely flower murals on the walls. All meals are open to the public. The inn will put up box lunches on request.

Although The Asticou attracts guests of all ages, including families with well-behaved children, most of its clientele are retired people who often stay at least two weeks. They reserve the same bedroom year after year, and they appreciate the excellent service provided by a cheerful, uniformed staff.

If guests ask to have the furniture rearranged in "their" rooms, it is done. If guests want to bring their small dogs on vacation (and many do), it can be arranged. If guests would like afternoon tea in their bedrooms, it will be brought. Those who want to ride to the village in the inn's car on its twice-daily mail trip have only to ask.

The bedrooms have flowered or striped wallpaper patterns, white curtains, and white bedspreads. They are on the second, third, and fourth floors of the inn and in two separate former homes the inn also runs for guests. Most of the bedrooms have private bathrooms that feature claw-footed bathtubs without showers. Eight have working fireplaces. All have room telephones. The most coveted bedroom is Room 3 with both a working fireplace and a private balcony overlooking the harbor. It has twin beds and a bathroom. It (and six other bedrooms) is in Four Winds, a white-clapboard house with green shutters and its own living room.

There are six more bedrooms in the inn's "Topsiders." These are octagonal modern cottages with living rooms and kitchenettes. They are available on the European plan from mid-April through late November.

In the dining room the menus are resort style, with many courses consisting of small portions. There are meal-order pads on which to write your order. When we were here, dinner began with a broiled grapefruit, unwrapped crackers presented on a china plate, and a cup of consommé. The half a dozen entrees included broiled lamb chops, boiled corned beef brisket with cabbage, and steamed finan haddie. The desserts ranged from Camembert and Swiss Gruyère cheeses to fresh fruits, ice creams, and several pies.

The inn's wine list has about eight domestic and imported wines. The bar is in the lounge. There are two living rooms, one with a television set.

Directions to the Inn: From New York or Boston, take I-95 and the Maine Turnpike north to Me. 3 east to Me. 198 toward Northeast Harbor. At the junction of 198 and Me. 3, turn onto Me. 3.

The inn is on the right side of the road. Note: you can fly to Boston and take Bar Harbor Airlines to Trenton, Maine, or take Delta Airlines to Bangor. People do come here by plane, arranging beforehand through the inn to be met by taxi. The cost of taxi service is substantial.

SKY LODGE

Moose River, Maine

There is a saying people use a lot in northwestern Maine: "This is God's country." The fact is that if anything could convert a nature-loving atheist into a Bible-peddling preacher overnight, this is it.

Moose River, two miles north of Jackman and twelve miles from the Canadian border, is surrounded by the finest wilderness in New England. This unspoiled and remote back country stretches from the Connecticut Lakes region in northern New Hampshire along the Maine-Canadian border into northern Maine. It is an area of vast forests, mountains, lakes, old logging roads, and trails.

There are three paved roads that cross this extensively forested and rugged corridor into Canada. One is U.S. 3 in northern New Hampshire (see The Glen); another is Me. 27 from Kingfield, Maine, to Lac Megantic in Quebec; the third and most northern route is U.S. 201 from Skowhegan, Maine, to Quebec City.

U.S. 201 goes through Jackman and Moose River (population 255) and right past Sky Lodge, set back on a treeless bluff easily seen from the road. Sky Lodge is more like an inn than a sporting camp, but it is a product of northwestern Maine, so it is different from southern New England inns. It is a solid spruce-log lodge with working fireplaces in six of the eleven bedrooms, handmade pine furniture, and pewter ceiling lamps. There is also a motel unit with another fourteen bedrooms. Each bedroom in the lodge and motel has a private bathroom. Sky Lodge is warm, personal, rustic, and well run by Ruthie and Ed Landgraf. All in all, it is a wonderful destination for an interesting trip. The lodge is open from May 30 through November 24. Three meals are served daily both for guests and the public. On request, the lodge will put up box lunches.

The most romantic bedrooms are those with both a working fireplace and a double bed. One suite, accommodating four to eight persons, has the only bathroom we know of in New England with a working fireplace. The suite has two bedrooms and a glass-enclosed sunporch facing the distant mountains ringing the horizon to the west and south.

Built as a summer home in 1929, the lodge apparently housed contraband liquor smuggled over the Canadian border during Prohibition. In Room 1 there is an immense walk-in closet behind the chimney fireplace. The closet door looks like part of the wall except for the doorhandle, which, at first glance, seems humorously out of place. If you examine the door carefully, you will find the secret latch that still releases at the touch of a finger.

The central space in the lodge is a huge living room with two stone ceiling-to-floor fireplaces and graceful stairways leading like arms to the second-floor balcony encircling the lodge. Most bedrooms are off the balcony. The living room has comfortable sofas, reading lamps, bearskins above the fireplaces, and snow-shoe chairs made in Maine. (The chairs are sold at the lodge's gift shop.)

For dinner the lodge has two menus. One is à la carte with sandwiches, hamburgers, and broiled steaks. The other is a full dinner menu with half a dozen entrees such as pan-fried rainbow trout, roast pork, veal cutlet, Parmesan cheese omelet, and braised beef in a casserole. During our visit dinner came with braised red cabbage, whipped potatoes or French fries, and a tossed salad or cherry jello with cottage cheese. The dozen desserts included cheesecake, German chocolate cake, apple pie, strawberry-rhubarb pie, éclairs with chocolate sauce, ice cream, and an extremely sweet Canadian maple syrup pie. The lodge has a wine list and a taproom.

This far north the maple trees start turning red around

Labor Day weekend. The height of the foliage season comes between mid-September and the first week in October. Here, the dark green spruce trees blanketing the mountains form a backdrop for the magnificent color display.

The sunrise over the mountains is so intense that we were awakened from a sound sleep by the brilliant oranges and deep blues stretching on the horizon. Guests who would prefer to sleep through the sunrise have only to draw their shades at night, which we, hoping to witness the morning spectacle, did not do.

Sky Lodge is set on 200 acres, with trails through the woods. There is a swimming pool, badminton, shuffleboard, archery, horseshoes, and a rifle range on the grounds. A nine-hole golf course is nearby.

The Environs: We have not been to Moosehead Lake, but when people talk about Maine's largest lake (forty miles long and two to ten miles wide) they use words like "majestic," "fantastic," and "paradise." You can picnic or swim at Lily Bay State Park on the lake's eastern shore. (A road from Lily Bay leads north to Baxter State Park and the Allagash Wilderness Waterway.) You can also hire a small plane to fly you over Moosehead Lake. Those who have taken this short ride say the scenery is spectacular.

Scenic Drive: Sky Lodge is especially popular with Massachusetts families and honeymoon couples who, while driving the five to six hours from Boston, have the bonus of traveling up U.S. 201. This was the route used by Benedict Arnold and his soldiers in the Revolutionary War for their attack on Quebec. It is a breathtaking scenic drive, with mountains rising to the west and north at almost every turn. When you get to Jackman, a ramshackle town with a population of 848, you will pass a general store that, when we drove by, had an interesting array of signs. The largest says, "If you don't stop, smile on the way by." The others say: "Muhammad Ali will rise again"; "Good! Old Fashion Cheese"; "Mens Work Clothes"; "Postcards and Films"; "Lottery Tickets Sold Here"; "Bienvenue Canadien."

Directions to the Inn: From New York or Boston, take I-95 and the Maine Turnpike to U.S. 201 north. Note: although U.S. 201 is the most direct route for motorists, at Sky Lodge the registration card asks for "Make of Car or Plane." Just outside, there is a 1,750 foot grass runway where private planes can land, refueling with 80/87 octane fuel available here. The Sky Lodge Airport is shown on the Lewiston sectional aeronautical chart.

New England Islands

Islands are so special. They create their own presence, and charge it with an atmosphere quite different from any mainland.

JOHN N. COLE
The Maine Times [1974]

Islands tease the imagination. They tantalize travelers, spell doom for lost ships in snow storms and gales, and even in New England they figure in stories of buried bars of silver.

New England's islands were first described by Italian, English, French, and Dutch explorers. In the sixteenth century, Giovanni da Verrazano, the Italian navigator in the service of France, was searching for the West Indies and gold. But when he scanned the horizon, he saw New England's islands instead.

In 1524 Verrazano reported to the French king, Francis I, that Block Island (off Rhode Island) was "full of hills, covered with trees, well-peopled, for we saw fires all along the coast." Block Island is almost treeless today, and the Indians who lived there then are gone. When Verrazano sailed past Martha's Vineyard off Massachusetts, he named it Louisa. The name did not stick.

In May 1605 Captain George Waymouth observed Monhegan Island off Maine from a distance. The captain's narrator, James Rosier, wrote, "This Iland is woody, grouen with firre, Birch, Oke, and Beech, as farre as we saw along the shore; and so likely to be within." Waymouth also explored the Maine coast, but he sowed the seeds of Indian hostility by kidnaping five Indians whom he took with him to England.

For thousands of schooners, barks, and brigs, the rocky

ledges and sandy reefs around New England's islands have been death traps. While a vessel filled with water, the sailors who could not abandon ship climbed the rigging. Sometimes islanders were able to row out through stormy seas and rescue everyone before a sinking vessel rolled over. In snow storms, sailors sometimes froze to death, caked with ice, still clinging to the rigging. A two-mast schooner, the *Warrior*, sank off Block Island in a heavy gale in 1831. Benjamin T. Coe, the island's inspector of customs, wrote, "It is impossible to describe the awful situation of that vessel when she first came on shore, the sea breaking over her masts, and seven souls hanging from the rigging, not more than 150 yards from us, and completely out of the power of man to render them any assistance." Coe reported that "some cotton and calico drove ashore here, one sack of hides, something like forty dozen carpenter rules, &c. What goods were saved I delivered to Mr. Charles Brown, the agent from Boston, and Mr. Charles M. Thurston, of Newport."

Other ships that ran aground off New England's islands in the 1800s carried molasses, sugar, spices, iron, cut stone, coal, coffee, lime, ice, salt, lumber, and barrels of apples.

Not all of the shipwrecks meant certain death. On October 12, 1865, a schooner captained by George Sawyer struck the Great Point Rip off Nantucket Island (in Massachusetts). In spite of a heavy gale, Sawyer, his wife and three children, and the crew launched the ship's long boat and rowed ashore safely.

When the schooner U.B. *Fisk* was caught in an ice floe near Nantucket's Great Point Light on February 1, 1881, the lighthouse keeper waded out in freezing water up to his armpits. He threw two lines to the crewmen who were trying to reach shore. The vessel was lost but the men survived.

For travelers on calm seas in the late 1800s, sighting offshore islands after a long voyage stirred up excitement. On ocean liners approaching the United States, first-class passengers interrupted their card games long enough to toast the glimpse of land. To immigrants in steerage, offshore islands meant an uncertain future was close at hand.

For people on the mainland, islands have been provocative, stimulating myths and novels. In classical and Celtic legend, the Fortunate Isles, or Isles of the Blessed, were the eternal home for the souls of mortals favored by the gods. Two Englishmen, Daniel DeFoe and Robert Louis Stevenson, wrote books about islands that are now literary classics. In 1719 DeFoe created Robinson Crusoe, a castaway on a desert island, and Crusoe's man, Friday. Stevenson wrote *Treasure Island* in 1883 and introduced to the English language the refrain, "Yo-ho-ho, and a bottle of rum!"

Islands have inspired land-locked balladers to celebrate phantom ships in songs and fables. One New England legend was immortalized by Massachusetts-born John Greenleaf Whittier. His poem, "The Palatine," which tells of a ship supposedly set afire in Block Island Sound in the 1750s, was written in the 1800s. Since then, some people have claimed they have seen the light of the *Palatine*'s flames still burning.

During wars, New England's islands have been pawns on the strategic chessboards of generals. Soldiers have plundered them. Their waters have been tactical zones for ships, battles, and blockades.

In the Revolutionary War the entrance to Nantucket Island's harbor was besieged with English warships. The effect was an embargo, crippling the island's whaling industry. Nantucket lost over sixteen hundred men during the Revolution, but whaling revived with the end of the war.

So many deserters from both armies in the Revolution hid on Block Island (and threatened the women) that the islanders set up an early warning system. When "refugees" were spotted offshore at night in small boats called "shaving mills," barrels of tar or oil were lighted on two prominent hillocks. They signaled the islanders who picketed the coast.

During the War of 1812, residents of Monhegan Island gathered on the highest bluff to watch a battle at sea. On September 5, 1813, the American privateer *Enterprise* defeated the British brig *Boxer*. Both captains were killed. Two days later when the men's bodies were rowed to the mainland at Portland, guns boomed and boats in the harbor formed a funeral cortege. The American Lieutenant William Burrows and the British Captain Samuel Blyth were buried side by side in Portland's Eastern Cemetery.

The Nantucket Lighthouse lanterns were extinguished in the War of 1812. And off the Maine coast, Islesboro Island maintained a forced neutrality because the British occupied nearby Castine (on the mainland) for eight months.

Block Island, also neutral, was free to trade with both the Americans and the British. The British on men-of-war stopped at the island to get fresh water and bought cattle, sheep, poultry, and other supplies. They were excellent customers and earned a reputation for propriety as well. When one British commodore gave the islanders a dinner party on his seventy-four-gun ship, many accepted his invitation.

During the Second World War, American soldiers were stationed on Peaks Island in Maine's Portland Harbor. Their abandoned garrisons, overgrown with weeds, still stand today.

In times of peace the artists flock to islands. The famous and the obscure have tried to capture on canvas the sand dunes, rocks, and weathered buildings well-scrubbed by salt spray. Winslow Homer (1836–1910), best known for his dramatic water colors of the sea, painted Monhegan Island's wharf. Rockwell Kent (1882–1971), who started Monhegan's first art school, is represented in New York's Metropolitan Museum with his *Winter Monhegan*.

To work-weary people, islands conjure up the idea of being cast adrift from twentieth-century anxieties and, once there, of being isolated from a crisis-ridden world. News, of course, travels to islands too. So some dream of retiring to uninhabited islands, prompting cartoonists to depict stranded couples who bring their problems with them like so much baggage.

Some people are bored by islands. "What do you want to waste your time going over there for? It takes one hour to see the place and then there's nothing, I mean nothing, to do!" A man said that in 1974 during a lively (and loud) argument with his wife on the Point Judith dock, where ferries leave for Block Island.

Still, lighthouse keepers and lobstermen call islands home, and travel advertisements claim that islands promise adventure, escape, and discovery. Marshall Shepard, the first president of the Dukes County Historical Society on Martha's Vineyard, was so taken with the island that in 1940 he wrote a paper trying to prove that "the Vineyard" was the island of Shakespeare's *Tempest*.

New England's islands have even participated in student exchange programs. In April 1974 the fifteen schoolchildren from Matinicus Island (Maine) visited their thirteen pen pals on

Monhegan Island overnight. Transportation was provided by the Maine Sea Coast Missionary Society, whose boat minister, Stanley Haskell, had suggested the children correspond as part of their English lessons. The Matinicus students were fascinated with Monhegan's deer population, but at least one child thought there was no place like home. As the Mission's boat, the *Sunbeam*, pulled away from Monhegan's dock, the child was heard to say, "Monhegan is fine, but I'm still glad I live on Matinicus."

New Englander Rachel Field spent her summers on an island. In 1926 she summed up the effect, pro and con, that islands have on newcomers in a poem, "If Once You Have Slept on an Island."

> Oh, you won't know why, and you can't say how
> Such change upon you came,
> But—once you have slept on an island
> You'll never be quite the same!

To island aficionados, the only real islands are the ones you cannot drive to. As soon as a bridge or man-made causeway connects an island to the mainland, the prospect of embarking for a distant port is gone. It can be complicated to get to an island by ferry, but some people even look forward to the trip. For them, the ferry trip is a rite of passage between a continent and land offshore, between everyday routines and the breaking of them, between a hurried pace of life and a more leisurely outlook on time, between the commonplace and the unpredictable.

Islands are highly vulnerable to the weather and the sea. Although you may have made a car reservation months ahead, you still run a slight risk of finding a sign at the ferry dock that says, "No Boat Today." There is no arguing with ten-foot waves no matter how long it has taken you to drive to the dock.

The sense of time is different on an island, and you may find some bus schedules and other set hours casually adhered to. If you are confronted by an unexpected wait, the best advice is to shrug your shoulders, forget it, and relax. That is what going to an island is all about anyway.

New England's most popular islands are Martha's Vineyard and Nantucket, both in Massachusetts. Since they are large and have demanding clientele, they are able to offer visitors the amenities found on the mainland.

Islesboro in Maine, although smaller and more private, attracts well-to-do summer residents and has an inn comparable to the best mainland inns.

On Monhegan Island, Maine, and on Block Island, Rhode Island, accommodations are simpler than on the other islands.

Although Peaks Island, Maine, is not especially interesting to visit, it is a convenient stop for travelers taking the ferry from Portland to Yarmouth, Nova Scotia, or to Canada.

The best of New England's island inns for food are The Chanticleer Inn on Nantucket and The Beach Plum Inn on Martha's Vineyard. For furnishings our favorite is The Jared Coffin House on Nantucket, which has five outstanding romantic bedrooms. The best all-around island inn is The Islesboro Inn on Islesboro.

BLOCK ISLAND, RHODE ISLAND

For eight weeks during the winter of 1973–74, this small, independent-minded island functioned in a time zone of its own.

When that winter's energy crisis hit New England, people here as elsewhere debated the merits of turning the clocks ahead an hour from Eastern standard time to daylight-saving time. The idea was that an extra hour of daylight in the late afternoon might result in decreased oil consumption.

The rest of the nation adopted daylight-saving time on January 6, 1974. But the town council of Block Island voted to start the experiment eight weeks earlier on November 11, 1973. So for two months, the daily ferry crossed from one time zone to another with each fourteen-mile trip from Point Judith on the Rhode Island mainland to Block Island.

It was not the first time people on this wind-swept island took an innovative course of action. In the 1960s Block Island (legally the town of New Shoreham) was the first Rhode Island town to ban the use of detergents to protect its abundant fresh water. The natural springs, for instance, that supply water for the island's town center produce at the extraordinary rate of over three thousand gallons an hour.

Some people consider Block Island (10.8 square miles in area) homely if not desolate. Others are enchanted with the small-scale landscape, the 200-foot Mohegan Bluffs at the southern end, and the bird sanctuary at the northern end near Sandy Point. (Swimming off Sandy Point is forbidden because it is dangerous.) Every spring and fall flocks of migratory birds take refuge here. In the winter the wind rages up to ninety miles an hour. In the summer there is a constant breeze, giving Block Island its nickname, "the naturally air-conditioned island."

During our visit, barbershop quartets from all the New England states came to Block Island for their one Saturday night concert a year. It was held in the small movie theater in Old Harbor, where a few of the stores, restaurants, and guesthouses are trimmed with Victorian gingerbread. The movie screen was rolled up that night and the barbershop quartets performed to a full house. There was so much enthusiastic applause, cheering, and whistling that even The Four Statesmen, who have sung throughout America, Canada, and England, looked mildly surprised. The audience called for encores and the quartet (representing Rhode Island, Connecticut, Massachusetts, and New Hampshire) obliged. Their exciting, polished, big-sound performance was the high point of the evening. But, then, we are hardly the first to praise them. In July 1967 The Four Statesmen were named International Champions of the SPEBSQSA. That stands for Society for the Preservation and Encouragement of Barber Shop Quartet Singing in America.

If you want to bring your car when you visit Block Island, you must make round-trip reservations in advance, and the cost is substantial. You really do not need a car here anyway. The island is highly bicycle-oriented because the terrain is fairly flat. The roads are usually full of bicycles, with the cars driving slowly behind them. Many people bring their own bicycles, but you can also rent them from shops near the ferry landing in Old Harbor. Taxis meet all the ferries and many offer island tours that take about an hour.

Ferry Schedules: For schedules, write to Interstate Navigation Co., Box 482, New London, Conn. 06320. The schedule lists trips from Point Judith, Rhode Island (year round); from Providence and Newport, Rhode Island (summer only); and from New London, Connecticut (summer only).

Airlines: New England Airlines flies from Westerly, Rhode Island, to Block Island. For schedules, write to New England Airlines, State Airport, Westerly, R.I. 02891.

Directions to the Ferry: From New York, take I-95 north to exit 3 in Rhode Island, then R.I. 138 east to R.I. 108 south to Galilee. Follow signs to the ferry dock. From Boston, take I-95 south to I-295 south to I-95 south to R.I. 4 south to R.I. 2 south to U.S. 1 south to R.I. 108 south to Galilee. Follow signs to the Point Judith ferry dock.

THE SPRING HOUSE

Block Island, Rhode Island

The Spring House on Spring Street, named for the island's natural springs, is a large white structure (with a separate guesthouse or annex) less than half a mile uphill from Old Harbor, where the ferries dock. Built in 1852, The Spring House overlooks the Atlantic Ocean and squarely faces the next landfall—the unseen coast of Portugal.

This island inn is open from the last weekend in June through the day after Labor Day. There are seventy-five bedrooms furnished in a plain manner with pale-pink or white walls, cotton bedspreads, dark painted floors, and simple straight-backed chairs. Most have twin beds, although some have double beds or one twin bed. The inn serves three meals daily and puts up box lunches on request.

When we arrived at The Spring House for dinner, we were greeted by a sign next to the dining-room door. It said, "It is requested that men wear coats and that ladies wear dresses or dress pantsuits for the evening meal." We turned to the head waiter and apologized for my husband's not having brought a jacket. He pointed toward an old-fashioned standing hat rack by the registration desk. There were several jackets suspended on wire hangers. "We have some loners over here," he said. The three of us walked to the hat rack. "It's been a tradition to keep some extras handy, but there's not much choice right now. It's been a heavy night on jackets," he said. The alternatives were a blue-and-white striped seersucker and a cotton black-brown check. The jacket with checks proved a closer fit and we entered the dining room, properly attired, wondering who else was wearing jackets belonging to innkeeper Doug Mott and his uncle.

The dinner menu changes every day and sometimes offers fresh fish and boiled lobster. Block Island is famous for its swordfish, so if the inn is serving that, we suggest you order it. The inn also serves an excellent beefsteak pie. It comes in an oval serving dish with chunks of beef, a little ham, fresh carrots, peas, a rich gravy, and a good pastry crust.

For our meal, we had a lukewarm chicken-noodle soup, baked stuffed shrimp with inedible bread stuffing, some whipped potatoes that tasted reconstituted, and a chocolate cream pie with a "whipped cream" topping that had the texture and flavor of something synthetic. But we also had a memorable blueberry pie that the waitress said was made in the inn's new kitchen. The crust was light and melted in the mouth; the filling was neither too runny nor too dry.

The wine list offers fourteen dinner wines, half California (Almaden) and half French (B & G). The inn also has a taproom.

Many guests at The Spring House have been coming here every summer for as long as twenty years. On weekends the guests include young couples and families; during the week most visitors tend to be middle-aged and retired people.

The most popular activities on Block Island are bicycling,

bird watching, fishing, and swimming. You can play tennis at The Spring House or park your bicycle in the rack on the wide veranda and board the inn's Volkswagen bus for the two-mile trip to State Beach.

Directions to the Inn: From the ferry landing, turn left onto Water Street for a few yards, then uphill on Spring Street to the inn.

MARTHA'S VINEYARD, MASSACHUSETTS

Martha's Vineyard, five miles off Cape Cod, is the largest of New England's islands and the most commercially developed. Its 108.7 square miles include beautiful beaches, six towns, a Coca-Cola bottling plant, and so much summer daytime traffic that some trucks unload food and freight at night. The year-round population of about six thousand swells to around sixty thousand in the summer.

It is generally thought that "the Vineyard" was named by the English explorer Bartholomew Gosnold, who had a daughter named Martha. He observed the island in 1602 and wrote of ". . . the incredible store of vines and the beautie and delicacie of this sweet soil. . . ." Gosnold also named the Elizabeth Islands (between Martha's Vineyard and the Massachusetts mainland), presumably for another daughter, Elizabeth.

In the last several years three vineyards have been started on this heavily wooded island. One, Chicama Vineyards, began selling its West Tisbury wines in island liquor stores in 1975. This marked the first time since at least 1933 that wine was made commercially in Massachusetts.

Martha's Vineyard, almost twice as large as Nantucket, seems more like an extension of Cape Cod than an island adrift from the mainland. If you cross the island on the West Tisbury Road, you can drive for twenty minutes without catching a glimpse of the ocean. But the Vineyard's size also means that nature has blessed this island with a great variety of protected harbors, salt marshes, and sandy beaches. There are myriad nature trails, renowned fishing, the weekly *Vineyard Gazette,* and the village of Edgartown, an exceptionally charming former whaling port.

Martha's Vineyard, like every island we have been to, has its aficionados. Among them is Sen. Edward W. Brooke of Massachusetts, who owns a home here. "Oh, I love the ocean! I love the wildness of it and the sound of waves crashing on the shore," Senator Brooke once said. "The sea, you know, is nature's perfect healer. It has a soothing, recuperative quality that's a cure-all. And I find myself greedily gulping salt air."

The six towns here are roughly divided between the eastern and western halves of the island. The eastern side, referred to as "down-Island," is made up of Edgartown, Vineyard Haven, and Oak Bluffs. The western side, known as "up-Island," includes West Tisbury, Chilmark, and Gay Head, where the multicolored Gay Head cliffs at the water's edge are one of the island's most popular scenic attractions.

Like "down-East" which has become synonymous with Maine, "up-Island" and "down-Island" are nautical terms. They derive from the days when Vineyarders used boats the way we now travel in cars. Since the prime meridian is at Greenwich, England, a vessel sailing east was running "down" its longitude. A ship heading west was running "up" its longitude. So when people on Martha's Vineyard spoke of going to New York, they said they were going "up," meaning west.

Deep-sea whaling at Martha's Vineyard began in 1738, when Nantucket fishermen launched their ships from here, but for some reason the Vineyard never became as prosperous a whaling center as Nantucket. In 1775, for example, there were 150 vessels, totaling 15,000 tons, that hailed from Nantucket, but Martha's Vineyard could claim only 12, totaling 720 tons. Farming was an important means of livelihood on the Vineyard, where sheep and cattle farms supplied both this island and Nantucket. In the late 1700s farmers who needed larger pastures for their sheep flocks migrated to Maine, New York, New Jersey, and the Carolinas.

In Edgartown, where the earliest residents voting in elections used corn to vote "yes" and beans to vote "no," Herman Melville shipped out in 1841 for his only whaling voyage on the *Acushnet*. Later, Melville stayed with the *Acushnet*'s captain, Valentine Pease, at his home on South Water Street.

Today Edgartown—with many old guesthouses, restaurants, and shops—is the most historically charming of the island's towns, several of which are not especially attractive. The ferries do not unload at Edgartown, though; they land at Vineyard Haven and Oak Bluffs.

Oak Bluffs is probably best known for its gingerbread cottages and for the State Lobster Hatchery (open to the public). In the ocean the mortality rate of the newborn lobster is very high, but at the hatchery the young lobsters have a much better chance to survive. When they are about three weeks old, they are put in the ocean off the coast.

Martha's Vineyard, in general, is very car oriented, although the cost of transporting a car is almost prohibitive. The ferries to both Martha's Vineyard and Nantucket resemble floating garages. Even so, they do not have room for all the cars people want to bring, especially to Martha's Vineyard. The best advice is to follow the example of summer residents, who often make ferry reservations for cars many months in advance. Unless you have round-trip reservations for your car, it is unwise to bring your car at all. Many island shops rent bicycles, and countless taxis meet the ferries.

There are many island tours. If you take one that makes a lunch stop at Gay Head Cliffs, you will be ahead of the game if you take your own sandwiches or picnic lunch. The tourist stands at the cliffs are shockingly commercial.

During the summer there is one ferry daily from Martha's Vineyard to Nantucket and back. Otherwise, ferries from Woods Hole go to one island or the other, but they do not stop at both.

Ferry Schedules: For schedules to Martha's Vineyard: from Woods Hole (year round), write to Steamship Authority, P.O. Box 284, Woods Hole, Mass. 02543; from Hyannis (summer only), write to Hy-Line, Ocean Street Dock, Hyannis, Mass. 02601.

Airplanes: Air New England operates regular flights to and from Martha's Vineyard, Nantucket, Boston, Hyannis, New Bedford, and New York's LaGuardia Airport.

Directions to the Ferry: From New York, take I-95 to Providence, then I-195 to Mass. 25 to U.S. 6 to Mass. 28 to Woods Hole. From Boston, take Mass. 3 to U.S. 6 to Mass. 28 to Woods Hole.

THE BEACH PLUM INN

Menemsha, Massachusetts

When guests arrive at this small romantic retreat, the first thing innkeepers Fred and Carol Feiner ask is, "What would you like for dinner?" There are usually about four entrees, each requiring extensive preparations, and dinner reservations here are highly prized.

Menemsha, part of the town of Chilmark on the island's western side, is a little fishing village on the edge of Menemsha Pond, a man-made harbor. The Beach Plum Inn is just up the road from the fishing community where, sheltered among trees, it overlooks the waters of Menemsha Bight.

The Beach Plum is one of our favorite inns, because it has imaginative food, cheerful bedrooms, and a friendly tone set by the Feiners. This is an excellent inn for couples who want a secluded atmosphere in which to eat well and relax. You can play tennis on the inn's courts or swim at the inn's beach, picking up shells as you walk barefoot in the sand.

The inn is open from Memorial Day weekend until September 20. There are twelve bedrooms, including attractively furnished cottages with fabric-covered headboards matching the striped and flowered wallpaper. The inn serves breakfast to houseguests only, puts up box lunches on request, and can seat fifty people (in addition to inn guests) for dinner by reservation.

From the dining room (where dress is informal), you can watch the sun setting behind nearby Gay Head and the Elizabeth Islands while you sit at a table covered with a blue-and-white checked cloth. There are garden flowers in little pottery vases, giving the dining room a refreshing appeal.

Our dinner began with a fresh tomato soup garnished with a tiny amount of grated orange. The salad was tender garden lettuce grown in the inn's vegetable garden. One entree caused more conversation and comment than the next: striped bass with lobster sauce, filet of sole bonne femme, tournedos with Béarnaise sauce, and chicken Alfredo. The vegetable of the day was a succulent ratatouille. Mr. Feiner, himself a Cordon Bleu chef, has another Cordon Bleu chef in the inn's kitchen as well.

Since Menemsha is dry, the inn is not permitted to serve liquor. You can bring your own, though, or ask the Feiners to purchase it elsewhere on the island for you. Before dinner, guests gather on the pleasant enclosed porch where setups are provided for those who wish to have cocktails.

The inn is named for the beach plum, a small pinkish purple tart fruit that grows close to the seashore on bushes sometimes four or five feet high. Too sour to eat raw, the beach plum is most often used to make jelly or jam. There are good years and bad years for beach plums. Since these plums grow wild and have proved stubbornly unresponsive to cultivation, they are considered a rare find even in New England.

Just as the beach plum often hides behind sand dunes, The Beach Plum Inn and its tennis courts are concealed down a one-lane dirt road. The inn's sign consists of the words, "Beach Plum Inn" and a single arrow painted on white boulders at the entrance.

This intimate inn attracts guests in all age groups. But the attention given to food here makes The Beach Plum a greater delight to adults who appreciate imaginative meals than to children whose concept of a memorable repast begins with hamburgers and ends with French fries.

Directions to the Inn: Drive from Vineyard Haven or Oak Bluffs "up-Island" to Chilmark. Take the Menemsha Cross Road to North Road and turn right onto North Road. The inn's sign is on the left.

THE MENEMSHA INN AND COTTAGES

Menemsha, Massachusetts

This compound of brown-shingled buildings, pink rambler roses, and a tall flagpole, all overlooking Menemsha Bight on the island's western side, is an unpretentious family-style inn open from mid-May until September 30. The Menemsha Inn has a camplike atmosphere. It consists of a dining and recreation hall, a seven-bedroom house, and fourteen cottages scattered among the scrub pine and oak that punctuate the hillside down to Menemsha Beach. The cottages, accommodating between two and four persons, are furnished motel style and have screened-in porches facing the water. Each has a private bathroom. The inn serves a robust breakfast for its guests and the public. (The cost is included in the overnight rate.) No other meals are served.

Near the main house a sign that says, "Beach," points you down a long path descending to the wide and sandy Menemsha Beach. It is a lovely walk. (It can also be reached by car in about two minutes.)

In the recreation lounge you will find a bulletin board covered with notices of things to do, restaurants to go to, deep-sea fishing trips to take, and current concerts, movies, and lectures to attend on the island. There are comfortable chairs in the living room, an old upright piano, an unabridged Webster's dictionary, and half a dozen jigsaw puzzles and games. From 4 to 10 P.M. you can help yourself to coffee or tea.

For guests who want to cook their own food (and many do), the inn provides outdoor fireplaces, picnic tables, and "condiment boxes" containing tools necessary for a cookout. Many people buy fresh fish nearby and keep their food in an assigned refrigerator. If your idea of a vacation rules out even the thought of cooking, there are many restaurants on the island, ranging from coffee shops to The Beach Plum Inn, which is almost next door. (Dinner reservations at The Beach Plum are required.)

The bedrooms in the main house are plain but pleasant, with painted chests of drawers, flowered curtains, green bedspreads, and yellow walls. None have private bathrooms. The community bathrooms have small neat signs saying, "In consideration of guests who are sleeping, it is requested that the tub or shower not be used before 7:30 A.M. or after 10:30 P.M." At 7:30 A.M. that polite request had been uniformly respected. The only sounds piercing the intense quiet were those of birds chirping and tennis balls plunking rhythmically on the tennis courts. (You can also play shuffleboard and Ping-Pong here.)

Breakfast is a hearty all-you-can-eat meal, starting with fruit, cereal, eggs, muffins, and ending with fresh fish fillets or whatever other daily special the inn is having.

The Menemsha Inn is popular with guests of all age groups, from families with young children to middle-aged couples. It is the kind of inn where people make friends easily, exchange addresses at the end of their vacations, and plan to return because The Menemsha is a relatively good buy on an expensive island.

The Environs: Besides lobster and fishing boats, Menemsha village has a good-sized beach, a wildlife sanctuary called Cedar Tree Neck (open to the public), and an out-of-the-way location on Martha's Vineyard. That is because the only road to Menemsha ends on the shore of Menemsha Pond, tucking the village into a corner of its own.

Directions to the Inn: Drive from Vineyard Haven or Oak Bluffs "up-Island" to Chilmark. Take the Menemsha Cross Road to North Road and turn right onto North Road. The inn's sign is on the left.

NANTUCKET ISLAND, MASSACHUSETTS

If we could visit only one New England island, our choice would be Nantucket. It is the most fascinating, inspiring, and consistently picturesque of this region's islands. Even now, Nantucket harks back to the days when New England's outpost island thirty miles at sea was the home port for one of the world's great whaling fleets.

From Nantucket Harbor, where the ferries dock today, ships hauled whale oil directly to England as early as 1720 to light London's streets. They brought back cobblestones as ballast to balance the ships on open seas and to build the streets in Nantucket Town. By 1760 Nantucket whalemen had killed all the whales in nearby waters and began sailing farther from home in search of the sperm whale.

Just as gold catapulted western mining towns into flourishing population centers, the sperm whale was Nantucket's one commodity. It was the waxy sperm, spermaceti, in the whale's head that yielded an oil producing a brilliant smokeless light. Spermaceti candles and sperm whale oil were in demand as light sources in the world's best cities and homes. One unit of candle power still refers to the light given off by the spermaceti candle.

By all rights, Nantucket today, like the mining towns that prospered and died, should be a ghost town. It peaked as a whaling center in 1842 when 9,712 people lived here and Nantucket's women ran the town while their husbands and sons went to sea on the eighty-six ships and barks, two brigs, and two schooners hailing from the island.

By then, Nantucket men (who routinely signed "death warrant" forms absolving a ship owner from responsibility for their lives) had sailed all over the world: north to the Davis Straits and south to the Bahamas and Brazil. In 1791 the 240-ton *Beaver* rounded Cape Horn and entered the Pacific Ocean. In 1818 the *Globe* discovered whaling grounds off Chile's shore. The next year the *Maro* found whales off Japan.

Not all of Nantucket's men returned. When the harpooner in the open boat nearest a whale hurled his iron through the air, he and his men never knew whether the wounded whale would take them on a wild "Nantucket sleigh ride" at up to twenty knots over the open seas.

If a Nantucket man escaped death on a "sleigh ride," there was still the danger of mutiny. Captain Thomas Worth saw Nantucket for the last time when he sailed the *Globe* out of the harbor in 1822. The ship came back on November 14, 1824, but Captain Worth had been murdered, along with three of his officers, when the crew mutinied in 1823.

Sometimes the men returned but their ships did not. On October 1, 1807, the *Union* had only been out of Nantucket for twelve days when it was struck by a whale and sank. The crew spent seven days in small boats before safely landing at the Azores. But some crewmen of the *Essex* were not so lucky. On November 20, 1820, the *Essex* was also sunk by a whale, but its survivors resorted to cannibalism to stay alive.

While some men risked their lives and died, other men grew rich. Joseph Starbuck, who in 1837 built three identical brick houses for his sons on Main Street, claimed that six of his twenty-three whale ships supplied the world with $2.5 million of whale oil.

Nantucket lost its stature as a whaling center for these reasons:

• The sand bar (which today has an outer curve of twenty-four miles at Nantucket Harbor's mouth) had built up over the years, making it impossible for the heavy ships to cross.

• The Great Fire of 1846 destroyed the docks and a large part of the business district.

• The Gold Rush of 1849 infected Nantucket men with the same "gold fever" that lured young men from other New England towns to California.

• The importance of whale oil declined when petroleum (yielding kerosene) was discovered as a fuel source.

On June 14, 1870, the square-rigger *Eunice H. Adams* was the last whale ship to sail home into Nantucket Harbor. By then, the population had dwindled to 4,100.

In the 1870s the whalers were already being replaced by summer visitors who could have gone to Newport, Rhode Island, or Bar Harbor, Maine, but chose Nantucket instead. In 1913 a vacation guide to Nantucket stated, "Nantucket has so many special charms of its own that it is easy to account for the preference shown the island by many who are so well off financially as to have practically all the world to choose from."

Today the entire island (fifty-seven square miles in area) is an historic district. Even its current architectural style is linked to its history as a whaling port. All new buildings on Nantucket must conform in materials, design, and color to one of the architectural styles in vogue around 1850. This intense commitment to the past means that if you want to paint your window shutters bright green, the chances are excellent that the five-man Historic District Commission will forbid you to do so. It also means that the more than four hundred buildings in Nantucket Town have been preserved. Now they are used as homes, shops, and guesthouses.

Nantucket has one of New England's most outstanding main streets. Bordered by red-brick sidewalks and many expensive shops, it looks more like a European square than a traditional New England village with a town green. It is a wide street with a canopy of elm trees arching gracefully over the cobblestones. Since Nantucket is so far from the mainland ("Nantucket" means "far off among the waves"), the disease that has blighted elm trees in one New England town after another in recent years has not reached this island. Hopefully, the canopy of elm trees will remain undisturbed.

Besides its historic buildings open to the public, Nantucket is known for its sandy beaches and for its heather-strewn moors, rutted roads, russet swamps in the fall, and more than two hundred acres of cultivated cranberry bogs. There were 3,774 year-round residents in 1970 but the population has increased since then.

The highlights among things to see on Nantucket include the Whaling Museum near Steamboat Wharf; the Jetties Beach on North Beach Road (buses go from Nantucket Town); Joseph Starbuck's "Three Bricks" at 93, 95, and 97 Main Street; and an island tour (there are many to choose from). The Nantucket Historical Association has a superlative booklet for a self-guided tour on foot or by car, and the Town Information Bureau, at 25 Federal Street, distributes the booklet free.

Since buses go to the beach and to Siasconset, a summer colony on the eastern shore, a car is less important for a short stay here than on Martha's Vineyard. If you do take your car, the best advice is to have a round-trip car reservation before leaving the mainland. There are many taxis on the island, and shops in Nantucket Town rent bicycles. For walking on the old brick sidewalks, bring comfortable shoes.

Ferry Schedules: For schedules from Woods Hole (year round), write to Steamship Authority, P.O. Box 284, Woods Hole, Mass. 02543; from Hyannis (summer only), write to Hy-Line, Ocean Street Dock, Hyannis, Mass. 02601.

Airplanes: Air New England operates regular flights to and from Nantucket, Martha's Vineyard, Boston, Hyannis, New Bedford, and New York's LaGuardia Airport.

Directions to the Ferry: From New York, take I-95 to Providence, I-195 to Mass. 25 to U.S. 6 to Mass. 28 to Woods Hole. From Boston, take Mass. 3 to U.S. 6 to Mass. 28 to Woods Hole.

THE CHANTICLEER INN

Siasconset, Massachusetts

When Nantucket men wanted to get away from it all in the 1700s, they often went to sea on whaling ships for several years. But when they were home and got restless, they traveled the eight miles from Nantucket Town to Siasconset to fish for cod.

Siasconset, usually shortened to 'Sconset or Sconset, is on the island's eastern shore. It earned the nickname Patchwork Village because the first fishermen built crude dirt-floor shacks with wood brought from town or salvaged from shipwrecks. Today those makeshift shanties are rose-covered cottages divided by privet hedges and narrow lanes strewn with broken scallop shells. The small-scale dimensions established by the fishermen still characterize every corner of this tiny summer village.

Two of the silvery-shingled cottages belong to The Chanticleer Inn, where Jean-Charles Berruet, the chef and innkeeper, oversees the excellent dinners and luncheons that alone make a trip to this out-of-the-way spot worthwhile. The food is superb, the setting is romantic, the dining room is intimate and elegant, the service is excellent, and the pink and white rambler roses are lovely.

The Chanticleer ranks so high on our list of favorite inns that whenever we fantasize about extravagant trips, one of us invariably says, "Wouldn't it be fun to fly to Nantucket for the sole purpose of eating at The Chanticleer and then fly home again?"

The inn is open from early June through early October, serving luncheon and dinner daily for the public. A Continental breakfast is served for inn guests only. The two cottages (each has two bedrooms and two bathrooms) accommodate eight people. They are behind the inn, assuring quiet for those who wish to go to bed before The Chanticleer's Chanty Bar closes at 1 A.M. The bedrooms are furnished in a plain manner, with twin beds and small flowered wallpaper patterns. Each cottage has a porch with rugged wooden furniture and rose-covered trellises.

The à la carte menu offers about twenty-one entrees, most requiring a great deal of preparation. They include roast pheasant with sautéed apples, heavy cream, and Calvados sauce; chicken breast stuffed with prosciutto ham and Swiss cheese; calf's brain with black butter; fresh lobster meat sautéed in cognac and heavy cream; and veal kidneys sautéed with mushrooms, shallots, and Madeira wine.

We began dinner with a bubbly hot crêpe filled with lobster, scallops, and mushrooms in a white-wine sauce. But you can also order cherrystones on the half shell, escargots de Bourgogne, pâté maison, smoked Gaspe salmon, lobster bisque, fresh consommé, onion soup, homemade vichyssoise, or clam chowder.

We had the Nantucket Bay scallops cooked with garlic, mushrooms, and tomatoes; and the bluefish Chanticleer, which was baked with onions, white wine, and mushrooms. The inn was also having ratatouille niçoise and a fresh salad. The wine list is extensive.

The dozen desserts included a Gateau Moka (a light, sweet cake with buttercream filling), chocolate mousse, assorted French cheeses, and fresh fruit salad with kirsch. We ended dinner with espresso coffee brought to the table in an espresso pot.

Everyone dining on a Saturday night has a choice of two

sittings for dinner. When we were there, both sittings were fully reserved early in the day. There were no children at the inn but the couples spanned all age groups. The women were wearing casually elegant clothes from long, colorful skirts to fashionable dungaree suits.

The Environs: Compared to Nantucket Town, there is not much to do in Sconset. Most people who come here are renting cottages by the week, stretching their legs on an island tour, or eating at The Chanticleer. Sconset does have its own post office and zip code, but it is almost entirely a residential village.

You can walk from the inn to Sconset Beach at the foot of Gulley Road. The beach, said to be good for surfing, has a lifeguard during the summer and playground equipment. Off the shore you can see the rip tide—a white seam on the water's surface—where two currents clash, creating an extremely dangerous undertow.

For a pleasant walk, take the foot path extending along the bluffs to the lighthouse. Although there is a public nine-hole golf course nearby, you need your car to get to it. A wide bicycle path, parallel to but separated from the main road, goes from Sconset almost to the center of Nantucket Town.

Service to and from Nantucket Town and Sconset is not frequent. Still, a bus does go and the driver entertains passengers by talking about the island the entire way. When we took this bus, it left about an hour late. Some people visiting Nantucket only for the day were positively outraged. But we have not been to one New England island where absolutely everything, including ferry departures and arrivals, happened just when it was supposed to. With a minority of other passengers, we thought the incident was memorably humorous.

Directions to the Inn: From the Steamboat Wharf at Nantucket Town, proceed straight on Broad Street for a block, turn left (opposite the Whaling Museum) onto South Water Street, turn right onto Main Street, then left onto Orange Street. Continue on Orange to the Milestone Road to Sconset, which is so small you will easily find the inn.

THE JARED COFFIN HOUSE

Nantucket, Massachusetts

Mrs. Jared Coffin was living in a simple square house on the corner of Pleasant and Mill streets during the 1830s and early 1840s when she decided that "Moor's End" was too far out of town. Besides, she was sick of the stench from her husband's tryworks in back of the house. These were used to render the whale oil that made Jared Coffin a wealthy man.

To please her, Mr. Coffin built a stately brick neoclassic house that not only was in the middle of town but also was bigger than anyone else's. He spared no cost in the construction of Nantucket's first three-story house. But, apparently, Mrs. Coffin still was not satisfied. Soon after the house was finished in the spring of 1846, the Coffins packed their belongings, put the house up for sale, and moved to a bigger town, Boston.

The house that Mrs. Coffin did not want is now a beautifully furnished inn. It has antique-laden living rooms, lovely bedrooms, and an intimate outdoor terrace where you can have sandwiches and drinks in the summer.

The Jared Coffin House, owned by the Nantucket Historical Trust, serves three meals daily for guests and the public. There are forty-one bedrooms, each with a private bathroom, telephone, and television set. Rooms, food, and beverages are offered 365 days a year, making The Jared Coffin House an island inn where you can spend Christmas.

Innkeeper Philip Whitney Read likes to make a celebration of the "Twelve Days of Christmas," when a tree is decorated in the living room and greenery is draped down the main staircase, around the fireplaces, and from the chandeliers. Some wreaths on the doors in Nantucket Town are made with cranberries. There is an annual "sing" at a place called Caton's Circle, and after dinner at the inn, coffee is served in the library.

But you can enjoy the Embroidery Rooms any time of year. They are the five most romantic bedrooms we have seen in an island inn, and they are popular with honeymooners. These rooms are called Phoebe Coffin 1, 2, and 3 (all reached by a separate entrance on the side of the inn), and Rooms A and C (in the main building). The largest room is Phoebe Coffin 1.

The Embroidery Rooms are sumptuously furnished, with canopy-covered double beds, Oriental rugs, and engaging china plates on the walls. The embroidered curtains match the bedspread and canopy. The three rooms in the Phoebe Coffin annex have unobtrusive kitchenettes.

The furnishings in the living rooms and dining room are also lavish, with Chippendale, Sheraton, and American Federal furniture, a Chinese coffee table, a lacquered Japanese cabinet, Oriental rugs, and chandeliers that give the inn an elegant air.

Although The Jared Coffin House is better known for its furnishings than its food, the Sunday buffet attracts both visitors and many Nantucket residents who look forward to the variety of beautifully presented dishes. During our visit the buffet included a delicious fresh lobster salad, some good fried potatoes, a tangy celery soup, tossed salad, sliced roast beef, tomato aspic, and hot fried chicken. A watermelon shell with scalloped edges contained fresh blueberries and balls of watermelon and cantaloupe. The buffet is a relatively good buy on Nantucket. (At breakfast the inn's menu included a daily special: grilled bluefish, hash-brown potatoes, and bacon.)

You do not have to stay at The Jared Coffin House to have a drink and a sandwich or a pot of tea on the flagstone terrace. Covered by a gray, white, and black awning, the terrace is refined, bordered with pink begonias and set up with decorative cast iron tables with marble tops.

The inn's attractive wood-paneled taproom used to be a billiard salon and gentlemen's smoking room when The Jared

Coffin House opened for business in 1847. The proprietors, as they called themselves, changed over the years, but from 1847 until 1961 (when the Nantucket Historical Trust bought the inn), the inn was called The Ocean House.

In 1862 Eben W. Allen advertised The Ocean House: "This commodious Hotel has, during the past winter, undergone a thorough repair; been essentially altered and re-furnished, and is now open to the Public as a First Class House. No pains will be spared to render it a pleasant and comfortable house to all. Connected with this House is a Billiard Saloon, Livery Stable, and all other equipments of Hotels of its class."

In September 1873 tourism was starting to replace whaling as a Nantucket industry. New owners of The Ocean House bought a 6½ ton, sloop-rigged yacht for guests to take cruises on. She was named *Salus* for the Roman goddess of health and prosperity, and she was fitted in black walnut with silver mountings. The *Salus* had two skippers who took the hotel employees on board for sails in the harbor. In September 1874 the employees said thank you by giving each skipper an elegant silver cake basket.

And what did it cost to stay at The Ocean House in those days? From 1872 to 1892 the price remained the same: $3 per day for transient boarders; $2.50 for permanent guests.

By 1913, The Ocean House and adjoining buildings accommodated 200 people. There was a ballroom, an orchestra, grounds for lawn tennis and croquet, and almost every room had running water.

Ironically, when Jared Coffin bought this property in 1845, there was a structure on the site that Mr. Coffin demolished before erecting his impressive house. That building was an old inn.

The Environs: Turn down the red-brick sidewalk along Centre Street and you will wind up on Main Street. Here, you can browse in needlework shops, buy ice cream cones, or sit on the benches beneath the elm trees, watching the world go by in the cobblestoned square.

Directions to the Inn: From the ferry, walk along Broad Street past the Whaling Museum and you will find The Jared Coffin House at the corner of Broad and Centre streets.

PEAKS ISLAND, MAINE

"Look! There's the fire boat," Mrs. Maggie Tunstall said, pointing toward a flashing blue light that was moving rapidly across the four-mile stretch of water between Portland and this island. "Oh, good," someone said. "Maybe Dickie's sister is going to have her baby at last."

Legally part of the city of Portland, this not particularly attractive island is serviced by the Portland Fire Department's little boat when emergencies call for one of the island's twelve hundred or so year-round residents to be taken to the hospital. Most people who live here work in Portland and use the island as a suburb, commuting by ferry. During the summer the population expands to about five thousand on Peaks, which is 2 miles long and 1½ miles wide.

For visitors who have come a long distance to see Maine, this island is by no means the first place we would recommend visiting. But it is a convenient stopover if you are en route to Nova Scotia. The ferries to Peaks Island leave from wharves in Portland very near the International Ferry Terminal, where boats set out for Nova Scotia. The M.S. *Bolero* and the M.S. *Prince of Fundy* make the ten-hour trip to Yarmouth, Nova Scotia, daily all year and twice a day during the summer. They carry cars and offer travelers private cabins, restaurants, bars, tax- and duty-free shops, and casinos.

Compared with other New England islands, Peaks Island lacks picturesque charm, and there is relatively little to do. The town center has a disappointing appearance because the buildings along the main street are not homogeneous either in building materials or in design. Even a bicycle trip (it takes thirty minutes to circle the island) rewards you with little more than the physical exercise.

One day when visitors to Peaks are sometimes involuntarily detained is Wednesday. Although there is frequent ferry service to the island during the summer, there is no car ferry on Wednesdays, a fact that is not well-publicized. Some people have brought their cars, planning to return on a Wednesday, only to find that they can leave but their cars cannot.

Ferry Schedules: For schedules to Peaks Island and the other Calendar Islands, write to Casco Bay Lines, Custom House Wharf, Portland, Me. 04101. For schedules to Nova Scotia, write to International Terminal, Portland, Me. 04101.

Directions to the Ferry: From New York or Boston, take I-95 to Portland, follow signs to the waterfront, and exit at the ramp for the International Ferry Terminal. After passing this terminal, continue on the same street, watching for small signs designating Portland Pier and Custom House Wharf, where boats leave for Peaks and for the Calendar Islands cruise. These are among New England's most interesting working wharves with old signs, bent piles, two brick streets, and buildings covered with metal in quasi clapboarding.

THE INN ON PEAKS

Peaks Island, Maine

If you plan to go to Nova Scotia and want a place near Portland to stay, The Inn on Peaks would be a good choice. The inn is open from late May through early September. There are twelve bedrooms. Three meals are served daily for houseguests and the public. Reservations are essential, both for meals and for overnight lodgings.

Everything about the inn, the year-round home of Margaret and Howard Tunstall, is personal. The atmosphere is more like that of a guesthouse than an inn, reflecting the fact that this was first a home. The small living room has the flavor of a den, with comfortable chairs, family photographs, and knickknacks here and there.

Mrs. Tunstall takes an interest in catering to her guests. When we said we would like to rent bicycles, she telephoned ahead to make sure the rental office was open. And when we were ready to catch a noon-time ferry, Mrs. Tunstall said, "You're going to miss lunch, so you'd better have some milk and cookies before you leave."

The great feature of the inn is the unusual view of Portland Harbor's twinkly lights strung out along the far shore, which can be seen at night from the dining room and four of the bedrooms. (Two of these bedrooms have picture windows.) The immaculate bedrooms have speckled-patterned wallpaper, white curtains, white bedspreads, wall-to-wall carpeting swirled in shades of yellow, plastic flower bouquets, and neatly placed books. (The half a dozen books in our room included *The Story of Baseball*, *The World of Jimmy Breslin*, and *Serpico*.)

About thirty people can be seated in the dining room, where local artists' paintings—portraying such scenes as sea waves dashing against rocks—are displayed on the walls. Dinner for us began with a delicious, hot cream of carrot soup made from scratch with fresh carrots, beef stock, spices, and milk. The entrees included the inn's baked lasagna, charcoal-broiled steak, and broiled scallops. The menu was handwritten on the back of a gilt object resembling a hand mirror.

You do not need to bring your car to Peaks. The Tunstalls will meet you at the ferry if you telephone the inn from the mainland before boarding the boat. And if you do not want to rent bicycles to see the island, you can hire the island taxi.

The Environs: One side trip that starts from Portland (you can also get on the boat at Peaks) is the cruise around the islands in Casco Bay. They are named the Calendar Islands because, it is said, there are 365 of them. Many are minuscule. Some of their names are Junk of Pork, Whale Boat, Sow and Pigs, Pound of Tea, Irony, and Stepping Stones. We did not take this cruise because heavy fog made the trip pointless; people say, however, that it is very enjoyable.

Directions to the Inn: From the ferry landing, turn left onto Island Avenue to the inn.

MONHEGAN ISLAND, MAINE

We were waiting on the weathered dock at Port Clyde for the *Laura B.* to take us the ten miles to Monhegan Island. "We hadn't planned to take our car on the ferry. Is Monhegan very big?" we asked a taxi driver who was squinting in the sun. "Can't take cars to Monhegan," he said. "Can we rent a bike over there?" we asked. The taxi driver half smiled. "Nope," he said, "and you won't need to either."

To say the very least, we were not prepared for Monhegan. It is a small, rustic, unspoiled, different place, and, all in all, a fascinating experience. The island, only .8 square miles in area, is unlike any other New England island with an inn. There is no good sandy beach, no main street, no paved roads at all, and no buildings with gingerbread trim and pretty plantings.

What Monhegan has instead is character, New England character. It is hard to imagine Monhegan off any coast but Maine's. There are seventeen miles of dirt trails that criss-cross the dramatic cliffs, the thick pine woods, and the village, where awkward gray-shingled buildings cling to the southwestern hillside near the inn. These wooden structures, buffeted by the salty air and swept clean by the wind, have appealed to artists since Rockwell Kent (1882–1971) started the island's first art school.

What is there to do on Monhegan? First, walk. The trails are delightful, the scenery is unusual, the pine scent is piquant, and the salt spray from waves crashing against the rocks is refreshing. If you go to a church service, you will find the Monhegan Community Church lit by gas lamps and four kerosene chandeliers. Deep-sea fishing boats leave almost every day; you can check The Island Inn's bulletin board and ask innkeepers Robert and Mary Burton for details.

Ferry Schedules: To visit Monhegan, the only sensible plan is to stay overnight. (Going for the day is inadvisable because the morning boat from Port Clyde is usually fully reserved ahead of time and the afternoon boat stays at the island for only half an hour.) When you write to The Island Inn, the Burtons will send you a ferry schedule and ask you which ferry you want to take. Then they will make reservations for you either from Port Clyde or Boothbay Harbor.

Directions to the Ferry: From New York or Boston, take I-95 to exit 9 on the Maine Turnpike and continue on the east branch of I-95 north to Bath. Follow U.S. 1 north to Me. 131 south to Port Clyde. There is a parking lot near the dock, for which a parking fee is charged.

THE ISLAND INN

Monhegan Island, Maine

After the hour-long ride on the tiny ferry, a truck from The Island Inn met the boat. "I can take your luggage for you," the driver said. We handed him our suitcases and climbed in the back of the truck. The driver scratched his head and frowned. "Do you want to ride to the inn?" he said. "Well, how far is it?" we asked. He turned around slowly and pointed to a building forty feet uphill from the dock. "Is that it?" we asked. He nodded. We laughed sheepishly. "We'll take our suitcases back," we said. Then we climbed out of the truck and walked uphill.

The Island Inn, open from mid-June through mid-September, has forty-five bedrooms. The inn serves three meals a day, puts up box lunches on request, and charges reasonable rates. Reservations are required for both accommodations and meals.

Since one-third of The Island Inn's bedrooms are single rooms, an individual traveling alone here is not an oddity. Most single guests are retired men and women, but, old or young, you will not feel out of place if you come to the inn by yourself. For the best view from the inn, ask for a bedroom overlooking the harbor. On a clear night the star-studded sky twinkles like minia-ture white Christmas tree lights over the lobster boats and sail-boats anchored here.

The inn is not unusual in itself. The furnishings are func-tional and the food is plain. What is striking about the inn are the contented smiles and the cheerful remarks of the inn's guests who are devotees of the Monhegan Island experience.

During our visit there was a water shortage. Handwritten signs around the inn said, "Water to the entire island will be off between the hours of 2 to 5 P.M. and 10 P.M. to 5 A.M." As it turned out, the water was still off at 9 A.M., but that did not seem to bother any of the guests. At breakfast one man shrugged and smiled. "It's the best excuse in the world not to have to shave before breakfast." When the island water is shut off—which hap-pens not infrequently—the inn switches to its own well for cook-ing purposes.

Monhegan has electricity, but The Island Inn generates its own, and many cottages have none at all. If you stroll on the darkened paths in the evening (as many people do), the cottage windows seem to glow from the kerosene lamps inside. You have to take a flashlight with you or risk stumbling on the hilly paths. But it is a wonderful sensation, part of the Monhegan experience, to walk along the dirt trails with small groups of people slowly passing by in the night. It is like being suddenly submerged in the early nineteenth century, before the electric lightbulb made such peaceful strolls in anonymity obsolete.

Every island has its own band of loyal summer visitors— and sometimes detractors. About Monhegan three separate peo-ple asked us to say that Monhegan is cold, boring, windy, and does not have a golf course. That is true. It does not have a golf course, and it will not appeal to anyone who wants to relax in the lap of luxury or, even, convenience.

For instance, if you need to make a telephone call between meals, you can use the inn's telephone in the kitchen. Otherwise, a sign states, "At any other time the necessary noises of kitchen work render hearing too difficult. Other public phones on the island are: Post Office (available post office hours), Monhegan Store (during store hours), Monhegan House porch (2½ hours a day), Sherman Stanley (at his discretion), Elva Nicholson (at her discretion), Mrs. Cyril Nelson (at her discretion)."

Since Monhegan is dry, drinking is not allowed in the inn's public rooms. You can bring your own liquor, get ice by the reception desk, and have a cocktail in your room. Smoking is prohibited on the island except in the village. The shoreline is unsafe for swimming except for one or two small places that the Burtons will point out on a map to any guests who ask.

For all that, Monhegan is a well-loved island, to put it mildly. The 1970 census counted forty-four year-round residents (the number has increased since then), but many more people than that are possessive about Monhegan and do not want to see it change. It is an island for bird watchers, for artists, for adventurous travelers, for fishermen, for hikers, and for families. It is an island for people whose idea of fun is to read a good book when it rains.

There is a tradition that when you leave Monhegan Island for the first time, you must throw some flowers from the ferry into the water to ensure that you will return. There are many signs on Monhegan, but one of the first you will see when you arrive on the dock says, "Do not pick the flowers."

ISLESBORO, MAINE

Everybody knows there are divided opinions about the best inn, the best meal, the best view, the best locale, be it mountains or sea. But for our money, the best ferry ride to an island with an inn is the one that goes from Lincolnville, six miles north of Camden, to Islesboro.

It is a short ride—only about fifteen minutes—but it is fifteen minutes you will never forget. The long-range views of the Camden Hills and the countless islands named only on navigational charts are superlative. The ferry ride lets you see the Maine seascape at its best, from a vantage point on the water, and for a minimum amount of time or money spent.

Islesboro is primarily a summer colony of large, expensive homes with formal gardens. In 1970 there were 421 residents here. The island is about three miles wide and fourteen miles long. The northern half is called Islesboro and the southern half is called Dark Harbor.

Many of the island's access roads to the water are marked Private Way, but there are two areas open to the public. They are at the extreme northern and southern ends. At Turtle Head, the northern tip, Great Blue Herons live in nests atop dead trees.

These prehistoric-looking birds are three to four feet tall and fish in nearby waters each afternoon. At the southern tip there is a tiny pebbly beach.

People who come by private boat and do not rent a mooring from the The Islesboro Inn often anchor offshore or go to nearby Warren Island State Park for the night. The state park, a seventy-acre island accessible only by private boat, is open from late May to mid-September.

If you would like to take your car on the ferry, the rate is very reasonable. Bear in mind that taxis do not meet the ferries and no bicycles are rented on Islesboro. If you want to explore the island, the best advice is to take your car or bicycle.

Ferry Schedules: If you make ferry reservations ahead of time, you will be charged extra for doing so. It is not necessary to make reservations anyway; the ferries go frequently. A sign at the dock says, "The ferry makes ample trips to handle all traffic. However, the last trips, especially on Sunday nights, are crowded. Patrons are advised that those who use last trips may possibly be left, due to an overload." For schedules, write to State of Maine Department of Transportation, State Office Building, Augusta, Me. 04330.

Airplanes: You can take Downeast Airlines to Rockland, Maine, and then a charter shuttle flight to the landing strip on Islesboro.

Directions to the Ferry: From New York or Boston, take I-95 and the Maine Turnpike to Me. 17 to Me. 90 to U.S. 1 to Lincolnville. The ferry dock is well marked.

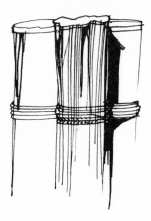

THE ISLESBORO INN

Islesboro, Maine

The view from The Islesboro Inn at Dark Harbor is breath-taking.
You can sit on the terrace in the white-wicker chairs, which are
filled with pretty pink and yellow cushions, and sip tea in the
afternoon or eat dinner in the evening. From the terrace you may
see windjammers skimming across West Penobscot Bay, their
unfurled sails silhouetted against the hills. For these beautiful
schooners plying Maine's coastal waters in the summer with vaca-
tioners on board, The Islesboro Inn is a frequent, if unscheduled,
stop.

This inn has the winsome combination of the dramatic
view, lovely public rooms, good food, and bedrooms with working fireplaces that overlook West Penobscot Bay. The inn is on
the southwest side of the island and, like the island, it has a
definite feeling of privacy. There is less to do on Islesboro than
on most New England islands with inns. But if what you want is
time out from a busy trip and an excellent environment—with a
strong touch of romance—in which to relax, The Islesboro Inn
would be a good choice. The inn does have a tennis court, there
is a nine-hole golf course open to the public next door, and if you
are feeling hardy, you can swim in the bay.

The inn, open from mid-June to mid-September, has fourteen bedrooms, and offers three meals a day both to its guests and
the public. Lunch, afternoon tea, and dinner are served on the
terrace as well as indoors in an intricately paneled dining room.
At dinner you may order breakfast to be served in your room. On
request, the inn puts up box lunches.

Many of the inn's visitors are boaters, who may rent one of five moorings and row ashore to the inn's private dock. The cost of a mooring includes the use of showers and clothes washers and dryers. In the living room, guests who come by sea sign a "Log Book," noting the name of their boat; others sign a guestbook.

When we visited the inn in August, the well-groomed flower beds were filled with marigolds, impatiens, and dusty miller. While we ate dinner on the terrace, we watched a magnificent sunset over the bay against the backdrop of the Camden Hills. By the time dessert arrived, dusk had fallen. The soft candlelight on the terrace tables flickered, and you could hear the seasoned birch and apple logs crackling in the indoor fireplaces.

There were citrus fruits, watermelon, and lime sherbet to start the meal, followed by a hearty clam chowder and English cream biscuits presented on a china plate. The salad was a mixture of fresh greens and sweet red onion slices. A little loaf of whole-wheat bread was fresh, full-bodied, and flavorful.

The menu had about ten entrees, from broiled lamb chops to lobster. The meat specialty of the day was roast ribs of beef, and the fish was a succulent piece of swordfish. The inn often serves broccoli, squash, cabbage, and snow peas grown in its garden.

For dessert, there were several pies, a coffee liqueur parfait, and a variety of ice creams. The blueberry pie, made by the same Islesboro woman who bakes bread for the inn, had a flaky golden crust. The wine list offered about a dozen wines, from Almaden Chablis to Pouilly-Fuissé Latour Burgundy.

The inn requests that men wear jackets and ties to dinner, although it is not mandatory, since sailors sometimes do not have jackets and ties on board.

On Friday and Saturday nights a pianist performs in the bar, an ordinary room that caters mostly to local people and to the visitors from the windjammers.

If you want to go to the inn for lunch, you can leave your car in Lincolnville, telephone the inn in the morning, and ask to be met at the ferry.

Compared with everything else, the bedrooms are on the plain side, but the best one is Room 15. It has a working fireplace and a private balcony. Four other bedrooms also have working fireplaces and a view of the Camden Hills. The rest of the bedrooms are not especially cheerful. All have pastel-painted walls, white-painted bedsteads, and small armchairs.

Directions to the Inn: From the ferry landing, take Ferry Road (it is the only road) to Mill Road. Go right onto Mill, left onto Creek Road, right onto Main Road, and right onto West Shore Drive to the inn.

A man travels the world over in search of
what he needs and returns home to find it.

GEORGE MOORE
The Brook Kerith [1916]

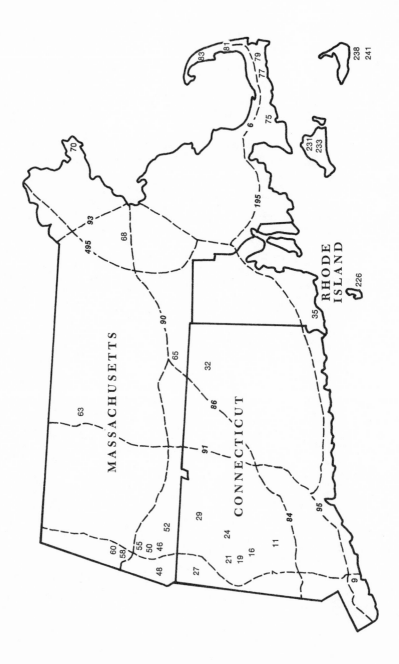

Numbers refer to text pages on which inns are described.

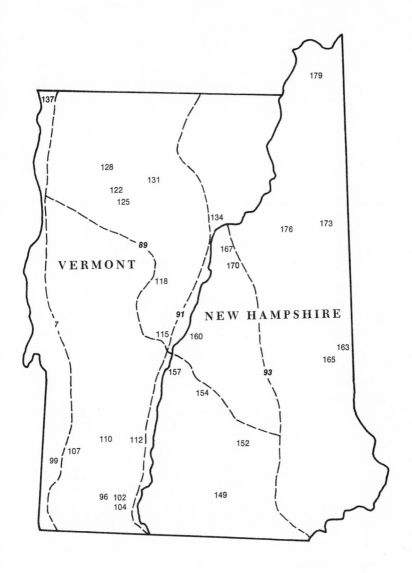

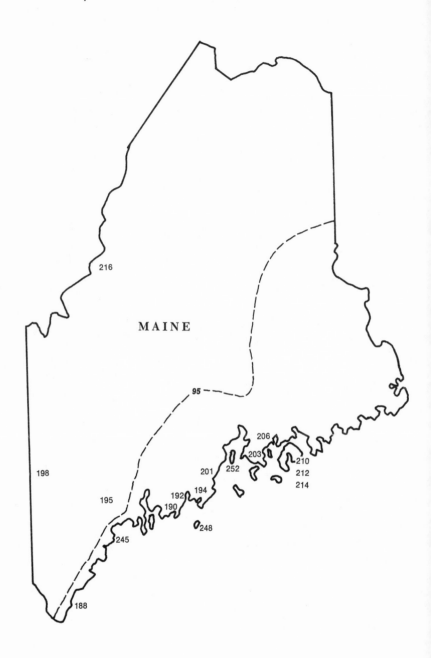

MAINE

95

216

198

195

245

188

192
190

194

201

252

248

206

203

210
212
214

Appendix

The following table is designed to provide a quick reference to the facts about each inn described in this book.

Under *season*, "all year" means the inn is open every day of the year except for some holidays. Seasons for each inn may vary from year to year depending on fall foliage, skiing conditions, and individual inn schedules. It is always best to call for reservations.

Under *bedrooms*, the total number of bedrooms given includes bedrooms in the inn itself, in motel units, and in cabins.

Under *rates*, all prices given are for double occupancy. They are current only as of the time of this writing. These abbreviations are used:

A—American plan
E—European plan
MA—Modified American plan

AE—American Express
BA—BankAmericard
CB—Carte Blanche
DC—Diners Club
MC—Master Charge

CONNECTICUT

Inn	Telephone	Season	Bedrooms	Bathrooms	Rates	Credit Cards
The Boulders Inn on Lake Waramaug New Preston 06777	(203) 868-7918	all year	24	24	$20–27, MA	
The Curtis House Main Street Woodbury 06798	(203) 263-2101	all year except Christmas	18	12	$10–20, E	
The General Lyon Inn Eastford 06242	(203) 974-1380	all year	7	3	$12, E	
The Hopkins Inn New Preston 06777	(203) 868-7925	May–Oct. except Monday	11	9	$13–20, E	
The Kilravock Inn Litchfield 06759	(203) 567-8100	Jan.–Oct.	23	22	$22–35, E	MC
The Mayflower Inn Route 47 Washington 06793	(203) 868-0515	all year	25	19	$45–53, MA	BA, MC
The Old Riverton Inn Riverton 06065	(203) 379-8678	all year except Monday, Tuesday & Christmas	12	12	$17–19, E	AE, MC
The Silvermine Tavern Perry Avenue Norwalk 06850	(203) 847-4558	all year except Tuesday Oct.–May	14	14	$25–28, E	

Inn	Telephone	Season	Bedrooms	Bathrooms	Rates	Credit Cards
The White Hart Inn Village Green Salisbury 06068	(203) 435-2511	all year	22	22	$17–24, E	MC

RHODE ISLAND

Inn	Telephone	Season	Bedrooms	Bathrooms	Rates	Credit Cards
The Weekapaug Inn Weekapaug 02891	(401) 322-0301	mid-June–early Sept.	80	80	$80–88, A	

MASSACHUSETTS

Inn	Telephone	Season	Bedrooms	Bathrooms	Rates	Credit Cards
The Col. Ebenezer Crafts House c/o Publick House Sturbridge 01566	(617) 347-3313	all year	9	7	$22–24, E	
Cornwall House Pond Road North Truro 02652	(617) 487-1881	late June–early Sept.	4	4	$25, E	
The Country Inn 86 Sisson Road Harwich Port 02646	(617) 432-2769	all year	7	6	$16–22, E	

Inn	Telephone	Season	Bedrooms	Bathrooms	Rates	Credit Cards
The Craigville Inn Craigville 02636	(617) 775-1265 775-1269	all year	63	32	$30–46, MA	
The Deerfield Inn Main Street Old Deerfield 01342	(413) 774-3147	all year except Dec. 23–25	12	12	$24–26, E	BA, MC
The Egremont Inn South Egremont 02158	(413) 528-2111	all year except several weeks in spring	25	25	$25–30, E	
The Fairfield Inn Route 23 Great Barrington 01230	(413) 528-2720	all year	11	11	$35, E	MC
The Flying Cloud Inn New Marlboro 01246	(413) 229-2113	mid-May–late Oct.; late Dec.–mid- March	10	8	$36, MA	
The Holden Inn Wellfleet 02667	(617) 349-3450	late June–Labor Day	24	12	$18–24, E $32–38, MA	
The Ivanhoe Country House Undermountain Road Sheffield 01257	(413) 229-2143	all year	5	4	$14–20, E	
Longfellow's Wayside Inn Sudbury 01776	(617) 443-8846	all year except Christmas	10	10	$20, E	AE, CB, DC, MC

The Melrose Inn Harwich Port 02646	(617) 432-0171	early May– mid-Oct.	75	50	$60–70, A	
The Publick House Main Street Sturbridge 01566	(617) 347-3313	all year	21	19	$24–26, E	AE, BA, CB, DC, MC
The Red Lion Inn Main Street Stockbridge 01262	(413) 298-5545	365 days a year	106	75	$24–44, E	AE, BA, DC, MC
The Village Inn 16 Church Street Lenox 01240	(413) 637-0020	all year	19	15	$29–39, E $53–59, MA	
The Williamsville Inn Route 41 West Stockbridge 01266	(413) 274-6580	all year	16	11	$22–32, E	BA
The Yankee Clipper Inn 127 Granite Street Rockport 01966	(617) 546-3407	April–Oct.	26	26	$50–60, A	

VERMONT

Inn	Telephone	Season	Bedrooms	Bathrooms	Rates	Credit Cards
The Four Columns Inn Newfane 05345	(802) 365-7713	late May–Oct.; late Dec.–April; except Monday	12	12	$25–35, E	AE, BA
Grandmother's House Covered Bridge Green West Arlington 05250	(401) 375-2328	all year	4	3	$40, MA	
The Green Mountain Inn Main Street Stowe 05672	(401) 253-7301	Memorial Day– early Nov.; mid-Dec.–mid-April	61	61	$22–26, E $48–56, MA	
The Green Trails Inn By the Floating Bridge Brookfield 05036	(802) 276-2012	Memorial Day–Thanksgiving; late Dec.–March; efficiencies: all year	10	8	$20–24, E	
The Inn at Sawmill Farm Box 8 West Dover 05356	(401) 464-8131	Jan.–mid-Nov.; early Dec.–Jan.	16	15	$70–90, MA	
The Inn on the Common Craftsbury Common 05827	(802) 586-9619	early May–mid-Nov.; Christmas–March	6	3	$50, MA	
The Lodge at Smugglers' Notch Mountain Road Stowe 05672	(401) 253-7311	mid-June–mid-Oct.; mid-Dec.–mid-April	45	35	$60–94, MA	AE, BA, CB, MC
The Norwich Inn Main Street Norwich 05055	(401) 649-1143	all year	27	24	$16–22, E	

Inn	Telephone	Season	Bedrooms	Bathrooms	Rates	Credit Cards
The Old Newfane Inn P.O. Box 101 Newfane 05345	(802) 365-4427	mid-May–late Oct.; mid-Dec.–March	10	10	$25–30, E	MC
The Old Tavern at Grafton Grafton 05146	(802) 843-2375	Jan.–March; May–Dec.	36	36	$20–35, E	
The Rabbit Hill Inn Lower Waterford 05848	(802) 748-9766	all year	20	20	$17–30, E	AE, BA, MC
The Reluctant Panther Inn Manchester Village 05254	(802) 362-2568	Memorial Day–early Nov.; late Dec.–Easter	8	8	$20–30, E	
The Three Clock Inn South Londonderry 05155	(401) 824-6327	mid-Dec.–early April; Memorial Day–mid-Oct.	4	4	$46, MA	
The Tyler Place Inn Highgate Springs 05460	(802) 868-3301	late May–Labor Day	50 units	50	$30–44, A	
The Windridge Inn Jeffersonville 05464	(802) 644-8281	all year	5	5	$18, E, summer $36, MA, winter	

NEW HAMPSHIRE

Inn	Telephone	Season	Bedrooms	Bathrooms	Rates	Credit Cards
The Colby Hill Inn Henniker 03242	(603) 428-3281	all year except 2 weeks in Nov. & April	8	6	$14–16, E	BA

Inn	Telephone	Season	Bedrooms	Bathrooms	Rates	Credit Cards
The Glen Box 77 Pittsburg 03592	(603) 538-6500	mid-May–mid-Oct.	20	15	$36–44, A	
Hide-Away Lodge New London 03257	(603) 526-4861	mid-May–mid-Oct. except Tuesday in July & Aug.	8	8	$48, MA	
The Homestead Sugar Hill 03585	(603) 823-5564	late May–early April	17	12	$18–22, MA	
The John Hancock Inn Main Street Hancock 03449	(603) 525-3318	all year except Christmas & 1 week in spring & fall	10	9	$20, E	MC
Lovett's Inn by Lafayette Brook Profile Road Franconia 03580	(603) 823-7761	mid-June–mid-Oct.; Christmas–early April	29	21	$10–29, E $30–52, MA	
The Lyme Inn On the Common Lyme 03768	(603) 795-2222	all year except last 3 weeks in March & first 3 weeks in Dec.	15	10	$16–24, E	AE
Pinkham Notch Camp and Lodge Appalachian Mountain Club Gorham 03581	(603) 466-3994	lodge: 365 days a year huts: mid-June– Labor Day	105	6	$30, MA	

Inn	Telephone	Season	Bedrooms	Bathrooms	Rates	Credit Cards
Rockhouse Mountain Farm Inn Eaton Center 03832	(603) 447-2880	mid-June–mid-Oct.; mid-Dec.–April	17	10	$34–38, MA	
The Spalding Inn Club Whitefield 03598	(603) 837-2730	June–mid-Oct.	65	65	$60–68, MA	
Stafford's-in-the-Field Chocorua 03817	(603) 323-7766	Memorial Day–Oct.; late Dec.–March	22	14	$42–48, MA	

MAINE

Inn	Telephone	Season	Bedrooms	Bathrooms	Rates	Credit Cards
The Asticou Inn Northeast Harbor 04662	(207) 276-3344	*inn:* late June–mid-Sept. *cottages:* mid-April–late Nov.	66	50	$56–82, MA	
The Bethel Inn Bethel 04217	(207) 824-2175 (212) 247-1233	late May–late Oct.	65	65	$25–38, E	
The Blue Hill Inn Box 403 Blue Hill 06414	(207) 374-2844	all year	8	7	$28, E	
The Cranberry Lodge Northeast Harbor 04662	(207) 276-3702	Sept.–May	9	7	$25, E	

MAINE (cont'd)

Inn	Telephone	Season	Bedrooms	Bathrooms	Rates	Credit Cards
David's Folly R.R. 1 Brooksville 04617	(207) 326-8834	mid-June–early Oct.	13	8	$275—300, A (per week)	
The Island House Perkins Cove Ogunquit 03907	(207) 646-8811	June–early Oct.	6	5	$28–30, E	
McKay Cottages 243 Main St. Bar Harbor 04609	(207) 288-3531	all year	30	15	$6–8, E	AE, BA, MC
Migis Lodge South Casco 04077	(207) 655-4524	late May–mid-Oct.	31	33	$52–72, A	
The Newcastle Inn Newcastle 04553	(207) 563-8889 563-8893	all year	23	13	$9–18, E	
Rock Gardens Inn and Cottages Sebasco Estates 04565	(207) 389-1339	mid-June–late Sept.	29	24	$42–46, A	
Sky Lodge Route 201 Moose River 04945	(207) 668-2171	late May–late Nov.	25	25	$20–26, E	AE, BA, DC, MC
The Squire Tarbox House RD 2, Box 318 Wiscasset 04578	(207) 882-6793	May–early Nov.	7	5	$35, MA	
Wells Wood RR 2 Windsor, Vt. 05089	(603) 675-5360	all year except several weeks in spring	4	3	$19–39, E	

ISLANDS

Inn	Telephone	Season	Bedrooms	Bathrooms	Rates	Credit Cards
The Beach Plum Inn Menemsha Martha's Vineyard, Mass. 02552	(617) 645-2521	Memorial Day– late Sept.	12	9	$58–72, MA	
The Chanticleer Inn New Street Siasconset, Mass. 02564	(617) 257-6231	early June–early Oct.	4	4	$36, E	
The Jared Coffin House 29 Broad Street Nantucket, Mass. 02554	(617) 228-2400	365 days a year	41	41	$30–45, E	AE, BA, CB, DC, MC
The Inn on Peaks Peaks Island, Me. 04108	(207) 766-5525 766-5004	late May–early Sept.	12	4	$15–30, E	
The Island Inn Shore Road, Box 96 Monhegan Island, Me. 04852	(207) 372-9681	mid-June– mid-Sept.	45	13	$34–50, MA	
The Islesboro Inn Islesboro, Me. 04848	(207) 734-2221	mid-June– mid-Sept.	14	10	$68–88, MA	
The Menemsha Inn and Cottages Menemsha Martha's Vineyard, Mass. 02552	(617) 645-2521	mid-May–late Sept.	21	16	$36–48, E	AE
The Spring House Block Island, R.I. 02801	(401) 466-2633	late June–early Sept.	75	30	$38–48, MA	AE